BOGART AND HUSTON

THEIR LIVES, THEIR ADVENTURES, AND THE CLASSIC MOVIES THEY MADE TOGETHER

NAT SEGALOFF

PEGASUS BOOKS
NEW YORK LONDON

BOGART AND HUSTON

Pegasus Books, Ltd.
148 West 37th Street, 13th Floor
New York, NY 10018

Copyright © 2025 by Nat Segaloff

First Pegasus Books cloth edition August 2025

Interior design by Maria Fernandez

All rights reserved. No part of this book may be reproduced in whole or in part without written permission from the publisher, except by reviewers who may quote brief excerpts in connection with a review in a newspaper, magazine, or electronic publication; nor may any part of this book be reproduced, stored in a retrieval system, or transmitted in any form or by any means electronic, mechanical, photocopying, recording, or other, or used to train generative artificial intelligence (AI) technologies, without written permission in writing and appropriate credit to the author and publisher. Excerpts from non-auctorial interviews and other such material appear under a Fair Use Rights claim under US Copyright Law, Title 17, U.S.C. with copyrights reserved by their respective rights holders.

Material from *No Green Bananas: The Life and Times of a Filmmaker* by Pancho Kohner is used by permission of Mr. Kohner. ©2024 Pancho Kohner.

Many of the designations used by manufacturers to distinguish their products are claimed as trademarks or service marks. Where those designations appear in this book and the author and/or publisher were aware of such a claim, the designations contain the symbols ®, SM, or ™. Any omission of these symbols is not intended as an infringement. Oscar®, Academy Award®, and AMPAS® are registered trademarks of the Academy of Motion Picture Arts and Sciences ©AMPAS.

The Author attempted to source all the photos appearing in this book. Anyone feeling his, her, or their photo was used incorrectly should contact the author with proof of ownership and it will be removed from future editions. YouTube links were accurate as of the writing.

Library of Congress Cataloging-in-Publication Data is available.

ISBN: 978-1-63936-931-7

10 9 8 7 6 5 4 3 2 1

Printed in the United States of America
Distributed by Simon & Schuster
www.pegasusbooks.com

For Gerry Herman
It's about time

Contents

	Introduction	vii
	Prologue: On the Twentieth Century	xiii
1	Becoming Bogie	1
2	The Impossible John Huston	11
3	The Ornery Jack L. Warner	19
4	The Black Bird	26
5	All This and World War Two	38
6	*The Treasure of the Sierra Madre*	52
7	Comparing Script and Novel of *The Treasure of the Sierra Madre*	69
8	*Key Largo*, HUAC, and Betrayal	91
9	*The African Queen*	111
10	*Beat the Devil*	129
11	Life After Death	141
Appendices		147
	Appendix 1: Henry Blanke: A Filmmaker's Secret Weapon	149
	Appendix 2: Walter Huston Appreciation	152
	Appendix 3: The Gold Standard	157
	Appendix 4: The Elusive B. Traven	162
	Appendix 5: John Huston, B. Traven, and the Mexican Connection	172
	Appendix 6: *The Bridge in the Jungle*	178
	Appendix 7: Dashiell Hammett and Sam Spade	182
	Appendix 8: The Rat Pack	187
	Acknowledgments	191
	Selected Bibliography	193
	Notes	195
	Index	213

Introduction

Director-star alliances were not uncommon in Hollywood: Alfred Hitchcock and Cary Grant, Frank Capra and James Stewart, Clarence Brown and Greta Garbo, George Cukor and Katharine Hepburn, Preston Sturges and Betty Hutton, John Ford and John Wayne, etc. Studio moguls knew that one plus one equaled more than two when gifted artists were paired in the same film. Some stars—no fools, they even had director approval.

But Humphrey Bogart and John Huston were more than creative partners, they were friends who together produced an extraordinary screen legacy. Between 1941 and 1953 Huston directed Bogart in six films, some of which are bona fide classics: *The Maltese Falcon*, *The Treasure of the Sierra Madre*, *The African Queen*, *Beat the Devil*, *Key Largo*, and *Across the Pacific*.

At the same time, both men led fiercely separate lives—except when they were making pictures together. Sometimes they agreed and sometimes they argued, but they always kept their eyes on the results.

What did each man bring to the collaboration, and how did their six motion pictures reflect their disparate personalities?

They were close friends who didn't spend much time together between films. They read each other's signals. Their relationship was one of love and mutual respect, but it was tinged with exploitation, opportunism, and manipulation. Their pictures stand on their own, but the escapades and ordeals that went into making them must be seen against the background of their lives away from the camera. This is what I wanted to explore not only through researching the facts of their productions but also by seeing the outcomes on the screen. With each successive picture, Huston and Bogart reached for the stars.

John Huston's life was as exciting as any of his films, and that's saying something. Bogart was nowhere near as adventurous as his friend and best director, but he knew a good thing when it came along, no matter how uncomfortable the journey was getting there. Each of the six films covered in this book involved a stretch of their talents that revealed different sides of both men. In *The Maltese Falcon*, Bogart and Huston are serious but not stuffy; Bogart is clearly at ease and having a great time. Come World War II and *Across the Pacific*, there is tension, and no wonder: Huston left the picture before it was finished, so he could fight in the war. For *The Treasure of the Sierra Madre*, both men are back on the same beam and elevate the many levels of the production.

Key Largo enjoys the tension of the story as well as the reunion of two great stars, Bogart and Edward G. Robinson. Their perfectly matched performances recall their gangster heyday at Warner Bros., and Huston pulls superlative performances out of them using their professional backstory. As for *The African Queen*, as magnetic as Bogart and Hepburn are as the mismatched Charlie and Rosie, there is the additional joy in simply watching these two great performers ply their craft, and Huston lets us come along for the voyage. Finally, *Beat the Devil* is *The Maltese Falcon* turned on its head, a crime story that doesn't want to be a crime story, and actors who, like the characters they play, are trying to figure out what's going on. It's a cult movie before there were cult movies.

One of the joys of writing this book was having the excuse to watch and rewatch the films, catching throwaway moments and studying the faces of great screen personalities who know they've been given solid material and want to play it to the max. There are no malingerers in a John Huston film. They wouldn't dare.

It has been noted that Huston's films are dominated by stories of losers, that is, people whose dreams do not come true, whose efforts are for nought, who wind up on the wrong side of the law or of fate, and others whose schemes variously fail to come to fruition but who, if they're lucky, find victory in defeat. Huston held fascination in such constructs, perhaps as a reflection of how he lived his own life, poised at the edge of the abyss on many occasions. He was constantly in debt, went through five marriages, tempted death with astonishing frequency, and yet managed to die in the sack. In his explorations, he hit on the mother lode: actors love playing flawed characters, and most actors (except those signed to franchises) love a good death scene.

Bogart, an actor who struggled through dozens of crummy parts before he was able to display his singular screen persona, was also a portrait of persistence. He survived Warner Bros. These similarities and contradictions suggest why the team of Humphrey Bogart and John Huston was so effective. Their work runs the emotional gamut and, however many ups and downs their personal lives took along the way, when they made movies together, they were in creative sync.

There is also a measure of personal discovery in what follows. I had the briefest of exchanges with both John Huston and Humphrey Bogart, the former directly, and the latter through his widow, Lauren Bacall. As a reporter, I had met Huston on two occasions. The first was in 1980 in the Plaza Hotel in New York when I stepped into the elevator to find a tall presence dressed in a white linen suit. Huston was in the city to do interviews for his just-published memoir, *An Open Book*. I stammered the usual banalities about how much I liked his work, he asked me to be sure to buy his book, and then we hit the lobby. Our second meeting was in summer 1987 in Newport, Rhode Island, where he was preparing to appear in the film that his son Danny was directing—*Mr. North*—and which he and writer Janet Roach had adapted from Thornton Wilder's novel, *Theophilus North*. His publicist, Ernie Anderson, had arranged with my newspaper, *The Boston Herald*, to give me full access to the production in exchange for running daily stories about it. Admittedly, some days were more interesting than others. Worse, Huston never made it to the set, because he was too ill. Dying, in fact.

On the day of my arrival, Ernie, who didn't drive and wore eyeglasses as thick as headlights, had me bring him to the rented home where Huston was ensconced on location. The large, level house was oddly devoid of rugs, for which I reasoned that anything on the floor would have hindered Huston's wheelchair and mobile oxygen tank from gliding around. We found him playing poker with actor Harry Dean Stanton, film editor Roberto Silvi, and producer Steven Haft. He wore a plain white T-shirt that draped formlessly over his narrow shoulders. He was, at the time, in the advanced stages of emphysema and was connected to an oxygen tank whose tubing snaked all around the rustic cabin. Hearing us enter, he laid his cards on the table, shook my hand, and wheezed a few perfunctory words about "how nice to meet you." I warranted that polite temporary smile that he flashed at people he knew he could dismiss. Ernie said a few words, Huston assured him softly that things were fine, and we were off. As soon as we got in the car, Ernie said, "He doesn't look well. He survived pneumonia and his fifth wife, and he doesn't look well."

Huston died during production. I broke the news to the world's press under my *Herald* byline. Later I revised and collected my location stories into a book, *Mr. Huston/Mr. North: Life, Death, and Making John Huston's Last Film*.

During this adventure I spent a far greater amount of time with Lauren Bacall, who was in the cast, although our encounters were cautious (on her part) and careful (on mine). I won't lie; we were polite to each other, but she didn't trust me. After all, I was a reporter. Even though Ernie vouched for me, Bacall's movie star self-preservation kicked in and our exchanges were confined to small talk and the occasional interview.

I wasn't the only person on the shoot whom she kept at a distance. One of the producers, thinking her to be a friend, called her "Lauren" which, as anybody knows, is not her first name. (It's Betty; I always called her Miss Bacall.) She even, I was told by someone who witnessed it, stuck her tongue out at me and flipped me the bird once as I walked some length in front of her. And it was fine with me because at least it meant she knew I was alive.

Throughout the following book I refer to John Huston as "Huston" and occasionally as "John" when I need to separate him from his father, Walter. I call Humphrey Bogart "Bogart" except when other people refer to him as "Bogie." This is the result of my contact with Bacall during that summer now nearly forty years ago. When she spoke of her late husband, she would say "Bogie and I did this . . ." or "Bogie always said . . ." I don't think there's anybody still around who knew Bogart well enough to call him Bogie, and I'll be damned if I'm going to pretend that I can.

—Nat Segaloff,
Los Angeles, California

PROLOGUE

On the Twentieth Century

Humphrey Bogart eyed the reporters with uncharacteristic apprehension. His twenty-three-year-old wife, Lauren Bacall, stood at his side, taking her cues from him. Hollywood's favorite acting couple was usually happy to see the press. They knew the fame game, they shared the same ribald humor (which never saw print, of course), no bullshit passed between them, and, if it did, the studio could clean it up. The newspaper boys admired Bogie's talent and honesty. But this time was different.

The setting wasn't a Warner Bros. soundstage, a function room at the Waldorf, or a booth at the Smokehouse grill across from the studio. Chicago's LaSalle Street Station wasn't any of the celebrity-friendly places where the stars hung out and reporters knew what was on and what was off the record. This was a dingy railroad depot where the Bogarts were connecting between New York's Twentieth Century Limited and the train for Los Angeles, heading for the shelter of the studio walls.

It was December 2, 1947. Two months earlier, on October 27, the Bogarts had made a very public visit to Washington, DC, with a score of other high-profile Hollywood elites. They had attended hearings by the House Un-American Activities Committee into alleged Communist influence in the movies. They were there to show support for their subpoenaed colleagues who were under suspicion as Reds. Now their own loyalty was being questioned. Bogart, shorter in person than he looked on the screen, compelled attention as he nervously read from a wire that had met him on the train.

"We went to Washington because I thought fellow Americans were being deprived of their Constitutional rights," he began, "and for that reason alone. That the trip was ill-advised, even foolish, I am very ready to admit. At the same time, it seemed the right thing to do. I have absolutely no use for communism nor for anyone who serves that philosophy. I am an American. And very likely, like a good many of you, sometimes a foolish and impetuous American." He stumbled over the word *impetuous* as if someone else had put it there, which they had: "We went in green and they beat our brains out."[1]

What had happened between October 27 and December 2 to frighten the man who had shot Major Strasse? The detective who had found the Maltese Falcon? The hero who had held off the German tank corps and uncovered Japanese plans to bomb the Panama Canal? What had made Humphrey Bogart go back on his principles and distance himself from his friends?

When one of those friends, John Huston, learned of Bogart's capitulation, he was shocked. After all, they had gone to Washington together and stood for the same freedoms—or so he thought. They had made three films together and would make three more over the next six years.

Or would they?

Humphrey Bogart and John Huston were more than friends, they were creative partners and inveterate provocateurs. Both men were key players in the heyday of the Warner Bros. studio and, later, in the burgeoning arena of independent production. They loved working together, drinking together, and giving Jack L. Warner a hard time together. Although Bogart was older than Huston, it's tempting to think that Huston, as one of his best directors, became a kind of surrogate father, as directors tend to do. This was not the case; as Lawrence Grobel, Huston's biographer, counters, "I don't think it went that far. John was too much of a prankster and mischief maker to be anyone's surrogate father." He then adds playfully, "Except maybe to me!"[2] Huston did, however, have the gifts of insight and manipulation, and he endlessly wielded them whenever he wanted to get something out of his friend, the movie star who got his pictures financed.

There have been enough books written singly on Bogart and Huston to fill a library. They had the kind of colorful personalities that were loved and loathed by the people who ran the studios. Each was talented in his own way, both were iconoclasts, and it's a good thing that they were united against the same system or else they might have found themselves at odds with one another (as they sometimes were anyway). On those occasions when there was friction between them, it was always for the good of the movie they were making.

Except for the Washington gambit.

Between films, they went their separate ways. "I didn't see very much of Bogie in Hollywood," Huston said. "He liked his own circle. He was a wonderful host, gave great parties. He didn't mix into the Hollywood circuit. Usually, we were kicking around the world or some other place together."[3]

That's why this book looks at their work through the lens of their personalities, histories, interests, and the noteworthy times they spent together when those moments entered the record. Yes, they used each other to get what they wanted, but it was a collaboration based on friendship, respect, and an awareness of each other's limitations. In other words, what counts is what's on the screen, and this is the story of how it got there.

CHAPTER 1

Becoming Bogie

Humphrey Bogart spent his life rebelling against the very kind of person he was born to be: a privileged, pampered, self-possessed member of the landed gentry. Even before he achieved stardom and the deference that comes with it, he enjoyed popping the bubbles of pretention that affected so many Hollywood egos. He abhorred phoniness, which grows freely in Hollywood, and took pride—which those who knew him confirmed—that he had none of it.

The well-born son of Belmont DeForest Bogart, a successful New York City surgeon, and Maud Humphrey, an even more successful advertising illustrator, he lived in stylish upper Manhattan and summered with his family in equally tony Seneca Point, near Willow Brook, New York. His parents were well-settled when they finally conceived him; Belmont was thirty-four and Maud was thirty-three. A few years later Humphrey was followed by sisters Catherine Elizabeth (Catty) and Frances (Pat).

Although Humphrey's Christmas Day 1899 birth date might lead to fanciful sentimentality, this was not an accessible emotion in the Bogart home. Comfortably old-line Republican in the way that the upper crust was expected to live and vote at the turn of the century, the Bogarts' outward gentility masked disturbing private undercurrents. Maud and Belmont drank and, in the days before morphine became a controlled substance, both were driven to addiction: he to quell the pain from an improperly set leg following a carriage accident, and she as palliative for a chronic skin condition. Even if neither parent had been chemically distracted, the fashionable home at 245 West 103rd Street might as well have been an ice box. Dr. Bogart was wedded to his practice, Maud was devoted to her career, and neither had time for their children. Often they would go off on trips, leaving Humphrey and his sisters in the care of servants who, according to reports, mistreated them.[1]

This is not to say that Bogie (he inherited the nickname from his father) was ignored. Far from it; he was doted on, but only in charcoal, as his mother's model for the baby food advertisements she drew. From infant to toddler, he was the face of Mellin's Food—not Gerber, as was often reported—a British company that produced dietary supplements for babies and the elderly. But when it came to the closeness he might have craved had he known it existed, there was none. The Bogarts were a career family of workaholic alcoholics. It may be a casual observation, but among Bogart's major film credits, it's hard to think of any in which he played a family man, and only one—*Beat the Devil*—in which he was married. Even his personal life, until he met his fourth wife, Lauren Bacall, and had children with her, could hardly be called domestic.

As was expected of his social class, Bogart attended the Trinity School in New York where he struggled to fit in, even as a boy of eight and nine. He lived for his summers in Seneca Point where he enjoyed sailing and being on the water, and it depressed him when his family decided to leave the Point for Fire Island when he was a teen. By then he was destined for Phillips Academy Andover, and it was only through his father's connections that the elegant prep school accepted him despite his poor Trinity grades. The legacy admission didn't help; he lasted two years and was asked to leave for a combination of academic and behavioral reasons.

It always pained Maud Humphrey, who had studied with James McNeill Whistler, that her son never went to college, but it didn't seem to bother the boy. After leaving Andover he toyed with a business career and did a little writing but showed scant passion for anything. (Such youthful indulgences as "gap year" hadn't been invented yet.) With little to command his time—and reaching the age when he could do so without parents' consent—he enlisted in the United States Navy in May 1918, more than a year after America entered the Great War. He saw everything but battle; on January 8, 1918, the first armistice was signed between Germany and Russia, and ongoing peace talks continued through November 9. This meant that young Bogart would spend his time ferrying servicemen back to America from Europe aboard the USS *Leviathan*.

It was on one of these crossings that his life was changed by an event that didn't happen. As an actor, Bogart would become known for a slight lisp that resulted from a partially paralyzed upper lip. Various stories were floated over the years about the cause of this condition; a favorite of the Warner Bros. publicity department and his friend Joe Hyams was that it came from a splinter blown into his face during a U-boat attack. Another was that his father had once beaten him. A third was an assault by a captured German prisoner. More likely (according to his biographers A. M. Sperber and Eric Lax) it happened during a fight in a speakeasy during prohibition. Whatever the cause, it gave Bogart a distinctive speech pattern that would not only enhance his tough guy image but has kept impressionists busy for the better part of a century.

Although studio publicity claimed he was a disruptive sailor, Bogart was given an honorable discharge in June 1919 with the rank of petty officer, second class after which he returned to the walk-in freezer that was his home.[2] By then both his parents had been slowed to uselessness by alcohol and other drugs. Bogart himself was no stranger to alcohol which, on January 17, 1920, became outlawed under the 18th Amendment. Considering how many speakeasies he would enter for his movie gangster roles, it's easy to believe he gained experience in the real thing during the Great Experiment.

Acting was not as great a passion for Bogart then as was sailing, yet he was drawn to performing almost by accident. Looking for work, he was connected by a mutual friend with theatrical producer William A. Brady. The mutual friend happened to be Brady's daughter, Alice, an actress who had begun in silent films and who would survive the transition to talkies. Bogart was given the job of stage manager in one of Brady's plays and was asked to double as a replacement actor. His roles were not auspicious; as a handsome but bland young man he was invariably cast as the juvenile whose major moment was coming on stage with a racquet and asking, "Tennis, anyone?" to button the scene. In these early days, he sometimes professed that acting was a less-than-noble profession, an opinion shared by his earliest critics. "He really loathed being an actor," recalled fellow thespian Rose Hobart. "He really thought it was sissy—it wasn't something you did if you were a man."[3] Over the years, his acting, his opinion, and his reviews vastly improved.

In 1922 he met actress Helen Menken while he was stage managing a touring company of Alice Brady's play *Drifting*. Helen was a last-minute replacement for Alice, who had gone into labor, and Bogart had his hands full just dealing with the production let alone recasting the lead. Opening night didn't go well; the curtain went up but some of the sets fell down, and Menken lost her temper at stage manager Bogart. In return, he lost his temper and kicked her in the butt. Once she stopped crying, they started dating.

There was some deceit involved. Helen was a friend of critic Alexander Woollcott who was known for unashamedly championing the careers of players he liked. Bogart may have hoped that Woollcott's affection for Helen would extend to him. It was a long courtship—four years—until they finally married on May 20, 1926, at the Gramercy Park Hotel in New York. The wedding did not go well. Menken's parents were hearing-impaired and so was the minister, who insisted on speaking the ceremony and simultaneously signing it. This upset Menken, who dodged the reporters who had been invited to cover the event. The marriage itself fared no better as her star ascended on Broadway and her husband Humphrey's never ignited.

While living in New York, Bogart did what many out of work actors did in the early talking picture days: they made movies. For Paramount he traveled to their Astoria, Long Island studio to film the short *The Dancing Town* (1928) as little more than an extra, and to Brooklyn for a more substantial role in *Broadway's Like That* (1929) for Vitaphone (Warner Bros.). His costars in that endeavor were torch singer Ruth Etting and a future Warner Bros. colleague, Joan Blondell. Subsequently signed to a Fox contract, he made a few features such as John Ford's *Up the River* (1930) with Spencer Tracy and Claire Luce. He was hired as voice coach for silent actor Charles Farrell on *The Man Who Came Back* (1931) but raised no eyebrows at the studio as an actor and was soon dropped.

The Bogart-Menken union lasted a year and a half.

In April 1928 he married another actress, Mary Philips, between her matinee and evening performances in *Saturday's Children*. The young marrieds pursued their separate careers, though she had more success than he, but as the Depression struck, times became tough for them both. For a while he augmented her paychecks by playing chess in an arcade window for a dollar a game. In early September 1934, Bogart was summoned to his father's bedside. Belmont's health had steadily declined to the point where he had become an invalid. Maud had become his caretaker, a position she resented. At the Hospital for Ruptured and Crippled in New York City, Belmont died in his son's arms and the young man found himself surprised at the affection he suddenly felt for the man. This emotion was not shared by his mother, and an estrangement developed between Maud and Humphrey. Belmont died in debt and Bogart vowed to pay off every penny of it from his earnings—as soon as he had some.[4]

Bogart was now fully committed to acting, but as he neared age thirty-five, he could no longer pass as a juvenile, and casting became a challenge. Rescue arrived when playwright Robert Sherwood recalled seeing him in a stage production and thought he would be perfect for the role of an escaped killer in his new play *The Petrified Forest* that was set to open at the Broadhurst Theatre in January 1935. Director Arthur Hopkins agreed, as did producer Gilbert Miller and star/producer Leslie Howard. Wearing a three-day stubble, spitting insults and threats, and holding the patrons of an Arizona desert café hostage, Bogart's Duke Mantee was a sensation. The play cast Howard as philosopher-traveler Alan Squier who passes through an isolated roadside diner and falls for waitress Gaby Maple (Peggy Conklin) who shares with him her dreams for escape. By the final curtain, Squier has financed Gaby's dreams by having Mantee kill him so she can claim Squier's insurance money.

The confined set, the rising dramatic tension, and the downbeat yet affirmative ending made the play a 197-performance hit and earned positive reviews for everyone, including Bogart. Although Mantee had barely ten pages of dialogue in the entire play, he spent much of it seated on stage holding a machine gun, ready to fire it at any moment, commanding attention when he wasn't saying a word. Both the play and the lead actors came to Hollywood's attention, and when Jack Warner bought the film rights, Bogart seemed poised at a second chance at a film career, if not stardom. Not so fast.

It has become well known that Leslie Howard, who shared film rights to the play with Sherwood, Miller, and Hopkins, was adamant that they were not for sale unless Bogart was hired to play the movie's Mantee. Jack Warner turned a deaf ear and offered the role to his studio's resident gangster, Edward G. Robinson, and the part of Gaby to Bette Davis. Even had Howard consented, it would have created a billing problem in that he would have received top billing above Davis and Robinson; Robinson, who had become a star with *Little Caesar*, refused to take third position. Howard resolved the matter and forced Warner's hand when he cabled Jack Warner from Scotland and told him, "No Bogart, no deal."

The Petrified Forest rolled November 26, 1934, and came in two weeks late on February 19, 1935, with delays attributed to everyone except Humphrey

Bogart. His performance in the rushes, however, did not win him a studio contract. Not until the film previewed off the charts in early 1936 did Warner Bros. finally offer him a seven-year agreement that started off at $550 a week and increased in twenty-six-week options that could escalate to $1,250 a week by its end. These were hardly king-making numbers but, coming out of the Great Depression, they were all that the notoriously parsimonious Warner was prepared to offer, and Bogart signed.

He might not have bothered. Once the paperwork went through, he was assigned to a relentless string of B-pictures that fed the studio's factory production schedule but did nothing to enhance his craft. Besides, the estrangement from his wife, who continued to live and work in New York, was maddening. "This is the first time I've really been able to support you," he told her. "We could never afford to have children before. [Come] here and let's start a family. Anyway, the play isn't any good and you're wrong in it." Bogart was right on both counts—Mary's play lasted seventy-two performances and she was miscast—but it hardly mattered. By this time, he had become attracted to another woman: the fiery actress Mayo Methot.

Mayo and Bogart were such a poorly kept secret that Mary Philips heard about them clear across the country. Complicating matters was that Mayo was more formally known as Mrs. Percy T. Morgan, the wife of a California restaurateur. She owed her early stardom to her discovery by George M. Cohan and had grown into a sassy presence onscreen as well as a violent alcoholic offscreen. She had first met Bogart in 1936 while acting in the Warners film *Marked Woman*, a Bette Davis vehicle in which Bogart played a crusading district attorney (do the movies have any other kind?) trying to bust the rackets. All their friends knew about the affair and reasoned that it would be just a matter of time before their spouses did, too, predicting that both marriages would make way for a single new one. It finally happened on August 11, 1938, when Bogart and Philips divorced. It wasn't a fait accompli that he would marry Mayo, but it was either that or give up films and go back to New York and stay wedded to the far more successful Mary. Bogart and Mayo married on August 20, 1938.

The marriage between Bogart and Warner Bros. was likewise unstable. Although the publicity department loved him for his affability with reporters, the front office wasn't sure what to do with him, and their scattershot casting attempts demonstrate their uncertainty.[5] There weren't many roles for unshaven escapees like Duke Mantee, not with the likes of Edward G. Robinson, James Cagney, and George Raft ahead of him. His passing resemblance to real-life gangster John Dillinger may have informed the studio's casting instincts. Bogart played all-purpose mobsters (*Bullets and Ballots*, 1936), racists (*Black Legion*, 1937), prisoners (*San Quentin*, 1937), and even a cowboy (*The Oklahoma Kid*, 1939). He was a standout under William Wyler's direction in *Dead End* (1937), made on loan to Samuel Goldwyn, and returned to Warners to play scoundrels in the more successful crime films *Angels with Dirty Faces* (1938) and *The Roaring Twenties* (1939). In the four years following *The Petrified Forest*, Bogart appeared in an astonishing twenty-eight films, none of them as a significant lead.

He did not do so without griping. Before the Screen Actors Guild secured protection for its members, actors (not to mention crews) were often required to work six-day weeks. Bogart, among others, complained to studio management that it was physically impossible for anyone to deliver the goods when they were overworked; from typical 6:00 A.M. calls, production frequently continued well into the night. Nevertheless, at a time when stars such as Bette Davis and James Cagney were taking suspensions rather than appear in unworthy scripts, Bogart kept his eyes open for opportunity, strategically distancing himself from studio infighting.

His patience paid off with *High Sierra* (1940). The novel by W. R. Burnett concerned an aging gangster who is induced to pull off one last job which, of course, goes wrong. The plot, seen by current standards, sounds beyond hackneyed, but it still had shelf life in 1939 when Jack Warner sent it to George Raft. Raft, whose taste in scripts was famously myopic, passed on it because he didn't want to die at the end. Then Warner gave it to Paul Muni, who rejected it as well, even though, or perhaps because, he had risen to stardom playing a gangster in *Scarface* a decade earlier. Muni's arrogance so angered J. L. that the mogul fired him. James Cagney, John Garfield, and Edward G. Robinson also turned down the role of doomed gangster Roy "Mad Dog" Earle, not wanting sloppy thirds, fourths, and fifths respectively. Almost as a last resort, the script was assigned to Bogart.

Bogart was pleased to land *High Sierra*, even if his leading lady, Ida Lupino, got top billing. It was an "A" picture with the dynamic Raoul Walsh as director. The two men had worked together in 1931 on *The Man Who Came Back*—the picture on which Bogart had been Charles Farrell's voice coach—but this was now the major leagues, and he would be acting, not coaching. The only question was some guy hanging around the set watching, a tall fellow by the name of Huston. Warner writers were usually restricted to the writers building where they would hide while the director mangled their words on the soundstage.

Bogart and Huston were not total strangers. They had developed a nodding acquaintance on *The Amazing Dr. Clitterhouse*, in which Bogart played a gangster whom sociology professor Edward G. Robinson studied for academic purposes. The script had originally been written by the book's author, the prolific W. R. Burnett, but production supervisor Hal Wallis felt it needed a polish, and he turned it over to Huston.

Huston wanted to be a director and, given that Walsh was one of the best, the lanky, brooding Irishman decided to watch him work. *High Sierra* was shot in Lake Arrowhead, Mount Whitney, and other scenic California locales with interiors filmed at the Burbank studio. During lunch breaks, Huston and Bogart would go to the Lakeside Country Club, less than a mile away, and among the cocktails a friendship began to develop between them. Roy Earle was yet another gangster role, but in Huston's talented writer's hands and Walsh's forthright direction it was rich enough that Bogart could allow the man's decency to leak through Earle's hardened, unshaven façade.[6] It was solid work and it alerted Warner that Bogart could carry a picture.

As for Huston, unsure of his future as a screenwriter, he found himself in New York in spring 1940 where he directed the play *A Passenger to Bali* by Ellis St. Joseph. It opened March 14 at the Ethel Barrymore Theatre. The fact that his father, Walter, was in the cast might have had something to do with his landing the assignment, but it didn't help the production and it closed in two days.

When *High Sierra* premiered to high acclaim at the end of 1940 and went into general release in January 1941, Bogart was celebrated as an emerging star. This drove a wedge between him and Mayo, whose lack of progress as an actress embittered her against her husband's ascent. Their marriage had been unraveling, but it was still in place during filming. Drinking was also an issue. While his was recreational, hers had become profound, and she grew suspicious of his long absences on location. Her knowledge of the illicit way in which they had begun their romance drove her to believe that he was cheating on her. Their discord was no secret to their friends who called them "the battling Bogarts" but who were powerless to intervene.

Their marriage survived until May 1945 with details of its bellicosity occasionally hitting the gossip columns. Meanwhile, the friendship between Bogie and Huston caught fire and the two men searched for a film they could make together.

CHAPTER 2

The Impossible John Huston

With all that John Huston did in his long and productive life, it's a wonder he found time to make movies. It could also be said that movies were what allowed him to pursue his other goals. In his lifetime he was also a fine artist, an art collector, a club boxer, a big game hunter, an equestrian, a soldier in the Mexican army, and even a dancer. Like so many other filmmakers from Hollywood's golden age, he brought actual life experience to the screen rather than a rehash of adolescent pop culture nostalgia.

His father was Walter Huston, a Vaudevillian when he could find stage work and a civil engineer when he couldn't. His mother, Rhea Gore, was an editor and sportswriter. Born John Marcellus Huston on August 5, 1906, he was their only child. Although he arrived in Nevada, Missouri, he left town with his parents when only a few months of age as the family bounced around the country from job to job.

At the age of nine his parents divorced, and he remained with his mother. Three years later, he was diagnosed with an enlarged heart and nephritis, and his mother moved to Arizona and confined him to bed, monitored his diet, and prepared both of them for his early death. Being bedridden did not sit well with young John.

"I'd sneak out at night," he recalled. "I'd been kept in bed. I remember one time I was whistling, and the doctor told me I mustn't whistle, it's an exertion. Whistling! That's how bad it all was. It was unbearable."[1]

Figuring that the end was inevitable, he decided one night to flout death. "I'd been swimming in the Arizona Canal which ran through Phoenix. I'd go out at night when no one was there and go swimming. They had locks on the canal, and when they were irrigating, why they'd open these locks and they'd be[come] waterfalls. And one night swimming, I was swept over one of these waterfalls. And went under water for a little while and came out. I discovered it was great sport. So I went up on the bank and went over the waterfall again. I had nothing to lose, God knows. Finally, there was the doctor who said I should remember not to walk around the block, and I found I could go in swimming. I went down and swam with other people there and I went over the waterfall and then everybody began going over the waterfall. The doctor didn't know about it."[2]

Not long afterward it was discovered that the diagnosis had been in error: his heart was large in preparation for him to grow to six-foot-two, and the nephritis was hereditary and non-life-threatening. But by then John was inoculated against fear, and his life would be spent tempting love, death, poverty, fame, and failure until it ended at eighty-one. Without seeking greatness, he became a great man as well as a greatly flawed one.

After Walter and Rhea's divorce, John managed to stay close to each of them, albeit separately. He was bored at boarding school and, on vacations, traveled to sporting events with his mother and from city to city with his father on the vaudeville circuit. These diverse adventures supplied more than sightseeing; thanks to his parents' disparate lives, he got to sample a range of arts, sports, and the colorful characters associated with such endeavors. Staying with his father in New York in the 1920s, he gleaned knowledge of the craft of acting as well as its uncertainties.[3] John was tempted to try a few stage roles and performed in two plays for the Provincetown Players: *Ruint*, by Hatcher Hughes, that ran April and

May 1925, and *Adam Solitaire*, by Emjo Basshe, that opened and closed in November of that same year.

He had found success in his late teens as a writer, publishing occasional stories in H. L. Mencken's highly regarded literary journal, *American Mercury*. He was able to afford to live because he and his father made a deal: Walter would support John if John agreed to give him half his future earnings. How long this arrangement lasted is not known. It did, however, enable John to take his first trip to Mexico. Stuck in New York and bored, Walter told him to get out of town for a few months. John decided to head to Mexico and, with a $500 stipend from Dad, he did just that, sailing to Vera Cruz where the post-revolutionary poverty was crushing. Taking the train to Mexico City, he was accompanied by soldiers who were stationed on the train in case of attack by marauding bandits. He later dramatized the possibility of a train attack in *The Treasure of the Sierra Madre* after learning from the soldiers that the trains before and after his had in fact been assaulted.

While in Mexico, he took up dressage and became an excellent horseman. When he ran out of money, his trainer offered him an honorary post in the Mexican Army, and he became Lieutenant Huston. During this period, he wrote a play (title unknown). When the movies learned to talk, he moved back to Los Angeles where playwrights and journalists were valued as dialogue writers for the newly invented talkies. At the same time, it was also the Great Depression, and studios were cutting back on budgets and payroll as audiences fell away. Huston spent six months working for Samuel Goldwyn Productions, where his talent was not utilized, then followed his father, who had left a rapidly disappearing vaudeville for roles at Universal Pictures.

Universal was in the throes of a corporate upheaval after the studio's founder, Carl Laemmle, turned over production to his son, Carl Jr. (known as Junior Laemmle). Junior momentarily saved the studio by adding horror films such as *Dracula*, *Frankenstein*, and *The Invisible Man* to the company's release schedule to augment their bread-and-butter, low-budget westerns. Huston wrote dialogue for *The Storm* (1930), *A House Divided* (1931), and *Murders in the Rue Morgue* (1932), the first two of which were directed by William (Willy) Wyler, who was likewise getting his start. The two men became lifelong friends.

Back in October 1926 Huston had wed for the first of five times. This one was to Dorothy Jeanne Harvey, a young woman he had seen in a school production of *Prunella* by Laurence Housman and Harley Granville-Barker. He found her merely attractive at the time, but nothing more, and set off building his career. He met her again through friends and they became besotted with each other, deciding on an immediate private wedding. John was twenty; Dorothy's age goes unreported. Neither set of parents approved when the couple naively informed them the next day, but Walter sent them occasional stipends as there was never enough money to suffice. At first it was romantic; they took a cottage in Malibu where Dorothy would read John the classics while John drew portraits of her. When writing and acting didn't provide income, he brought in money club fighting until he was beaten so decisively by one opponent that he gave up that knockabout profession.

The marriage was tested by John's infidelity and Dorothy's drinking. Rather than face the burden, Huston returned to Mexico. When he got back to California, nothing had changed between him and Dorothy, so he arranged for her to stay with a friend of his in England in hopes that she could resume writing and curtail drinking. Instead, the opposite occurred. They divorced on August 18, 1933. In retrospect, he wrote that he thought he could never again be as happy as he was when they were first married, adding that she was the first woman with whom he ever made love for whom he had actual affection.[4]

On September 25, 1933, a month after his divorce, Huston was involved in a motor accident in Los Angeles in which he struck and killed a woman, Tosca Roulien. He had picked up a hitchhiker and was distracted in conversation when Roulien ran into the street between parked cars and Huston, uncharacteristically sober at the time, ran her down. He claimed to police that he had been blinded by oncoming headlights. He escaped grand jury indictment for vehicular manslaughter, but the gossip columnists picked it up. Only the intervention of MGM's Louis B. Mayer, for whom Walter was under contract at the time, minimized the extent of the newspaper coverage. (In those days the studios controlled the press, if not also the police.) John was subsequently sued by Roulien's husband, Raul, and settled by paying $5,000 for her funeral expenses. It was later determined that the traffic signals had, in fact, been improperly placed so as to block a driver's view, and an accident was ultimately inevitable, but his culpability haunted him forever.

Lesley Black, an attractive Irish lass, became Huston's second wife on October 3, 1937. Taken by a friend to see a production of a political play called *The Lonely Man* in Chicago, he was introduced to her by that friend and was smitten.[5] Shortly, Black left Chicago for San Francisco but, when she returned to the Windy City en route to Ireland, Huston intervened and proposed. The couple moved to Hollywood where Huston was hired as a writer at Warner Bros. His first major assignment was the screenplay for *Jezebel*. Three previous writers had labored on the script without pleasing its director, Huston's friend Willy Wyler, who asked him to add his touch. The story of a self-possessed Southern belle in antebellum New Orleans was the studio's compensation to their star, Bette Davis, for losing the role of Scarlett O'Hara to Vivien Leigh in *Gone with the Wind*. In those days the studios played fast and loose with writing credits, but if Huston's last billing as writer is accurate, it suggests that it was his fine hand that made the film camera-ready.

Meanwhile, his marriage withered as he spent time at work and Lesley gave birth to a premature child who died. Their union endured almost to the end of World War II; while John was off making documentaries, Lesley filed for divorce. It was granted on April 7, 1945.

Huston thrived as a Warner Bros. contract writer, working on loan-out to Samuel Goldwyn for uncredited rewrites on *Wuthering Heights* (1939).[6] Back at Warners he shared credit on *Juarez* (1939), the historical drama starring Paul Muni as the Mexican president who wrested his country from domination by German Emperor Maximilian in the 1860s. Working with writer-producer Wolfgang Reinhardt and historian Aeneas MacKenzie, the men had a cordial collaboration. Huston delivered a complex script that Warner production executive Hal Wallis deemed the best he had ever read. Muni, however, counted his lines and found them to be fewer than Brian Ahern's, the man who would play Maximilian. Muni demanded rewrites and the film's director, William Dieterle, capitulated. Huston was outraged, but Muni was the studio's prestige star and he prevailed. It was this incident that fueled Huston's desire to direct his own screenplays, something that was simply not done in the studio system of the 1930s. Working on *Juarez* did, however, codify a love of Mexico that would surface throughout Huston's life and career. It also alerted his agent, Paul Kohner, to get the studio to agree to let Huston direct a film as a condition of his upcoming contract renewal.

But *High Sierra* came first.

"With the exception of *Little Caesar*," John Huston wrote Hal Wallis, "all of [W. R.] Burnett has suffered badly in screen translation." He promised that his draft of Burnett's *High Sierra* "could be made into a fine and outstanding picture."[7] To that end, deeming the novel already film-worthy, he skipped writing the traditional treatment* and plunged directly into the screenplay.[8]

As noted earlier, the story follows an imprisoned gangster, Roy Earle, who is freed from the pen on a bribe from a mob boss so he and the boss's gang can pull off a jewel robbery at a mountain resort. Along with the gang

---

* A treatment is more than a story condensation. It is a narrative describing action and some dialogue as though the film is being watched in time-present.

is a woman named Marie (Ida Lupino) who falls for Earle even though he ignores her. Along the way, Earle is drawn to a different woman who has a clubfoot. He underwrites her medical treatment, but she does not reciprocate his attention. The robbery goes awry but Earle and Marie escape along with a dog named Pard. Police close in on the other gang members, one of whom identifies Earle. Earle sends Marie away for safety but is himself identified and pursued by police into the mountains. The police summon Marie to talk him into surrendering, but Pard draws him into the open where he is shot and killed.[9]

Huston tied together these seemingly diverse threads into a remarkable story of misplaced affection, betrayal, the intervention of fate, and the passing of an era. Meanwhile, the audience appeal was undeniable: it has a disabled girl (Velma), an unrequited love (Marie), and even a dog. Naturally, George Raft was offered the role. Bogart, recognizing the possibilities of showing the soft side of a man nicknamed "Mad Dog," talked Raft out of taking it by stressing that the character was "just rushing toward death" and would die at the end. Raft fell for it, though it's doubtful that he had the talent to pull it off had he held fast. The slow but sure development of a romance between Earle and Marie, his victimization by the fence to whom he expected to sell his booty, his shock at learning that one mob boss had been replaced by another, and the grim belief that death is preferable to returning to prison—all of these elements were kept in balance between Huston's writing, Walsh's focused direction, and Bogart's understanding of the highly conflicted character.

Before *High Sierra* was released, Warner assigned Bogart to make *The Wagons Roll at Night*, a tepid drama in which Bogart played an unscrupulous circus owner. Written by Fred Niblo Jr. and Barry Trivers, it was designed to cash in on the strong notices Bogart had received for 1940's story about truckers, *They Drive by Night*. When *High Sierra* came out, the praise heaped upon it enabled Huston to call in his directing marker with Jack Warner. Warner and Hal Wallis agreed, figuring that Huston would make his debut with an artistic bomb and skulk in shame back to the writers building. Huston had different ideas. He decided to make his first film the third version of an old property that the studio already owned and had twice flopped. But this time, he would make it right. It was Dashiell Hammett's *The Maltese Falcon*, and he wanted his new best friend Humphrey Bogart to play the hero, Sam Spade.

CHAPTER 3

The Ornery Jack L. Warner

Jack Leonard Warner (born Jacob Wonskolaser) was not a sophisticated man. He was also not a fool, although he often played one for strategic business purposes. A mediocre singer who fancied himself a virtuoso, a teller of lousy jokes at which those in his employ felt compelled to laugh, and a vulgarian (Joan Crawford once said he should be fed out of a trough), he—like his fellow founding Hollywood moguls—knew what the public wanted before the public knew they wanted it.[1] Love him or hate him, and many people did both, he added immeasurably to American popular culture.

He wasn't alone. To date, no one has been able to explain how the Warners, Mayers, Cohns, Laemmles, Goldwyns, Laskys, and their brethren did it—certainly not today's Ivy League, Wall Street, risk-avoidant executives who use focus groups and data analysis in place of guts and instinct. Neal Gabler, in his landmark book, *An Empire of Their Own*, posits that, when the Eastern European Jewish immigrants were blocked by antisemitism from taking part in the American dream when they got to California, they invented an idealized America in their films that the world came to believe was the real thing, and they called it Hollywood.[2] Despite being shunned socially, they benefited so much financially that they became politically conservative, essentially joining their oppressors, routinely rejecting projects that spotlighted the very shortcomings they had faced when they first came to America. (The rare exception to this reactionary ethic was Darryl F. Zanuck, whose tenure as Warner Bros.'s and then as Fox's production head, created a string of socially relevant pictures. Notably, Zanuck was a US-born Protestant.)

Budgets were always a consideration at Warner Bros. where financial disaster was always one or two flops away. In those days, pictures had to go into profits routinely from the box offices where people laid down their ticket money. There was no television, home video, action figures, or other ancillary markets to bail out losses. In what is now called the Golden Age of Hollywood (the 1930s), feature films seldom cost more than $1 million, unlike today's budgets of $200+ million just for the production and another $50 million for marketing. But it was still a struggle, quarter by quarter.[3]

In other words, guys like Jack L. Warner had to keep their fingers firmly up the pulse of the public. Like the other moguls, somehow, in the long run, he had a sense of what worked. He seldom mixed with the rabble (except at sneak previews), but he knew what they wanted because what they wanted was what he wanted.

The brothers Warner were as diverse as the films they made. Sam, Harry, Albert, and baby Jack had begun in the exhibition end of the business at the turn of the twentieth century. Their father, Benjamin Wonskolaser, a peddler, brought the four boys and eight other children to America from Krasnosielc, Poland, in 1883. Arriving in Baltimore, Maryland, they roamed throughout the northeast United States and lower Canada (Jack was born in London, Ontario, on August 2, 1892), eventually settling in Youngstown, Ohio. Here the boys became enamored of movies shown in the Nickelodeons that were then popping up throughout the country. In 1903 they went into the theatre business by selling Benjamin's gold watch and his faithful horse, Bob. Brother Sam managed to find a used primitive kinetoscope projector and, with his brothers' help, installed it in the Cascade Theatre in New Castle, Pennsylvania. Their sister Rose played piano to accompany the films, which were obtained from regional distribution offices called "exchanges." When audiences refused to leave the auditorium to make way for the next wave of patrons, eleven-year-old Jack would sing at them (badly) until they fled into the street. He never lost his love of singing, much to the distress of employees who could not flee.

For frères Warner as for other early filmmakers the hypnotic allure of flickering images soon gave way to a fascination with the money the images brought in. It didn't escape them that people paid cash up front to see the show and couldn't demand a refund if they didn't like what they saw (this has not changed in 130 years). It soon dawned on the brothers that the real money wasn't the literal nickels and dimes earned showing films, it was in making and distributing the pictures themselves. Doing this, however, involved more than financial risk. The Motion Picture Patents Company, a trust formed by Thomas A. Edison, controlled all the equipment and had ways of intimidating anyone who refused to rent from them, including sending thugs to harass and beat people and damage their non-Edison cameras. This drove the Warners, as it did other enterprising independents, to California to escape the reach of Edison's process servers and, in some cases, his sharp-shooting thugs.[4] They opened an office in Culver City in 1918 and, that year, produced their first hit, *My Four Years in Germany*, from the 1917 memoir by American Ambassador James W. Gerard. Its success financed other productions including a string of twenty-seven films starring Rin-Tin-Tin, a German shepherd rescued by American GIs during the first World War. Many of these were written by Darryl F. Zanuck, himself newly arrived from Wahoo, Nebraska, who quickly rose through the Warner Bros. ranks.

In 1923 the entity widely known as Warner Brothers Pictures was formed with Harry in New York as the president, Sam and Jack running the studio in California, and Albert as treasurer (and peacemaker between Jack and the rest of the family). Everything was possible and nothing was certain. Said one of the brothers, probably Albert, the treasurer, no doubt apocryphally, "When we started, we owed two thousand dollars and were considered a failure. Now we owe two million dollars and are considered a success."

Like most immigrants, the Warner brothers wanted respectability. For the first filmmakers, prestige came from the legitimate theatre. It was tough getting successful stage material for the movies. For one thing, theatre was talk, and movies were pictures. For another, stage actors considered movies a professional comedown, if not an outright disgrace, and wouldn't appear in them. Although their dog pictures were paying the bills, the Warners wanted more. The breakthrough came in 1923 when Jack persuaded stage impresario David Belasco to sell him the film rights to *Girl of the Golden West*, a potboiler about a young woman who gives herself to the town sheriff to save the life of the cowboy she truly loves. This marked the company's arrival.

But they were still just another studio turning out pictures as the twenties roared on. The existing gaggle of struggling film companies began congealing into what became the studio system. Smaller companies faded as bigger, wiser, or luckier firms survived. Eventually major studios emerged such as Metro (MGM wasn't formed until 1924), Paramount (founded in 1912), and Universal (1915), which was a consolidation of nearly a dozen independent companies. By this time such long-forgotten studios as Selig, Essanay, Mutual, Keystone, Lubin, Vitagraph, and Biograph had vanished.

Jack Warner saw the sea change throughout the 1920s and didn't want to be swept away in the tide. Moved by brother Sam's fascination with technology in the blossoming medium, he urged all his brothers to back the experimental Vitaphone system of talking pictures. This came to fruition on October 6, 1927, with the debut of *The Jazz Singer* with music, dialogue, and talking on separate synchronized discs. (The previous year had seen a dry run with *Don Juan* featuring music and sound effects only.) *The Jazz Singer* was advertised as "Warner Bros. Supreme Triumph," but there was no triumph for Jack, Harry, and Albert: days before the film opened, Sam died of a heart attack, and his brothers were at his funeral instead of the premiere of the breakthrough film he nurtured.

Soon all Hollywood was converting to talking pictures with most studios using the more dependable sound-on-film system developed by RCA (Photophone) and Fox (Movietone). As the first company out of the gate, however, Warner Bros. dominated the industry. (They, too, switched over to sound-on-film by 1931.)

The Great Depression didn't hit Hollywood at first; the public needed escapism so much in 1929 that they found a way to scrounge 35¢ cents to see a show. When the fallout arrived, the studios' first move was to cut ticket prices by a dime in hopes of making them more affordable.[5] When that failed to compensate for losses, studio grosses began falling and staff cutbacks were ordered. After President Roosevelt declared a bank holiday on March 6, 1933, Warner Bros. joined Fox, RKO, and Paramount in cutting everyone's salary by fifty percent. At Warner Bros., where Darryl F. Zanuck was head of production, he halved his $5,000 weekly paycheck out of solidarity with his staff and assured them that their cuts would be restored once the studio was back on its feet. When FDR reopened the banks on March 13, Jack and Harry Warner kept the cuts in place for their employees but not for management. Unable to reverse their morale-crushing decision, on April 15, Zanuck quit.[6]

Zanuck's noisy departure set the stage for a feud between Jack and Harry Warner that was settled only on Harry's death in 1958. Jack's relationship with labor was also combative. In the years before unions, it was standard practice for studios to work not only on weekdays but half-day on Saturdays. In the late 1930s there was an effort to organize labor, but the advent of World War II stalled the movement, though not the passions behind it, in solidarity with the war effort.[7]

Like many illiterate or semiliterate people, Jack L. Warner didn't trust writers. He famously called those in his employ "schmucks with Underwoods" and continued the practice, which was rife in the pre-Writers Guild era, of having multiple writers work on the same project at the same time, unbeknownst to each other. In theory, this would enable the director to pick and choose the best of everything; in practice it meant that the material was wildly unrelated and scenes did not mesh into the same picture.

And yet look at the films that were made under Warner's reign.

Warner hired John Huston as a fourth writer on *Jezebel*, perhaps at the urging of William Wyler, the film's director, who had worked with Huston at Universal and knew of his talent. Huston and Warner developed a begrudging respect for each other. "There was a funny, childish candor to the man," Huston wrote in his memoirs. "He was never guarded in anything he said; words seemed to escape from him unthinkingly. He was accused—and there may be something to it—of playing the fool. He was anything but pretentious, and seemed to be constantly laughing at himself, but he was certainly a canny, astute individual when it came to his own interests."[8]

At least Jack got along better with Huston than he did with Harry. The brothers' relationship became strained as the years wore on. Harry took pride in community service and in helping others; Jack mainly helped himself and any public honors he won were arranged by the studio publicity department. Family and studio workers for years recalled the time when Harry, wielding a lead pipe, chased Jack through the studio streets shouting, "I'll get you for this, you son-of-a-bitch." The precise reason is lost to time, but Milton Sperling wrote that he found himself the truce-maker between his uncle and father-in-law. "I'd say, 'listen, you're brothers, and you're trying to kill each other. But you're killing the studio instead.' So I told him, 'Harry, why don't you go into a kind of quasi-retirement and not come to the studio?'"[9] Harry did just that, but Jack screwed him anyway when he later sold the studio out from under his brothers in a stock deal that benefitted only himself.

This was the backstory of the man who ran the studio and controlled the lives of those who worked for him, among them John Huston and Humphrey Bogart. Jack keenly watched the returns and the notices on *High*

Sierra. They were strong enough to open his mind to letting the two men work together, but the timing would have to be right. While Huston took his time searching for a project to direct, Warner filled Bogart's schedule by assigning him to *The Wagons Roll at Night*. When Huston finally decided on a property, Warner and production chief Hal Wallis gritted their teeth and prepared for failure.

They should have listened to a little birdie. A little black birdie.

CHAPTER 4
The Black Bird

Writers didn't become directors in the heyday of the studio system; they were too valuable chained to their typewriters. Preston Sturges was the first exception. He managed to cross over in 1940 at Paramount with his political satire *The Vagrant*, but only by offering to lower his high screenwriting fee to $10 in exchange for being allowed to direct it. Paramount ran the numbers, decided they could come out ahead whatever happened, and agreed. Retitled *The Great McGinty*, the film was a hit, and Sturges was off to auteurdom.[1] Sturges's success inspired his fellow Paramount writer, Billy Wilder, to push for the same thing, and Wilder won the privilege in 1942 with *The Major and the Minor*.

John Huston, under writing contract at Warner Bros., was aware of these transitions, and so was his astute agent, Paul Kohner, who negotiated a directing clause in Huston's new Warner Bros. contract. When the time came to direct, Warner and production chief Hal Wallis were relieved, if suspicious, when Huston declared he wanted to remake a property the studio already owned, *The Maltese Falcon*.

Warners had purchased the rights to Dashiell Hammett's book for $8,500 upon its 1930 publication and had already squeezed out of it two unremarkable screen versions: *Dangerous Female* (1931) and *Satan Met a Lady* (1936). The only reason *Satan Met a Lady* was made was that, when the studio tried rereleasing *Dangerous Female* in 1934, the Breen Office—Hollywood's official censorship unit run by Joseph I. Breen—had begun enforcing the strict 1930 Production Code and the reissue was denied a Code seal.[2] Huston's logic for choosing a third try was clever and flawless: it was silly to remake a good film, he argued, but why not remake two bad ones and finally get it right? Supported in his ambitions by the urbane and respected producer Henry Blanke, Huston arranged to adapt and direct Hammett's compelling mystery novel.

But there were no free rides in Hollywood, then or now. Before Huston could make *The Maltese Falcon*, he was ordered to do a script polish on Howard Hawks's in-preparation production of *Sergeant York*. Four other writers had already labored in the trenches on the story of America's World War I hero but, as with *Jezebel*, it was Huston's final touch that made the picture happen. His work pleased Hawks and Alvin York (who was a consultant) enough to move forward. Only then could Huston begin work on *Falcon*.

There is a legend that Huston never wrote the screenplay for *The Maltese Falcon*, that he merely handed the novel to a studio secretary and had her break it down into a scene-by-scene synopsis that included Hammett's dialogue. It was, it has been claimed, such an efficient job that, when it was prematurely circulated to the studio departments for budgeting purposes in anticipation of getting the final draft, everybody thought it was the actual script, and J. L. green-lighted the picture. Another version has Huston submitting his first draft screenplay that so impressed Warner that the mogul immediately put it into production. In truth, Huston did ask a secretary to break Hammett's lean novel into synopsis form, after which it was okayed to go to script, and that's when Huston sat down, fashioned the scenes, and wrote the dialogue.[3] He made changes along the way that not only streamlined the story but made it acceptable to the censors. Warner still minimized the risk by committing only $381,000 and six weeks to get it done, a tight schedule for any director, let alone a tyro.

Huston's first stroke of luck came when the studio's go-to tough guy, George Raft, turned down the role of Sam Spade because he felt it was "not an important picture" of the kind that Warner had promised him when he had renewed his contract.[4] He also didn't want to trust his career to a fledgling director. Jack Warner could easily have taken the picture away from Huston and gone with a director of whom Raft approved. Instead, he sent Raft across town to Fox on loan-out. This cleared the way for Bogart, who had been wasting his days on suspension for turning down yet another gangster role (in *Bad Men of Missouri*), to have a shot at Spade.[5] Huston considered it a blessing when Warner told Bogart to play Hammett's private eye. "Bogart, to my secret delight, was substituted," Huston beamed, "and that picture began a whole new career for Bogie."[6] Did Huston use his charm to manipulate Warner? It's not beyond him, but if he had, he was also not beyond taking credit for it, and he never did.

"John saw something in Bogie that worked early on," says Huston biographer Lawrence Grobel. "And Bogie liked the way John directed without many takes. John did speak about how Bogart wasn't all that impressive off screen, but how the camera loved him, and he came through vividly on screen."[7]

Regarding this screen appearance, it may be time to note Bogart's physicality. He was a compact five feet, nine inches tall, which hardly seems a disqualification for leading man when Kirk Douglas, James Dean, Marlon Brando, Fred Astaire, and Frank Sinatra were roughly the same height. What distinguished Bogart, and it's obvious when he is seen standing with others, is his unusually large head. Many great stars share this physical characteristic. It dominates the frame and draws attention away from whoever shares the shot with them.

In Bogart, Huston found an actor who could emanate Sam Spade's toughness as well as his intelligence. The former allowed him to keep audience sympathy when he turned Brigid over to the police and let them forget that he had cuckolded his business partner, Miles Archer. The latter explained his wisdom in hiding the wrapped bird in a locker, noticing that Gutman had palmed a $1,000 bill, and recognizing that Miles had been shot at close range. Audiences accepted the good and ignored the bad. The result was that *The Maltese Falcon* was the first "Bogart picture" that was truly a "Bogart picture." The effect was so powerful that Bogart has clouded Hammett's own description of Sam Spade. Hammett's Spade was over six feet tall, a "blonde Satan" with hair that came to a widow's peak, giving him the image of a malamute. "His jaw was long and bony," Hammett wrote, "his chin a jutting V. His nostrils curved back to make another, smaller V. His yellow-grey eyes were horizontal." The truth hardly mattered; Bogart so fit the role that with one film he obliterated his gangster image to the point that it was said that prisoners wrote him letters from jail complaining that he "went straight."

Once Huston had Bogart on the call sheet, he conferred with the studio's casting director, Steve Trilling, and obtained stage actor Sydney Greenstreet for his first film role as Kasper Gutman, the portly criminal dilettante, and paired him with Peter Lorre as Joel Cairo, tempting the censors by having Lorre play him as effeminate (Lorre's German accented English clouds the issue but his eye movements convey the idea). The duplicitous Brigid O'Shaughnessy was played by Mary Astor, who had begun acting in the silent days. Astor turned thirty-five in 1941 and was second choice after the younger Geraldine Fitzgerald, who was not available. Other Brigids proposed included Olivia de Havilland, Rita Hayworth, and a new arrival from Sweden named Ingrid Bergman.[8] Deciding on Astor, Bogart and Huston met with the actress at her home to present her with the script, which she accepted days later. The "chemistry meeting" between Bogart and Astor was essential, as was the fact that it was held away from the eyes and loose lips of the studio. Finally, John cast his father Walter in a small uncredited role—ship's captain Jacoby—for luck.[9] The final blessing came from producer Henry Blanke who told Huston, "John, just remember that each scene, as you shoot it, is the most important scene in the picture."

Reflecting on this advice, Huston said, "That's the best advice any young director could have."[10]

Before collaborating with director of photography Arthur Edeson, Huston used his artistic skills to produce sketches—today they would be called storyboards—of camera setups. Hundreds of them. These gave the film a look that would later be seen as the first stirrings of *film noir* as well as the director's emerging visual style.

Shooting began on June 9, 1941, and commenced largely in sequence. After a few days, Hal Wallis memoed Huston to speed up the actors' delivery; Huston either ignored him or was going to do so anyway.

As had happened with *High Sierra*, the actors formed a close ensemble. They frequently went to the Lakeside Country Club for food and drinks during lunch. Huston, though married to Edith Black (from October 3, 1937 to April 7, 1945), had affairs with Mary Astor and Olivia de Havilland. Bogart was still with Mayo and hating every moment. Principal photography ended on July 18 with the burning of Jacoby's ship, *La Paloma*. The shoot was planned so meticulously that it was brought in two days early and $54,000 under budget. After a September 5, 1941, studio sneak preview, Warner and Wallis ordered retakes and a rewrite of the opening sequence because audiences were having trouble following Miss Wonderly's fabricated story of her errant sister.[11] Otherwise, the preview was a sensation. By Warner's and Wallis's standards, Huston walked on water.

Less than three months later, it opened, but not before Jack L. Warner made one final change: instead of reading "*The Maltese Falcon* with Humphrey Bogart and Mary Astor," the studio chief changed the billing to "Humphrey Bogart and Mary Astor in *The Maltese Falcon*."

The Maltese Falcon begins with the telling of a legend in which, in 1539, the Knight Templars of Malta sent a golden, jewel-encrusted falcon to Charles V of Spain that was stolen in transit by pirates and "remains a mystery to this day."

Sam Spade (Humphrey Bogart) and Miles Archer (Jerome Cowan) are partners in a San Francisco detective agency, Spade and Archer. They are visited by Miss Wonderly (Mary Astor) who wants them to locate her missing sister, Corinne, who has run off with a dangerous man named Floyd Thursby. That night, when Archer follows Wonderly to investigate, he is murdered. Police Detective Tom Polhaus (Ward Bond) and Lieutenant Dundy (Barton MacLane) suspect Spade of killing Thursby and Archer but cut him slack when he explains Archer was on a case.

Spade tries to find Wonderly but she has checked out of her hotel. He tells his secretary, Effie (Lee Patrick) to break the news of Archer's death to Archer's widow, Iva (Gladys George).[12] In the morning, Iva shows up at the office, kisses Spade, and asks if he killed Miles so the two of them could marry. After Iva leaves, Miss Wonderly calls and tells Spade to meet her at an apartment. On the way out, Spade wastes no time telling Effie to move Miles's desk out of the office and remove his name from the door and window.

At her apartment, Miss Wonderly confesses that her real name is Brigid O'Shaughnessy and that she lied to him about having a sister, but that she and Thursby were partners and that Thursby probably killed Archer, though she has no idea who killed Thursby. Nothing else she says makes any sense, but Spade agrees to protect her and tells her to stay put. That night at Spade's office Joel Cairo (Peter Lorre) enters and offers Spade $5,000 to find the statue of a black bird. When Spade hesitates, Cairo pulls a gun and demands to search the room for it. Spade easily disarms Cairo, knocks him out, and searches him, finding nowhere near $5,000 in his wallet. When Cairo comes to, he tells Spade where he is staying and pulls out the gun again to search the office. Spade smiles.

Later, Spade is on the way to Brigid's apartment when he is shadowed by a young gunman, Wilmer Cook (Elisha Cook Jr.). He loses him and, when he sees Brigid, tries to get her to tell him what's going on. Spade arranges to meet Cairo at his (Spade's) apartment and brings Brigid with him. As they enter Spade's building, Iva sees him enter with Brigid and she glowers. From his office window, Spade looks down and sees Wilmer waiting in the street.

Brigid and Cairo are already acquainted and are worse than wary of one another. Spade watches their pas-de-deux and learns that they both wanted the falcon and that someone named "the fat man" also wants it and may be the one who killed Thursby. Brigid snarks that Cairo, whose behavior suggests homosexuality, may have seduced a previous gunman.[13] Cairo slaps her and once more pulls a gun. Spade disarms him again. Detectives Polhaus and Dundy show up to accuse Spade of involvement with Archer's wife as a motive to kill his partner. Spade blocks their entry until there is a scuffle inside between Brigid and Cairo and the police enter. Spade lies well enough to placate the cops, who leave, followed by Cairo. When they are alone, Brigid fills in Spade about how she, Cairo, Gutman, and Thursby all tried to get the falcon and betrayed each other. Spade doesn't buy a word of it, but he is falling for Brigid.

In the morning, Spade goes to Cairo's hotel to meet him but finds Wilmer nestled in the lobby. Spade gets the house dick to eject the gunsel, then sees Cairo returning from an all-night police grilling. At Spade's office (which now reads solely "Samuel Spade") Brigid awaits. He sends her to stay with Effie for a few days. Then Iva Archer arrives and pleads her love for him. Gutman calls and summons him to his apartment. When Spade arrives, he is greeted by Wilmer who is ordered from the room so Spade and Gutman may speak. Gutman (Sidney Greenstreet) offers Spade $10,000 to find the bird and is surprised when Spade admits he has no idea what it is. He and Spade verbally joust: Gutman won't tell Spade what the bird is, and Spade won't exactly tell Gutman he doesn't know where it is. At the impasse, Spade pretends to lose his temper and gives Gutman till 5:00 P.M. to come clean.

THE BLACK BIRD

Spade goes to see the District Attorney (John Hamilton) urging him to keep the police away so he can solve the murders and get himself off the hook. They reluctantly consent. Having bluffed the DA, Spade goes back to see Gutman. He is met by Wilmer, whom he again disarms, embarrassing him in front of his boss. Over cocktails, Gutman reveals the story behind the Maltese Falcon and offers Spade $25,000 and more to turn it over. Spade lies that he will have it in a few days. The drink Gutman has given him is drugged and he collapses. Gutman and Wilmer—and Cairo who was hiding in the other room—leave.

When Spade awakens hours later, he finds a newspaper notice that a freighter called *La Paloma* is arriving that night. He goes to meet the ship, but he finds the dock in flames. Later at his office, Spade opens the door and the ship's captain, Jacoby (Walter Huston), stumbles in holding a heavy bundle containing the Maltese Falcon. Brigid calls, gives her address, and screams. Spade stashes the package at a bus terminal and goes to the address Brigid gave him, but it's an empty lot. Again she has fooled him.

When Spade returns to his apartment, Brigid, Cairo, Wilmer, and Gutman are waiting. Spade accepts Gutman's offer of $10,000 advance payment for the bird but says he needs someone to give to the police for the murders of Thursby and Captain Jacoby. He nominates Wilmer. At first, Gutman objects, but later agrees. They wait together all night for the bus station to open. Come morning, Spade calls Effie to fetch the bundle and bring it over. On inspection, the falcon turns out to be a fake. Gutman is shaken but calms down and jauntily invites Cairo and Wilmer to join him in Istanbul to locate the man Kemidov, who presumably still has the real bird and sent them the fake. Meanwhile, Wilmer escapes.

Spade and Brigid are alone. Spade phones the police and tells them to arrest Cairo, Gutman, and Wilmer. He then tells the police to come to his apartment. While waiting for them, Spade tells Brigid that he knows she killed Archer with Thursby's gun to implicate Thursby and get Thursby off her back. Brigid begs Spade not to turn her in. He refuses to let her go but says he'll wait for her when she gets out of prison, explaining, "When a man's partner is killed, he has to do something about it." Even though he loves her, she is too dangerous for him to lie for. As the police take her away, Detective Polhaus asks Spade what the falcon was. Spade replies, "It's the stuff that dreams are made of."

Here the film ends.

There are several changes from the novel, all of them in service of simplification of the story and two instances of censorship. First, the story takes place over a six-day period from Wednesday, December 5 to Monday morning, December 10, 1928. The film is updated to 1941 with no anachronisms. In the novel, after Brigid fills in Spade on her background with the falcon and Cairo, she contrives to spend the night with Spade. From the point of view of the Production Code, this was unacceptable and was removed in the script stage. Also removed was a scene from the book in which Spade, in his apartment at 891 Post Street, forces Brigid to strip so he can search for a missing $1,000 bill.[14] This was included in the 1931 film that was made before the Code was enforced. In the novel, the police inform Spade that they have picked up gunsel Wilmer Cook, who has just shot Gutman as payback for offering to turn him in for Thursby's and Jacoby's murders. Spade, as in the novel, turns Brigid over to the police as Archer's killer and also gives them the $1,000 bribe he had secured from Gutman to lie about Wilmer.

As an epilogue, the next morning Iva Archer comes to Spade's office. Effie lets her in, and Spade (and the reader) are left to wonder whether he and the widow will resume their affair. Although scripted, Huston and Blanke determined that this coda was not needed, and it was never shot. Otherwise, the film slavishly follows to the novel.

Huston's mastery of style in this first film is already apparent. Working largely in unbroken takes, he seldom relies on traditional master shots—the camera stationed far away encompassing everyone in the scene—and daringly trucks in on close-ups and two-shots. He has his actors walk and uses their moves to motivate the camera, panning and handing off from one actor to another in a continuous take. When one of them stops to make a point, that cues the cut to the character who has been set up to react to it. This is an extraordinarily brave technique for a first-time director and would be so even for a seasoned director. It also ensures that the studio would have trouble recutting it, as there are no clearly evident places for cutaways. Having crackling dialogue makes it seem to move even faster, like a relay race as one actor picks up the cue from another.

Huston shoots much of it looking past Bogart from slightly behind him. This puts the audience in Spade's point of view. The camera is frequently below eye level as if sitting in a chair watching the scene play out, angling slightly upward. This device is used for comedic comment in the scenes involving Sidney Greenstreet, whose bulk dominates the frame. It would be easy to say that Huston's device of shifting from one character to another in a continuous take is his way of keeping the viewer off-balance about whom to trust, but in fact he often uses this technique to keep long dialogue scenes alive. Throughout his career, Huston would trust his actors and would photograph them in ways that support, rather than replace, their performances.

The Maltese Falcon has been celebrated for many things over many years, and its last line about "what dreams are made of" is particularly memorable. The line does not appear in Hammett's book and for years it was attributed to Huston, the writer. Speaking with his biographer, Lawrence Grobel, Huston generously clarified, "This would be in the way of a revelation. It's never come up, but that last line in the *Falcon* . . . it was Bogie's idea. It's been quoted a number of times, but this is the first opportunity I've had to tell where the credit for it lies. Before we shot that scene Bogie said to me, 'John, don't you think it would be a good idea, this line? Be a good ending?' And it certainly was."[15]

The Maltese Falcon allowed Bogart to be as tough as he had always been as a gangster but without having to chicken out, die, or end on some other

Code-mandated fate.[16] He could show masculine strength and it turned out that strength was his strong suit. The film remains endlessly watchable, even when one knows the plot. Details emerge with each viewing, including a mesmerizing performance by Mary Astor. All of this is supported by Adolph Deutsch's rich music that not only underscores the mood—hard-edged but with romance seeping through—but drops clues through leitmotifs. At times it veers into a playful riff on what sounds like the first few notes of *La Marseillaise* when representing the black bird's mythical lure.[17]

As for bravura filmmaking, the last twenty minutes are played in one room with five people talking and yet not once does tension or interest dissipate. What could have been the denouement of a standard, English country house mystery, in which the detective gathers all the suspects in a living room, instead becomes a game of cross emotions. It took a week to shoot after a day of rehearsal. At the end of his film, Huston even allows himself an obvious joke: as Brigid is taken away, the police lead her into an old-style elevator whose cage has bars like the prison cell to which she is headed. Sure, it's heavy handed, but by this point the audience is ready to grant Huston anything he wants.

"Bogart was a second-class star who then became a big star," Huston assessed years later. The film also made Huston a full-time director who Bogart said was "a mite teched with genius. You have to be a mite teched to be a genius."[18]

For a time there was talk of a sequel. Jack Warner himself asked Jacob Wilk, the studio's story editor, to ask Dashiell Hammett whether he would be interested in writing a continuation of his story using all the original characters (except Brigid O'Shaughnessy, who was sent up for murdering Miles Archer).[19] Apparently Hammett was agreeable, but the money he wanted was not. Warner refused to pay Hammett more than five thousand dollars and, "if he hasn't confidence in his ability to write an acceptable story, let's forget it."[20] Which they did.[21]

The Maltese Falcon has been labeled film noir, but it really isn't. The conniving heroine is not a blond, the hero is neither wounded nor doomed, and the crime is clear-cut rather than a symptom of paranoia. It has no overriding symbolic implications for society. What it is, and always has been, is a ripping great detective yarn with smart and varied characters told at full speed and with a satisfying ending that is both moral and cynical. It's the stuff that legends are made of.

CHAPTER 5
All This and World War Two

Huston and Bogart were paired again in the war picture, *Across the Pacific*, which was produced and released September 4, 1942, nine months after the United States was brought into World War II. Some of the cast from *The Maltese Falcon* (Bogart, Astor, Greenstreet, and supporting player John Hamilton) returned in this story, set before Pearl Harbor, of a disgraced Army lieutenant who ships out on a Japanese boat to the Panama Canal and learns on the way that Japan is planning to attack America.

The story was a morale-building fabrication with an ominous overlay of real war. Captain Rick Leland (Bogart), stationed in Panama, faces court-martial and is discharged from the US Army after being convicted of stealing. Notably, the proceedings take place on November 17, 1941 (and of course everyone in the audience knows what happened twenty days later). Turned down in Nova Scotia by the Canadian army because of his conviction, he declares in his pique that he is now going to fight for Chiang Kai-shek.[1] He books passage on the Japanese freighter *Genoa Maru* headed for the Philippines. Being loaded aboard the ship are crates destined for D. Morton, Bountiful Plantation. Aboard the boat, Leland is spied upon by the Japanese crew including his cabin steward, Sugi (Roland Got).

At sea he meets Alberta Marlow (Mary Astor), a Canadian woman who playfully rebuffs his advances but seems interested in him. Also on board is Dr. Lorenz (Sidney Greenstreet) and his valet, T. Oki. Rick, Alberta, and Lorenz discuss world politics while lounging on deck and weigh what will happen if and when America enters the war that's already raging in Europe. Lorenz praises the Japanese and admits that his support for them has made him unpopular in the Philippines. Rick announces that he will fight for whomever offers him money.

The ocean becomes rough. At first, Alberta thinks this is romantic and seems to melt to Leland's charms. Then she becomes seasick and takes to her cabin. Lorenz and Leland have no such problem and proceed to get drunk together. Leland gets too drunk and reveals his bitterness about America. Lorenz begins asking him secrets about the Canal Zone where he had served before his court-martial but Leland is too drunk to answer and staggers back to his cabin. There Alberta finds him and gloats that, this time, he is the sick one.

The *Genoa Maru* docks in New York City. Leland and Alberta alight and Leland goes to meet a friend named Hart. He is following by a man who wears a white scarf. In the meeting with Hart (Paul Stanton) it is revealed that Leland is a double agent who was purposely dishonorably discharged to make him attractive to a spy ring believed to be planning an attack on the Panama Canal. Leland asks Hart about Alberta, and Hart warns Leland to watch out for a Japanese man named Totsuiko (Victor Sen Yung). Leaving Hart, Leland sees the white scarf man bothering Alberta and punches him out. Alberta asks Rick what he knows about a planter in Panama named Morton who seems to be neutral.

Back on the ship, Leland surprises a Filipino man who is about to shoot Lorenz. Rather than turn the would-be assassin over to the authorities, the ship's captain has him killed while the ship is still moored.

The chatterbox Joe Totsuiko boards as a passenger before the ship leaves New York. No one notices that another man now appears using the name

T. Oki. Lorenz pays Leland for information about the defense programs for the Panama Canal.

Arriving in Panama, the *Genoa Maru* is forbidden use of the Canal because it is of Japanese registry. Leland, Lorenz, and Alberta wait at their Panama hotel. Lorenz demands from Leland current US plans for the air defense patrol of the canal. Leland meets with A. V. Smith (Charles Halton), his local intelligence contact, and obtains legitimate plans, arguing that Lorenz would know if they were fakes. Smith informs him that plantation owner D. Morton is a rich alcoholic and that Alberta is a buyer for a New York City department store and travels widely in that capacity.

Leland gives Lorenz the plans, but then is beaten for no apparent reason. After his assailants leave, he recovers enough to phone Smith to warn him to change the defense schedule, but Smith is killed as soon as he hangs up. The hotel manager, Sam (Lee Tong Fu), tells Leland to meet a contact at a local cinema. The contact tells Leland to go to the Bountiful Plantation, and then is killed. Assassins try to kill Leland in the theater but he escapes.

Arriving just outside Bountiful Plantation, Leland sees a small bomber being loaded with a torpedo on a secluded jungle airstrip. He is captured and brought inside the plantation house where he finds Lorenz, Totsuikjo, Morton (Monte Blue), Alberta, and the replacement T. Oki (Kam Tong) who is a Japanese prince proudly preparing to bomb the Panama Canal. Morton is revealed to be Alberta's father. When all the spies but Totsuiko leave to prepare the bombing, Morton gets up in an alcoholic haze and Totsuiko shoots him. This distraction enables Leland to take care of Totsuiko and race outside to stop the plane from taking off. He commandeers a machine gun and shoots the plane with its torpedo contents. Lorenz, in disgrace, lacks the nerve to commit seppuku and is held pending arrival of the US authorities. Leland and Alberta embrace.

The screenplay for *Across the Pacific* was adapted by Richard Macaulay from Robert Carson's *Saturday Evening Post* serial "Aloha Means Goodbye" that ran June 28 to January 26, 1941. Carson's story presciently had the

Japanese targeting Pearl Harbor, which might well have triggered a government inquiry on December 8, 1941, if anybody had a subscription to the *Saturday Evening Post* or was suspicious enough. In Carson's story the devious spy is named Dr. Barca, not Lorenz, and Alberta is Dan Morton's niece, not his daughter. Warner Bros. was sufficiently intrigued to pay Macaulay $12,500 for the screen rights.[2] Huston, coming off *The Maltese Falcon*, was assigned to direct but, surprisingly, was not told to do the adaptation; apparently, he was simply handed the script like any studio contract director. It was originally to star Dennis Morgan and Ann Sheridan.[3]

Shooting began in early December 1941 on the Warner Bros. soundstages decked out to represent the *Genoa Maru*. New York City exteriors were staged on the backlot, and ocean-going scenes involved rear projection. Although the film was edited by Frank Magee, house editor Don Siegel, later to become a major director, handled montages—except there were no montages, so Siegel very likely directed second unit inserts and drive-bys in which principal cast members were doubled. As he had on *The Maltese Falcon*, Arthur Edeson photographed *Across the Pacific*, although on this outing, aside from some complex crane shots early in the film, his camerawork is best described as serviceable.

Across the Pacific suffered a delay when Mary Astor contracted flu and dropped out for a few days. The major disruption, however, came when the Japanese attacked Pearl Harbor on December 7 and the picture shut down for three months while America reacted to being drawn into the war. By the time production resumed on March 2, 1942, the target of the spies had been rewritten from Pearl Harbor to the Panama Canal. Then on March 29, President Roosevelt's Executive Order 9066 was enacted and all the Japanese cast members, as well as all Japanese and Japanese-Americans living on the west coast, were ordered into internment camps. Japanese performers who had been in the film were replaced by Chinese actors.

During the shutdown Huston, at age thirty-three, enlisted in the US Army in a deal brokered by writer Sy Bartlett in which he was promised a commission in the Signal Corps. In April 1942, weeks after production resumed, he was called up. In league with Bogart who, at age forty-two, was too old to serve, he hatched a trick to play on Vincent Sherman, the director chosen to finish the film in his absence.

While Huston was preparing to leave Los Angeles on military assignment, across the country his play, *In Time to Come*, cowritten with fellow Warner writer Howard Koch, opened on Broadway. Directed by Otto Preminger, it ran from December 28, 1941 to January 31, 1942 at the Mansfield Theatre and was doubtless forced to close, as were many other shows at that time, by public concern over the war.

As Huston left the production of *Across the Pacific*, they were shooting the ending in Bountiful Plantation. As a prank on his fellow director Sherman, Huston arranged to have Bogart tied to a chair by Japanese spies and left in circumstances from which it was impossible to escape. When Sherman took over on April 22 and asked how he should pick up the story, Huston told him, "That's your problem. I'm off to the war." Another version of the story has Huston telling Sherman, "Bogie will know how to get out" and walking away.

Both iterations are publicity fabrications. In truth, Huston sat down with Sherman a week before he was scheduled to leave for the service and the two men rewrote the ending together, after which Sherman reshot scenes leading up to the revisions. In his memoir, Huston writes that there were no retakes and that Sherman had "one of the Japanese soldiers in the room go berserk. Bogie escaped in the confusion, with the comment, 'I'm not easily trapped, you know!'"[4] This, too, involves a little embellishment on Huston's part. In any event, the picture finished ten days over schedule.

Across the Pacific seethes with disinterest and contains none of the complexity of design that Huston showed in *The Maltese Falcon* (or even, for that matter, in his interim job, *In This Our Life*, which he also did not write). The film is an awkward mixture of intrigue and comedy, one contradicting the other. Unusual given the context of its time, Japanese culture is accorded respect, although the praise comes from the turncoat Dr. Lorenz. The film's true propaganda feelings emerge in the T. Oki plot point that calls on Japanese to be physically interchangeable except for one whose eyeglasses could do service on Mount Palomar.

As a spy drama, the film's big (but not surprising) reveal is that Leland is a double agent, although leading up to it Bogart shows not the least bit of shame at his condemnation, only irritation. When he meets Alberta, he drops his sullenness and becomes the tease, which makes their badinage seem almost goofy. The two moods don't mesh. While it's entertaining to watch Bogart and Astor joust, their obvious attempt to recapture their *Maltese Falcon* relationship contributes little to the plot and leads awkwardly to the clumsy resolution. No wonder Huston fled the country. Nevertheless, when the $576,000 picture was released on September 9, 1942, it was received enthusiastically and returned $2,375,000 in worldwide rentals.[5] At this early stage of the war, which wasn't going well, American audiences needed escape and reassurance.

Unlike Rick Leland in the film, for Bogart himself there was no escape from the enemy: Mayo. His marriage had degenerated to the point where she had convinced herself that he was having an affair when he was just out after work winding down with colleagues. Enraged on his return home one night, she began humming the Gershwin song, "Embraceable You." This was a signal Bogart had learned meant that trouble was coming. And it did; Mayo gave chase through the house and, before Bogart could make it out the door, she stabbed him in the back with a kitchen knife. Fortunately, she missed anything important and a doctor was paid $500 to stitch him up and not call the police. Like a trouper, Bogart reported to work the next morning.[6]

While Huston was balancing *Across the Pacific* and World War II he was preparing a dream project, *Moby Dick* (eventually realized in 1956). As with many of his personal projects, he used another writer, in this case Charlie

Gibson, to get the ball rolling after which he would revise. While Gibson was writing a treatment, Huston was asked by a Jewish organization to give a speech. This inspired Huston, with Bogart's participation, to play a trick on Gibson. In an escalating series of prank phone calls, Huston convinced Gibson that he, Gibson, would give the speech, that it would be at the Hollywood Bowl, and that he was to meet with two dozen rabbis to confer about it. Bogart played along by phoning Gibson and speaking in a New York Jewish accent to give him a pep talk about the appearance. Just before Gibson lost his mind in anticipation, Huston broke the news that was all a hoax.[7] Gibson's reaction is not known.

With Bogart fighting the battle of Warner Bros. and monsoon Mayo, Huston was engaged in the real thing. In April 1942 he spent several weeks in Washington, DC, waiting for assignment from the US Army Signal Corps. Although he doesn't mention it in his memoirs, Huston is credited with writing and codirecting (with Owen Crump) the short recruiting film *Winning Your Wings* in which Lieutenant James Stewart urges young men to apply to be flying officers in the US Army Air Force. Produced in eleven days, it hit theaters on May 28, 1942.[8]

Huston endured Washington's hot and humid summer and was sent to the Aleutian Islands where the weather was cloudy, rainy, and windy. There he and a five-man crew shot *Report from the Aleutians*.[9] With prints by Technicolor® and narration by Huston himself, it profiled the men of Adak Island who fly missions over Japanese-occupied Kiska, one of the Rat Islands that was, at the time, the Japanese outpost closest to US soil. Shot and edited in the wake of the Battle of Midway of June 1942 as Japanese domination waned in the Pacific theatre, its release was delayed while the Army fretted over Huston's inclusion of a sequence showing servicemen digging latrines. After recording the daily details of the men stationed at Adak, the film accompanies a bombing mission to Kiska and returns with all participants safe. This is contrasted later in the film by scenes of a plane crash landing and the pilot's subsequent funeral.

Huston insisted on shooting film himself during a bombing mission. The plane was attacked by Zeros while he was trying to get footage from behind the waist (side) gunner. His camera wound down and, by the time it was ready to go again, the gunner had been shot. The belly gunner, Huston wrote, told him to take over the post while he, the belly gunner, took over the waist gun. Huston did, adding that the plane was shot up but made it back to Adak.[10] Huston makes an indirect pitch for the audience to write letters to these and other servicemen to relieve them of their homesickness ("Ask any pilot. He'd tell you he'd gladly fly an extra trip over Kiska to get just one letter").[11] When he learned of resistance to releasing his film, Huston lobbied the War Department and eventually arranged a showing at New York's Museum of Modern Art. He would again rely on MoMA when he clashed with the brass in 1946 over *Let There Be Light*.

Huston's most chilling documentary was *The Battle of San Pietro* covering the catastrophic December 8–17, 1943, encounter between US and German forces at the "Winter line" near Naples in occupied Italy.[12] It remains starkly affecting. Narrated as well as written and directed by Huston (sans credit, as with the other films made by the Signal Corps unit), it allows the audience to witness soldiers being shot and shows their corpses placed in body bags. Two of Huston's crew were killed during its production, and the result so disturbed the Army that the film was not allowed to be shown until 1945 when it was liberated by act of General George Marshall who argued that men should be able to see the truth of battle.[13,14] When Huston was criticized by the Army of making an antiwar film, "I pompously replied that if I ever made a picture that was pro-war, I hoped someone would take me out and shoot me."[15]

Subsequent research revealed that, because Huston and his crew showed up after the battle had ended, portions of the film were restaged for the camera.[16] This is also what happened for the 1944 documentary *Tunisian Victory* which Anatole Litvak had shot in Northern Africa for Frank Capra's *Why We Fight* series. Some of the important footage was destroyed along with the ship that was carrying it, and the brass—concerned that they would engender President Roosevelt's ire if word got out—assigned Huston and Capra to recreate battle scenes in the Mojave Desert, doubling for Tunisia. Capra was, at the time, in charge of the entire US War Department motion picture unit and brought along Huston as his assistant.[17] Later they went to Florida to fake air combat using actual planes and ammunition. Huston disowned his participation in the result but did manage to get promoted to captain.[18] *Tunisian Victory* was released March 16, 1944.

While Huston was in Italy finishing *The Battle of San Pietro*, Bogart and Mayo were on a USO tour entertaining the troops. When they were near Naples, they arranged to visit Huston. This was the first time Bogart and Huston had seen each other since Huston left *Across the Pacific* to join the war. On their reunion, the first thing Bogart said to Huston was, "John, you sonofabitch, leaving me tied to a chair!"[19] Then the two men got therapeutically drunk.[20]

"He loved to drink and play the roughneck," Huston said. "Actually, I don't think I ever saw Bogie drunk. It was always half acting, but he loved the whole scene."[21]

In 1944 Bogart had met Lauren Bacall on Howard Hawks's *To Have and Have Not*. She was Hawks's protégé and both men eased the young former model from New York into becoming an actress. The attraction between them was gradual—Bogart didn't fool around, but his marriage to Mayo was crumbling—but consistent, as their screen chemistry clearly shows. As Hawks famously recalled, "Without Bogie's help I couldn't have done what I did with Bacall. Not many actors would sit around and wait while a girl steals a scene. But he fell in love with the girl and the girl with him, and that made it easy."[22]

Bogart and Bacall (friends dubbed them "Bogie and Baby") married on May 21, 1945, eleven days after Bogart's divorce from Mayo. They moved into a three-story house on King's Road above Sunset with a butler, cook, and handyman-gardener. This was how Bogart had been raised and to which Bacall, who had known a more modest upbringing, quickly adjusted. Mrs. Bogart, as did everyone who knew him, called him Bogie. He, like everyone else, called her Betty (her birth name was Betty Joan Perske; "Lauren Bacall" was a professional invention).

"[His] life was improved by Betty's presence," Huston proclaimed. "Oh boy, was she good for him." Under Bacall's love and regal bearing, Bogart cut back on his drinking and, to commemorate the way they met, he famously gave her a charm bracelet with a gold whistle reading, "If you want anything, just whistle."

Bacall finally connected with Huston at a New Year's Eve party at the Ira Gershwin's in 1945. They had met briefly at Jules and Joyce Buck's wedding at which Huston was best man. She remarked on how tall he was and that, "he adored Bogie and vice versa. He was very funny, but devilish and socially undependable. I discerned this gradually."[23]

But this came after the war. While hostilities continued, Huston was cowriter with Frank Capra and Carl Foreman on the documentary *Know Your Enemy: Japan* which Capra directed with career documentarist Joris Ivens for the *Why We Fight* series.[24] Released August 4, 1945, it had been conceived in 1942 by Ivens, who had portrayed the Japanese people as having been misled into war by their Emperor. This contradicted the propaganda position of the US Army and they removed Ivens and shelved the project in 1943.[25] Edited from stock footage, "borrowed" Japanese fiction films, and animated illustrations, *Know Your Enemy* was eventually released after V-E Day while the war in the Pacific raged on. There is every reason to believe that it was designed to arouse public sentiment against Japan at a time when the atomic bomb was being developed. At the same time, the Army, War, and State Departments were aware that they would have to deal with the postwar Japanese government, so the film begins with a disclaimer assuring viewers that "a great many [Nisei] share our love of freedom and our willingness to die for it" and extols Japanese-Americans for their patriotism (despite having placed thousands of them in camps since

1942). This is followed by an hour of incendiary racist footage narrated by Walter Huston and Dana Andrews. There are no screen credits.

Huston's most troublesome documentary was the controversial *Let There Be Light*, a painful but consistently compelling study of hospitalized soldiers overcoming battle fatigue.[26] Completed in 1946, it followed the eight-week journey of a group of psychologically damaged combat veterans at a recovery hospital. They suffer an assortment of maladies from neurotic paralysis to tics to constant tears. With a combination of treatments from hypnosis and counseling to electroshock they emerge apparently ready to face the world anew.

"These are the casualties of the spirit," says Huston's narration, spoken by his father, Walter, "the troubled mind, men who are damaged emotionally. Born and bred in peace, educated to hate war, they were overnight plunged into sudden and terrible situations. Every man has his breaking point; and these, in the fulfillment of their duties as soldiers, were forced beyond the limit of human endurance."[27] The film was so disturbing that the government refused to release it. In 1946 when Huston invited friends to a private screening at New York's Museum of Modern Art, Army MPs were tipped off and seized the print before it could be shown. Not until 1980 did Motion Picture Association of America president Jack Valenti and other industry leaders prevail on then–Vice President Walter Mondale to declassify *Let There Be Light* so the public could finally see it.[28] It was first screened publicly at Cannes in 1981 (although pirated copies had been circulating among film scholars for years).

War changed Huston as an artist, but he was still a kid, according to his then-wife, actress Evelyn Keyes. She and John met at a dinner party during which she tried to get his attention but failed until the party ended and he tracked her down as they both headed for their cars. Keyes was and is best known for playing Scarlett O'Hara's younger sister in *Gone with the Wind*. Bright and attractive, she drew Huston's eye even though he was carrying on at the time with Ava Gardner. One night Huston and Keyes were imbibing at Romanoff's when he decided, "let's do it." This constituted a proposal, and Mike Romanoff provided a wedding ring while Huston hired stunt pilot Paul Mantz to fly them all to Las Vegas for nuptials. It was July 23, 1946.[29]

Keyes provided Huston with a home that he enjoyed coming back to, but which he seldom stayed in. He was there on the night that they hosted Bogart, Bacall, Ida Lupino, Lupino's husband Collier Young, and writer Charlie Grayson. Bogart and Huston, already in their cups by the time the others arrived, decided to play catch with Huston's Ming vase. Joining the game, Grayson picked it up and tossed it at Bogart, who missed, and the priceless pottery shattered on the floor. Nobody seemed to care, and Bogart, who had removed his shoes and socks for better traction, stepped on the shards. Bacall duly picked the pieces out of his feet and the evening continued.[30] "John and Bogie were like children," Evelyn Keyes explained, relating that Bogart would say that he didn't trust anybody who didn't drink. She observed that Bogart needed alcohol to free himself, where Huston was content to be a social drinker.[31]

In his loving biography of Bogart, Joe Hyams places the vase incident at a post-Oscar® celebration for *Treasure of the Sierra Madre* at their home with Huston's pet monkey "clinging to his neck.'" Producer Henry Blanke and Bacall were referees, and the players were still wearing their tuxedos.[32]

With *Casablanca* (shot after *Across the Pacific* and released in January 1943), Bogart had become king of the Warners lot. He had been given a new contract that would pay him $467,361 with $199,999 minimum per picture, director approval, and an option to make one picture a year for another studio. This made him the highest-paid actor in Hollywood. It also included a specific provision that he was to star in *The Treasure of the Sierra Madre*, which had been on the studio's back burner and which he and Huston had been preparing for three years.

With Bacall, Bogart was finally able to have children. Their firstborn was Stephen who arrived January 6, 1949. The celebration started months earlier, however, when Bacall told her husband that she was pregnant. Bogart was forty-nine at the time. "He just got kind of quiet and emotional and put an arm around me as we walked into the house," Bacall remembered. The real hoopla started when Harry Kurnitz and others decided to throw a shower, not for Bacall, but for Bogart. The celebratory dinner started in an upstairs dining room at Romanoff's and ended on the floor with Bogart on his back with his legs up in the air as John Huston and Collier Young used fireplace tongs to deliver an imaginary baby from him.[33]

It was a good break for Huston who was going through marital stress. His and Keyes's relationship slowly eroded as work kept him away from home. He was highly sought after as a director, and she less so as an actress, hitting perhaps two films a year while he was making *The Treasure of the Sierra Madre*, *On Our Merry Way* (partly), *Key Largo*, *We Were Strangers*, and *The Asphalt Jungle*. He began an affair with Enrica Sonia "Ricki" Soma, a Russian ballet dancer, and it was with her that he conceived his first son, Tony. To avoid the stigma of the boy being born out of wedlock, his father divorced Keyes on February 10, 1950, and married Ricki on February 25 when she was seven months pregnant. Tony was born April 16, 1950. It was with Ricki that John also conceived their daughter, Anjelica, born July 8, 1951.

John's roving eye was not to be confined to Ricki. In the early Sixties he became attracted while in England to actress-writer Zoe Ishmail Sallis, whom he would cast in the role of Hagar in his 1966 film *The Bible: In the Beginning*. This is ironic given her place in the Huston lineage. She and John also fathered a son, Danny, who became an actor and director. Danny was born on May 14, 1962. John and Zoe also bore a daughter, Allegra, on August 26, 1964.

Understandably, John and Ricki were estranged during this period. Sadly, on January 29, 1969 in Dijon, France, she was killed when the car in which she was riding was involved in a collision. Huston was shattered and for years refused to tell Anjelica the details of her mother's death. Ricki was thirty-nine and John was fifty-five at the time. The two had never married.

On August 8, 1972, Huston married English beauty Celeste "Cici" Shane who was half his age. It was both a sensuous and tumultuous relationship; in his sixties, he was looking to restore his youth and she was looking to extend hers. She also had a special needs son from a previous marriage, and this may have fed John's savior complex (as it did when he adopted Pedro). The marriage to Cici lasted until July 21, 1975, and the fact that he refers to her only as "the crocodile" in his memoirs suggests his appraisal of the relationship. Huston did derive a major benefit from Cici, however: he met her maid, Maricela Hernandez. Maricela came to live with him and serve as his close companion for the rest of his life. It was she to whom he dedicated his last film, *The Dead*, and it was her hands he held in his when he died on August 28, 1987.

Huston never lacked for paramours (most notably Olivia de Havilland during the making of *In This Our Life* in 1942 and again later) and always charmed his way into the lives of any woman he sought, even while married to another. Tommy Shaw, his longtime friend and production supervisor, insisted that John always loved every woman he was with. Lauren Bacall, however, with more insight and less tolerance, was more observant in the documentary *John Huston: The Man, the Movies, the Maverick*: "I don't think John liked women very much. I don't think he had much respect for them. I think he respected the mother of his children as the mother of his children. He respected me because I was Bogie's wife, and I was the mother of Bogie's children. But I would hate to have been in love with him."[34] She was just as frank in her memoir, *By Myself*: "I was accepted immediately by him because I loved his friend. He didn't like women very much on their own."[35]

CHAPTER 6

The Treasure of the Sierra Madre

As clear as the paths were from script to screen for *The Maltese Falcon* and *Across the Pacific*, *The Treasure of the Sierra Madre* twisted and turned like the fortunes of the men whose story it tells. As the most profound and honored of the Huston-Bogart collaborations—as well as the one that most tested their friendship throughout its grueling production—it is deserving of more expansive consideration.

The Treasure of the Sierra Madre is the kind of film of which today's movie fans say "they don't make 'em like that anymore." In point of fact, Warner Bros. didn't want to make it in 1948, either. Its existence is a testament to the tenacity of Huston, Bogart, producer Henry Blanke, agent Paul Kohner, and the inscrutable author B. Traven.

A relentlessly grim moral tale about greed and fate, *Treasure* became a power play by Huston to make a film on location, away from studio scrutiny. Then there was Bogart's desire to play a complex, if unsavory, character unlike his heroic leads in *Across the Pacific* (1942), *Sahara* (1943), *Passage to Marseilles* and *To Have and Have Not* (both 1944), *The Big Sleep* (1946), and, of course, *Casablanca* (1943). Finally, there was the budget: $1.8 million at a time when the average studio film cost $730,000.[1]

The adventure began in 1927 when B. Traven's novel was published in Germany. It took eight years to make it to America not only because it had to be translated into English but because Traven, a fervent Marxist, refused to allow his book to be published in any capitalist country. Somehow this was resolved and, before it hit American bookstores, the publisher, Knopf, as was the practice, sent it around to all the film companies for possible acquisition.[2] Times have changed; nowadays the film companies rely on outside producers to bring projects. All of them passed, including Warners. But then came *The Maltese Falcon*, and Huston urged J. L. to give *Treasure* another look as a possible project for himself and his father, Walter, who, at the time, he wanted to play Dobbs, the role that eventually went to Bogart.

Wanting to keep Huston happy, Warner consented. The acquisition was complicated by several factors. First, Traven, in addition to his politics, was a recluse who could be reached only via mail to a remote post office box in Mexico. Second, he was vague about whether he had already sold the film rights to a Swedish company. Third, just who was B. Traven anyway? Was he an American born in San Francisco as he said? Was he English? Was he German? Perhaps he was Mexican. And was B. Traven even his real name? Traven himself was evasive about answering anything about himself, insisting that his work was the important thing.

Traven's agent, Paul Kohner—himself having to deal with his eccentric client strictly by mail—assured Warner that everything could be worked out, and the studio optioned *Treasure* for $1,500, reserving full acquisition until the rights issue was clarified. At about the same time, Roy J. Obringer, the studio's general counsel, alerted Hal Wallis, the studio's production chief, about Traven's odd behavior. On November 14, 1941, Obringer called Traven "some sort of a spook in Mexico" who refused to sign any documents himself and wanted everything done through a Power of Attorney.[3] In an industry as litigious as Hollywood, and with studios to this day being routinely sued by people who claim infringement or plagiarism, Obringer's caution was understandable. But Warner ordered the deal closed anyway.

The problem, as Obringer wrote Morris Ebenstein of the studio's New York legal department on January 15, 1942, was that Traven was being cagey about the translation rights he may have given to various publishers around the world, and not just to the party in Sweden.[4] The subject of citizenship arose again in Ebenstein's somewhat frantic return letter to Obringer on January 29. Not only did Ebenstein doubt Traven's claim that he was a native-born American ("He may be one, but he certainly does not write like one"), but he also said he sounded German, and he advised that no title company (insurer) would guarantee such a weak warranty. In his June 30, 1942, letter back to Ebenstein, however, Obringer threw caution to the winds by telling him that Colonel Warner wanted to make *Treasure* and insisted on doing so once the Swedish copyright matter was cleared up.[5] As for the rest, the studio would take a chance.

Meanwhile, Kohner arranged for a writer named David Commons to write a treatment (a condensed synopsis) of the novel to facilitate its studio development. When advised of this, Traven was skeptical: "I don't know any David Commons so I can't say whether he is the right man to work on the screen play," he wrote Kohner on April 9, 1941, "but if you say he is okay I have no objection."[6] Kohner's strategy was that a screenplay plus the book would could fetch a higher purchase price than the novel alone. On June 16, 1942, Kohner notified Traven that Warners was extending the option for $500.

Traven tried to clarify the rights issue by contacting Axel Holmstrom, Traven's Swedish publisher. He was not a producer, as was first thought, and, as of June 22, 1942, had not responded to Traven's inquiries.[7] Kohner advised Traven on June 28 that the studio had "no way to get mail thru to Sweden or back here" but that "Warners are very anxious to get this matter settled."[8] This was, after all, during World War II.

Regardless, on September 14, 1942. Kohner wrote Traven that Warner Bros. had exercised their option on *Treasure* for a total price of $6,500 minus the $1,500 they had already paid. There was, however, one hitch: David Commons. Commons's treatment was of no interest to the studio, yet they wanted his signed release so he couldn't make a future claim against them. Kohner offered Commons $500 for what he called "nuisance value." Commons demanded $750, and Kohner reluctantly agreed, deducting the amount from Traven's fee. With Kohner's commission and Commons's buyout, Traven received $3,750 for *The Treasure of the Sierra Madre*.

"What Commons did to us is little short of blackmail," an aggravated Traven wrote Kohner on October 28. "You may tell him so if you see him that I said it. He may have had a certain justification for asking $250 or, well, $300. The worst thinking he did was to ask fifty percent more than you had arranged when he felt that he could get away with it because we needed his release. In my opinion he is a loser by all means."[9] While this was going on, John Huston was finishing *In This Our Life* and was eager to begin adapting *Treasure*. He wrote to Traven, asking him to come to Los Angeles to discuss the script. Traven declined, citing weather and other reasons.

The *Treasure* rights question would be resolved in 1942 in a two-page "copyright agreement" signed by Axel Holmstrom, owner of the Swedish publishing rights, that transferred to Warner Bros. the "exclusive right to use, interpolate songs, music, sounds, words and dialogue in, translate, adapt, change, add to, and subtract from" the property *Der Schatz der Sierra Madre*. But not really, because, on November 3, Traven wrote Kohner expressing surprise that Holmstrom signed a conveyance of rights to Warner Bros. because "He cannot sell anything he does not own." Traven explained that he allowed Holmstrom only to publish the book in Sweden, not to control any other rights. He insisted that he had asked Holmstrom to sign a follow-up statement admitting that he did not own the rights he had just sold. He ended by assuring Kohner that only Kohner may sign documents representing his interest, and ends with a cordial, "Regards to everybody" and a typed signature, "T."[10] Presumably, this was sufficient to allow Warners to proceed.

There was one fly in the Holmstrom ointment: the publisher, in signing the release, referred to B. Traven as "Bruno Traven." This incensed Traven.

"My first name is given again as Bruno although I have repeatedly stated that this is not my name and the Warners know it," he typed in an October 18 letter to Kohner. "I can prove before any court including the US Supreme Court that my first name is not Bruno but were I to collect a check for as little as one dollar made to Bruno T., I would commit a felony and be sent up the river for a coupla years or more."[11]

Two opposing forces now went to work: Jack Warner wanted to make *Treasure* right away with Vincent Sherman directing instead of Huston. Producer Henry Blanke, Huston's champion, wanted to keep it for Huston's return from the war, whenever that might be. Blanke shrewdly placated Warner by trying to cast the picture, sending the book to a succession of other Warner Bros. contract players including Edward G. Robinson, Errol Flynn, and John Garfield, all of whom passed. Ronald Reagan was under consideration as Curtin and Zachary Scott, a contract player like Reagan, was assigned to play Cody.[12]

Whether anyone saw through Blanke's subterfuge is unknown. When asked for a progress report, Blanke insisted to Warner that the script was still being written and, to cover himself, assigned a series of contract writers to work on it, including Robert Rossen, apparently never intending to use anything anybody did.[13] All of this conspired to keep the picture on hold; Jack Warner trusted Blanke so much that he accepted his decisions.

Huston continued to write during his military service, although not on *Treasure*; in August 1942, he was working on *Background to Danger* while in the Aleutians shooting a documentary on the building of an air base.[14]

On February 10, 1943, Warner Bros., again eager to move forward, announced that Humphrey Bogart, Walter Huston, and John Garfield would star, but nothing happened for three-and-a half years until August 22, 1945.[15,16] By that time, Garfield was unavailable so Tim Holt was borrowed from RKO to play Curtin after Jack Warner and Huston dismissed the idea of letting Ronald Reagan appear as the decent dreamer.[17]

Once Huston was released from the service in 1945 (with a US Legion of Merit award for making films under dangerous battle conditions), he went back to writing *Treasure*, refusing to look at any of the previous scripts.[18] He wrote from March to August 1946 but, on finishing, had doubts whether he had made the characters rich enough, so he sent a copy to Traven in Acapulco. He also went to New York where he directed the debut production of Jean-Paul Sartre's stage play *No Exit*. The production ran from November 26 to December 21 of that year.

On December 16, 1946, Traven replied enthusiastically to Huston about *Treasure*, writing, "It goes as close alongside the book as a picture will ever allow." In particular, he approved of the scene in which Dobbs was trapped in a mine cave-in but suggested that Curtin should hesitate for a moment before going in to rescue him. The author also liked Huston's revised ending in which Curtin and Howard are left completely broke (Traven's book accords them a little money at the end), calling it "super excellent writing." As for casting, he liked Bogart as Dobbs but felt that Walter Huston was "too robust" for Howard and suggested Lewis Stone, the elegant elder actor popularly known as Judge Hardy in MGM's *Andy Hardy* series, as the grizzled prospector. (Traven later came around.)[19]

On February 17, 1947, Huston and a small crew went to Tampico, Mexico, where the story begins, to shoot background plates for the film's process shots. These would be rear-projected behind the actors on the Burbank soundstage where conditions could be controlled.[20]

While they were away, a problem arose that the Production Code Administration, Hollywood's official censors, had first warned about in 1942 but that had been put on hold along with the picture during the war. Henry Blanke sent the script to Geoffrey Shurlock in the industry's self-censorship office. Blanke's concern was how the story might affect the legacy of the "Good Neighbor Policy" of the Roosevelt administration because "I would not want to do anything in these days that would turn out to be a boomerang to a 'greater effort.'" Shurlock's boss, Joseph I. Breen, lost no time replying to Blanke's boss, Jack L. Warner. Except for having to consult with his Latin-American advisor, Breen decreed that the basic story "met the requirements of the Production Code" except for:

> Page 20: In handling these Mexican girls, please avoid any direct suggestion that they are prostitutes.
>
> Page 27: Please change the line, "For the love of God Almighty." Also, the expression "jerk" is now on the Association's list of forbidden words.
>
> Page 29: The same applies to the word "louse."
>
> Page 44: In this sequence, please make it clear that the bandits are attempting to rob the women, and nothing more. There should, of course, be no suggestion of attempted rape.[21]

Breen noted a few other, smaller breaches. Similar letters passed between the Breen Office and Warners over additional uses of the words *damn*, *hell*, *geez*, the phrase "three shots of rye," changing "white man" to "American," substituting "native" for "Mex," and other linguistic infractions. Not until June 12, 1947, would the final go-ahead be conferred by Breen. This was fortunate as *Treasure* had been shooting since April. Warner approved a $1.8 million budget that was higher than the studio's other current productions.[22] It bought Huston seventy-two days to shoot 143 pages and predicted a wrap date of June 9, 1947. (It would take until July 22.) June 9 is the date of the final Huston screenplay, suggesting that Huston made changes throughout the shoot.

The film's treatment of Mexicans, Mexico, and animals continued to be an issue. "May we again remind you of the vital necessity of getting proper technical advice to be certain that the picture is not offensive to the Mexicans," Breen began in his letter of January 13, 1947, to Jack Warner. "Unless this is done, we may not be able to approve the picture under Article 10 of the Code. Furthermore, with regard to all scenes in which animals are used, please follow standard industry policy and consult with Mr. Richard Craven of the American Humane Association."[23]

Breen reminded the filmmakers that the women should be dressed modestly and that their breasts should be fully covered at all times. Exhibits of American arrogance toward Mexicans were also a concern. "There are a number of items in this opening sequence on which we especially urge you consult your Mexican technical advisor," he continued. "Specifically, we call your attention to the scenes of the bootblacks diving for cigarette butts; the scene of Dobbs throwing water into the boy's face; also, the expression *hex* on page 5." Breen reminded the producer to change the expressions *helluva*, *damn*, and *geez* and to omit specific references to liquor drinking.[24] There was an even sterner caution urged about the sequence in which an alluring woman entices Bogart toward a hotel in Tampico once he's had a haircut and has a spare peso in his pocket. The script says that he realizes he doesn't have enough money to afford her but, in the film, he is nevertheless seen walking toward her apartment before a dissolve suggests that they will connect. The prostitute is supposedly played by an uncredited Ann Sheridan, Hollywood's sexy "oomph girl," but this has been disputed. Whoever played her, the Production Code censors completely missed the presence of a prostitute in the finished film.

Quite apart from Breen's admonitions, the film was put in jeopardy on February 18, 1947, when Mexico shut down Huston's location scouting expedition. An article appeared in a local newspaper criticizing the film's suspected treatment of Mexico. What more likely happened was that Huston failed to bribe the correct bureaucrats. While Warner Bros. used its political influence in Washington, DC, to obtain State Department assistance to clear up the snafu, Huston asked artists Diego Rivera and Miguel Covarrubias to speak on his behalf to Mexico's president. A discrete investigation was begun that implicated the editor of the critical newspaper. The man was eventually shot by the jealous husband of the woman he was seeing.

Meanwhile, Huston left town and went to San José Purúa to shoot what would today be called second unit scenes with extras. Once there, he engaged an employment agent to provide men. The wages offered by the production were sufficient to attract numerous volunteers. The agent told Huston that the men should be paid ten pesos a day if they were on foot, fifteen pesos a day if they rode horses, and twenty-five pesos a day if they were to fall off a horse. He also gave Huston the option of paying them fifty pesos if he wanted to actually shoot any of the men in the arm or leg, but was told, "mind you, no killing."[25]

Huston and his small crew returned to Burbank. On March 17, he, Bogart, and Holt shot the "bench scene" in which Dobbs meets Curtin and they lament the lack of work for riggers like them in Tampico, "even though the world needs oil." This was set in Plaza de la Libertad in Tampico but shot on the studio's process stage using the background plates that had just been made in Mexico. A week later, Bogart, Holt, and their stunt doubles would go to the Columbia Pictures ranch for the rigging scenes at a construction site after their characters were hired by McCormick (Barton McLane).

Shooting in the Black Bear (El Oso Negro) flophouse set began on April 2. It is here that Dobbs and Curtin meet Howard (Walter Huston) who fills their heads with dreams of gold and has the knowledge of how to mine it. Playing a small part in the scene is Jack Holt, Tim's father, who had been a major western star in his younger years. It is in this scene that the Mexican boy (Robert Blake) who earlier sold Dobbs the lottery ticket arrives to tell Dobbs that he has won. Other scenes were done on the studio's Burbank back lot and soundstages in an intricate blending of process shots and reverse angles shot weeks apart and designed to be intercut with each other to provide a seamless narrative. For five days, Bogart, Holt, McLane, and their stunt doubles fell about in an unusually violent barroom fight that would alarm the censors and force editorial trims.

An unusual makeup problem arose when Dobbs, spending money given him by the white-suited American (John Huston), gets a haircut, after which he notices that his hat sits too loosely on his head. Bogart, when seen from behind, is obviously wearing a short-hair wig, one of several hairpieces that were provided for him throughout the picture as he becomes progressively scruffier. Although Bogart was losing his hair naturally from male pattern baldness, his loss had been exacerbated by one of two reasons: one source ascribes it to hormone shots he was taking in order to conceive a child with Lauren Bacall, and another says it was a vitamin deficiency that caused alopecia areata.[26]

When Dobbs hits up the white-suited stranger for money, the script uses the popular Depression expression, "Can you spare a dime, brother." Bogart and Huston changed it to, "Say mister, can you stake a fellow American to a meal?" It was B. Traven who suggested that John Huston play the part of the white-suited American who gives Bogart three handouts after seeing Huston liberally cross the palms of people he had met in Mexico.[27] According to the Internet Movie Database this was Huston's fourth appearance in a film as an actor. In the way IMDb identifies people by their best-known credits, they continue to use *Treasure* to label him as an actor despite dozens of later, more substantial roles, including in *Chinatown*.

The outdoor camp scenes were shot for two weeks inside the massive Stage 7, the tallest such facility in Hollywood. After that, with the company having exhausted studio and California locations, they headed down to Mexico to continue principal photography. Early in April 1947 Huston and the crew boarded American Airlines at Burbank Airport for Mexico City. Although the desert and jungle conditions required for the film were formidable, the hostelry accommodations not far from them were quite the opposite. Everyone got to stay in the luxurious Hotel Balneario, San José Purúa-Zitacuaro, and commuted to location.

By April 23, Huston had shot for three weeks and had committed twenty-five pages to film. Then things started to slow down. Huston had decided to shoot in Mexico's rainy season to take a chance on clear weather versus what would have been intolerable summer heat. He lost his bet with Mother Nature and rain delays slowed down production. When Durango, Mexico, proved unsuitable for filming, they moved the company to San Francisco Coatepec de Morango near Veracruz; the move created more delays.[28] Even traditional six-day location work weeks did little to speed things along.

As delays piled up, so did Jack Warner's impatience. Although he wanted a prestige film, he didn't want an expensive one. Soon the $1.8 million budget was a memory.[29] On May 30 the company left Mexico nearly twenty days behind schedule, and there was still more to do.

"John wanted everything perfect," griped Bogart, who gave the director the nickname "Hard-Way Huston" because of his penchant for authenticity. "If he saw a nearby mountain that could serve for photographic purposes, that mountain was no good; too easy to reach. If we could get to a location site without fording a couple of streams and walking through snake-infested areas in the scorching sun, then it wasn't quite right."[30]

Location catering was a problem. The chef provided such unpalatable food that soon Bacall took over, at least to cook the principals' meals. Huston's wife, Evelyn Keyes, was there, as well, but was not as appreciated as was Mrs. Bogart, and drew steady criticism from her husband.[31] Bacall witnessed Huston picking on Keyes repeatedly; for example, if she said something, he would shush the room and demand that everyone listen to her as if she was about to make a pronouncement, braying, "What? What was that, Evelyn?"[32]

The mine and surrounding desert scenes were filmed from June 13–16 at Kelly's Rainbow Mine in Kernville, California, whose surroundings passed visually for those in Mexico. Other locations for the film were the Iverson Ranch, the California Sierras, Tucson Mountain Park in Arizona, and the Mojave Desert.

Bogart, who liked poking people's egos, found Huston's unexpectedly sensitive. Bogart would ride his friend about taking a long time to set up shots and taunt him about trying to make a masterpiece. As the July Fourth holiday approached, Bogart became increasingly restless. He had planned on taking his yacht, the *Santana*, to Hawaii for the Honolulu Classic boat race, and if shooting continued, he would miss the cherished event. One night over dinner he expressed his impatience to Huston who, by then, had had enough. Huston reached across the table, grabbed Bogart's nose between his thumb and forefinger, and gave it a painful tweak that shut up his star for the rest of the schedule. Bogart missed the race and finished the film.[33]

"We had a terrible row and were sore at each other for days," Huston recalled of it. "Then we had a few drinks of an ancient tequila laced with Scotch—his favorite local beverage—and anger melted into understanding and then sympathy."[34]

"One of the reasons they worked as well as they did together," Bacall said, "was that John needed Bogie to keep him paying attention. He tended to lose interest as a picture was coming to a close. And Bogie always said that if an actor normally went just so high, John would always make him go higher, find things in himself he never suspected were there . . . John told Bogie late one night, 'the trouble with me is that I am forever and eternally bored.' They'd been talking about life—John envied Bogie his. I always thought it was a sad and revealing remark, diagramming the eternal war raging within him."[35]

Huston had another adversary in Jack Warner. Although the studio boss had originally greenlit the picture and championed Huston, when he saw the rushes back in Burbank he was incensed at how scruffy Huston was making his top star look. His initial support for *Treasure* wavered and that, plus the budget overage, primed him to hate the results when they arrived.

The final showdown in the story between Dobbs and Gold Hat (Alfonso Bedoya) was among the last scenes to be shot in Mexico. Bedoya was a small-part actor whom Huston hired. One or more of his on-screen companions may have been actual bandits ("In those days, bandits weren't all that scarce in Mexico," Huston would say.) When he needed to bring Bedoya back to Los Angeles to reshoot a scene, there was a problem; bandits weren't allowed to cross the border.[36] In the scene, both Gold Hat and Dobbs know that Dobbs is going to die. The murder—a beheading—is carried out below the frameline and is further blocked from view by a burro in front of the camera. There is no mistaking what has happened, however, as Gold Hat watches Dobbs's head roll offscreen into the waterhole. Huston decided to shoot the waterhole scene with a hacienda set in the background, but despite the rain that had been holding up the production, there was no waterhole to be found, so he ordered the crew to dig one. At first there was trouble getting Bogart's burro to drink the water in the same frame that Bogart was refreshing himself, but the stubborn animal eventually did so without Huston having to tweak its nose too.

Before they left Mexico, Huston did something that perplexed his wife and still vexes those who hear of it. There was a boy hired to be an extra to whom John took a paternal liking. Pablo Albarran was an orphan living in a car, and one day Huston asked him, "How would you like to go to the States, boy?" No fool, Pablo agreed. This surprised Bogart who urged Huston to comprehend the effect that the dislocation would have on the lad. It turned out that not only was Pablo five years older than he appeared, but he also had a sister who he apparently left behind. "He attached himself to me," Huston said, "and when it came time to leave, I thought, why not? I didn't tell Evelyn anything about it. I inquired how difficult it would be to bring him to the States and they said not difficult at all."[37] When Evelyn learned of her husband's deed, it put additional strain on their marriage.

Back in Burbank, the last scene to be shot in the studio was in the soundstage at Warners: Dobbs, by now fully paranoid and talking to himself, returns to the spot where he shot Curtin and, seeing Curtin gone, wildly speculates that predatory tiger cats have dragged him away to devour him. Bogart artfully speaks a monologue—a contrivance that always looks artificial in the intimate medium of film—but because of his carefully gradated performance leading up to it, it works.

There were some small reshoots such as the moment at the very end when Howard, realizing that all their gold has blown off in a dust storm, can only laugh at the twist of fate. Huston thought he needed more footage to sell the idea that there was nothing Curtin could do but laugh along with him. The laughter was something Walter recalled after the disastrous opening of his 1937 production of *Othello* at Broadway's Amsterdam Theatre. In effect, when the news is bad—and his *Othello* closed after twenty-one days—sometimes all one can do is laugh.

With that, *The Treasure of the Sierra Madre* finally finished principal photography on September 19, 1947, nearly three months over schedule and at a cost of between $2.5 and $3 million versus the original $1.8 million allotted.

After the picture was edited and Max Steiner recorded his distinctive musical score, the picture was successfully previewed in Glendale, California, far enough away from Hollywood to discourage gossip but close enough for the studio brass to commute comfortably.

There remained the Production Code gauntlet. Although the censors had approved of the script at every stage, they still needed to view the finished film before issuing their seal of approval. The Breen Office's "analysis chart" for the film, filled out on August 8, 1947, adjudged the character of "Gold Prospector" (Bogart) played straight and unsympathetically; "His Young Partner" (Holt) played straight and sympathetically; and "His Elderly Partner" (Water Huston) played "comic." Mexicans and Mexican Indians were played straight and sympathetically—no mention is made of Gold Hat being neither—and there were scenes of drinking with one character (Bogart) "shown slightly high on beer." These ratings were acceptable enough to not require trimming, and on August 27, 1947, *The Treasure of the Sierra Madre* was awarded Code seal #12347 with the caveat, "this certificate is issued on the understanding that the picture will be released exactly as reedited and re-reviewed by us today, August 26, 1947."[38]

This domestic approval did not stop censors in other countries from demanding changes. Alberta, Canada, for example wanted to remove McCormick kicking Curtin during the saloon fight, and the bandit's machete blow that kills Dobbs offscreen. Australia and India also wanted cuts to the violence.[39]

The final word, of course, belonged to Jack L. Warner. On August 1, 1947, he sent the following cable to his sales manager, Benny Kalmanson, in New York:

> THIS IS THE FIRST TIME I HAVE EVER DONE THIS BUT LAST NIGHT I RAN IN 12,500 FEET THE TREASURE OF THE SIERRA MADRE. I WANT YOU AND THOSE ASSEMBLED TO KNOW THAT THIS IS DEFINITELY THE GREATEST MOTION PICTURE THAT WE HAVE EVER MADE. IT IS REALLY ONE THAT WE HAVE ALWAYS WISHED FOR. A FEW YEARS BACK THIS ONE PICTURE WOULD VIRTUALLY PUT OVER A WHOLE SEASON'S PRODUCT. THAT'S THE SIZE OF IT.

In Hollywood equivalence, this amounted to a papal encyclical. As Warner Bros.' publicity department prepared the film for its January 23, 1948, world premiere in New York, the studio duly invited B. Traven to attend, feeling that the publicity would help both him and the picture. He disagreed on both counts and stayed in Acapulco.

Meanwhile, Jack Warner gloated that the film he had championed was worth the effort. *The Treasure of the Sierra Madre* drew more positive attention than any recent Warner Bros. film, but it was not the expected box office smash. It grossed only $4.1 million in the days before ancillary markets, returning half that in theatrical rentals, making it a financial loss but a succès d'estime.[40] Along the way, it became a legend.

The trade papers were mixed in their reviews, not one positive and one negative, but within the same notice. *Weekly Variety*'s Herm Schoenfeld called it "radically different" and "a distinguished work that will take its place in the repertory of Hollywood's enduring achievements." In a solemn review, he praised the three main performers, and he carped that the film's ending is "a grim joke the film public will remember and won't laugh at."[41] *Daily Variety*, *Weekly Variety*'s sister paper, had said in an unusual, separate unsigned review the day before that the film was "action stuff with heavy masculine appeal" but added, carefully, that the film "would have to be sold strongly," a code phrase warning of minimal commercial appeal.[42] The *Hollywood Reporter* was picky, saying it was "insight into a man's world done in fascinating style and completely without self-conscious effort." The uncredited review also noted that the film's action flagged and "does not sustain interest completely," but later praised editor Owen Marks for "another splendid facet of a splendid motion picture."[43]

The mainstream press was more effusive, recognizing the film's mature themes. The *New York Times*'s Bosley Crowther wrote that Huston had "resolutely applied the same sort of ruthless realism that was evident in his documentaries of war."[44] Kate Cameron of the *New York Daily News* cited *Treasure* as "the best picture that has come from the Warner Bros. Studios since the war."[45] The *New York Herald Tribune*'s Howard Barnes called Walter Huston "nothing short of magnificent" and said John Huston had "staged the production superbly."[46] "This is one of the most visually alive and beautiful movies I have ever seen," wrote James Agee in *The Nation* (he would later script *The African Queen* for Huston).[47]

Treasure's most appreciated honor, though, would surely be the one that Walter Huston received on March 24, 1949, at the Academy Theatre in Hollywood. The film was nominated for four Oscars: best picture, best director, best adapted screenplay, and best supporting actor. Humphrey

Bogart, whom everyone had anticipated would receive a best actor nomination, was overlooked. John Huston won for his screenplay; he took the statuette from presenter Deborah Kerr, hoisted it in the air, smiled at the audience, and said nothing. When he was announced as best director by presenter director Frank Borzage, he was more vocal and thanked his producer, Henry Blanke. Later after Celeste Holm presented the best supporting actor Oscar to Walter Huston, the elder Huston said, "Many years ago—many, *many* years ago—I raised a son and I said if you ever become a director or writer, please find a good part for your old man. And he did all right."[48]

CHAPTER 7

Comparing Script and Novel of *The Treasure of the Sierra Madre*

T he differences between the novel and the screenplay of The Treasure of the Sierra Madre *are so profound as to require a separate chapter. Here the novel and film are compared to examine the additions, deletions, and compromises that were involved in what became Huston's only Oscar-winning screenplay.*

Synopsis of the Novel

A great deal of the novel's content was eliminated in bringing it to the screen, particularly three extended tangential stories that enrich the reader's understanding of the milieu but have scant effect on the plot. This synopsis compares how material that appears in both book and film was altered in the transition.

Mexico, 1920.[1] Dobbs, an American oil worker whose job has long since ended, is reduced to begging for tostóns from tourists, and repeatedly from a white-suited fellow American whom he hits up four times without recognizing it's the same man.[2] Out of desperation, Dobbs is ready to buy shoe polish and set himself up giving shines in the town plaza except the local kids already do this. Dobbs uses some of the tourist's handout to buy a small percentage of a lottery ticket from a pushy kid who promises him luck.[3]

Dobbs stays in the Oso Negro flophouse where no one steals anybody else's possessions because anyone who has any possessions worth stealing would be suspect. He meets another out-of-work laborer, Moulton, and together they venture into the jungle looking for itinerant work at oil drilling sites. They are accompanied by a local Indian who is afraid to enter the jungle alone. (There is an auctorial digression about the exploitation of the country's resources and the Indians' lack of desire to capitalize on their own land.)[4]

After a harsh journey, the men find no work and the Indian goes his own way. Dobbs and Moulton meet Pat McCormick, a labor foreman, who hires them for eight dollars a day to perform sweltering rigging work. Upon their return to Tampico, McCormick stiffs them.

At a bar, Dobbs runs into Bob Curtin, a fellow laborer, from California, who lectures Dobbs that they were foolish to be suckered by McCormick, who is known for cheating the men he hires.[5] Later, by chance, Dobbs and Curtin find McCormick and beat their back pay out of him.

Sitting on a bench in the Tampico town square, Dobbs and Curtin contemplate their futures. They hate oil and confess that they only wanted to do such work long enough to save up a stake so they could go out and look for gold. They split up; Curtin is staying in the Roosevelt Hotel while Dobbs is still in the poverty-level Oso Negro. There he hears an old man, Howard, enthralling two younger men with tales of gold and what it does to a man.[6] As an example of the destructive power of gold, Howard tells them "The Legend of La Mina Agua Verde" (the Green Water mine).[7]

The story of the Green Water mine (La Mina Agua Verde) originates with a former prospector, Harry Tilton, who was the sole survivor of a fifteen-man expedition to the mine, and who escaped carrying a fortune. Tilton passed the tale along to Howard (who enters the story at a later point).

As Howard relates it, when the Spaniards conquered the land between Arizona and Sonora, Mexico they enslaved the natives and forced them to mine the area's rich silver and gold deposits.[8] Anyone who refused to do so was tortured with the complicity of the Church of Rome. The gold was plentiful, but death befell the conquerors who took it—evidence that the Indians had cursed the lode. The government sent soldiers to enforce the labor mandate, but laborers kept escaping and retaliating. In 1762 the Indians forced out the armies and destroyed all evidence of the mine's location, and its existence faded into legend.

By the 1840s, when the United States took possession of northern Mexico, rumors began resurfacing of the rich Green Water mine and the curse that followed all who sought it. In the 1870s, three American college students make a copy of a map that supposedly reveals the mine's location. They forge a compact with experienced prospectors—among them Harry Tilton—to travel to where they believe the mine will be found. The search and mining party numbers fifteen men.

The search proves fruitless until three of the team, working away from the others, find a small trove of ore so rich with gold that its value is unmistakable. They contrive to hide this trove from their cohorts but are discovered and murdered. The remaining twelve men work the mine. Harry Tilton leaves early with $28,000 worth of gold, returns to Kansas, and builds a farm. Once he is gone, the other men are killed by natives.

Gold fever ravages the world at the beginning of the twentieth century and men approach Tilton, who is known to have survived the mine's curse, to lead a new expedition to rediscover the Green Water mine. Howard was one of the members of this new team. The new expedition departs for Mexico. When Tilton cannot find the mine—geology has done its job to erase it on top of the camouflaging done by the natives—the other men torture him, believing that he is withholding information. He has none to give. He survives and returns to Kansas where he finds that his farm has been burned. He rebuilds and it burns again. Tilton flees Kansas into obscurity, and the prospecting party he was forced to join returns empty handed but alive.

Back at the flophouse, the men listening to Howard all swear that gold would never affect them this way. Warns Howard, "I have seen quite a number of men get rich prospecting, but I haven't yet met one who stayed so."[9]

Dobbs repeats Howard's tale to a skeptical Curtin and echoes Tilton's decision that he would be satisfied with a finite amount of gold if they ever discovered any. After a week and a half of joblessness, Curtin and Dobbs are so desperate as to consider committing robbery, but then Dobbs sees in a newspaper that he has won 100 pesos in the lottery. With $200 each from Curtin and Howard, they set off for Durango to buy prospecting supplies and seek a score.[10]

The men buy supplies in Durango and head off. The younger Curtin and Dobbs are stunned at the older Howard's stamina as they climb into the hills of the Sierra Madres. After some false alerts, Howard discovers a skein of placer gold (gold that must be separated from other minerals but has great value). As a cover story, they create a fake campsite more than a mile away from their dig and tell the locals that they are hunters. At the locale of their discovery, they construct a sluice trough and begin extracting gold dust at a steady rate. The work is brutal; although the Sierra Madres are kin to the Rockies, the climate is tropical and there is no respite from the heat, humidity, and insects.

The men forage for food and work for months digging and filtering the ore. They debate registering their claim—doing so might attract others—and they weigh the risks of keeping it a secret and facing confiscation and prison if the government discovers them. They decide to risk breaking the law rather than be at the mercy of corrupt government officials, other prospectors, or mining companies who could come after them. Their debate shows them moving from being workers to becoming property owners, and Traven makes a point of saying that, despite their closeness, they never really become friends.[11] When Dobbs is buried in a mine cave-in, Curtin rushes in to save him. Afterward, Dobbs begins grousing at the conditions, and Howard finds himself mediating between Curtin and Dobbs, constantly reminding them that they need to work together for the common good.[12]

They begin to divide their gold equally every night and hide it from one another. Howard estimates they if they come away with $15,000 apiece, he'll be satisfied; both "Dobbsy" and "Curty" want to keep digging, especially Dobbs. When at last the vein seems to be thinning out, the men decide to leave in six weeks' time. The setting of a departure date calms them; they no longer get on each other's nerves.[13]

One day Curtin returns from a supply run to the village with news that a stranger, probably from Arizona, had been hanging around town asking about silver or gold deposits. The natives had said there were none, but while Curtin was at the trading post, the stranger tried to pump him for information. The partners debate what to do should the man show up and, as if on cue, he does. He introduces himself as Robert W. Lacaud from Phoenix, Arizona. He also challenges their explanation that they are hunters noting that there is hardly any game in the area.[14] Everyone is polite, yet cautious. At nightfall, Lacaud beds down away from the partners. Once he is out of earshot, the three men debate whether to kill him. They decide to do so.

The next day, after a dispute with Dobbs, Lacaud declares that he will stay and mine for gold with them. His extortion plan is that he will not claim any of their existing shares, but he will keep whatever he himself finds, and if they complain, he will go to town and reveal everything. He also says that he knows they were planning to kill him. Before any of them can move, however, the bandit Gold Hat and his men approach from below, having heard in the village about the strangers. Lacaud tells Dobbs, Curtin, and Howard the story of Gold Hat that was just told to him by Don Genaro Montereal.

In the story, a passenger train links the western and eastern areas of the republic, carrying mail and goods, an army contingent, and a few passengers. One Friday night more than twenty passengers, all mestizos, board the train without tickets.[15] This is not strange as the custom is that people may pay their fares to the conductor. They disperse among the train's passengers. When the train is moving at full speed these strangers whip out guns, shoot at the soldiers, and begin attacking the passengers. They work their way through the train, robbing, beating, and shooting those who resist. The engineer, hearing shots, speeds the engine to the next station.

The bandits continue trashing the train and begin to set the cars ablaze, then they jump off. When the train pulls into the depot, a hospital train is dispatched to go back and rescue the injured. In time, the federales hunt down the bandit-murderers, who insist that they were fighting for religious liberty on behalf of Jesus and the Roman Catholic church. Surviving passengers recognize two priests among the bandits. The army seeks the bandits, who are hiding among the peasants; anyone whose clothing does not match his income or social status is detained. Those men deemed to be guilty are not taken to court but, rather, to the local cemetery where they dig their own graves, are shot, and fall into them.[16]

Hearing this report, Dobbs and his partners cautiously shake hands with Lacaud and welcome him to their side. Lacaud describes the bandit leader, who is still at large, as wearing a gold-painted palm hat. This is the man whose gang is poised below to attack them. The prospectors leave their base camp and allow the bandits to enter it. One bandit finds Curtin at his post. It is a stand-off. The bandits lie that they are *policía montada*.[17] Curtin says, "If you are the police, where are your badges?" to which Gold Hat sneers, "Badges, to god-damned hell with badges! We have no badges. In fact, we don't need badges. I don't have to show you any stinking badges, you god-damned *cabrón and ching' tu madre!* Come out from that shit-hole of yours. I have to speak to you."[18] After many tense days and nights waiting for the attack, a battle is avoided when soldiers arrive to chase off the bandits.[19]

Howard now encourages Dobbs and Curtin to forsake more treasure, return to civilization, and leave Lacaud behind to do as he wishes.[20] "He is an eternal," says Howard, labeling the stranger as someone who will stay in one place and keep digging with eternal hope of finding gold. The partners spend a week restoring the land to the state in which they found it. They finally become friendly with Lacaud, whom they call "Laky."

Mindful that the real jeopardy now lies in transporting their riches to town, Howard tells his partners the story of Doña Catalina María de Rodríguez. It is a tale of religion, swindling, and riches:

The story begins in the late 1700s when a Northern Mexican chieftain named Aguila Bravo has a son who is blind. A corrupt monk entices him to give him money to effect a cure, and the cure involves prolonged, exhausting travels and religious sacrifices to the church by Bravo and his family. When nothing works, the chief renounces the church. The church declares him a blasphemer and threatens him with the tortures of the Inquisition. Arriving in Mexico City, the chief is swindled by a fraudulent doctor, Don Manuel, who offers to restore the boy's sight if the chief will tell him the location of a silver mine, but if the mine turns out to be barren, the doctor will reverse the operation. Surprisingly, the doctor manages to give the boy sight, and the mine proves to be full of silver, though less so of gold.

Don Manuel is wary that the church will get wind of his riches, so he hides them. He also abuses his Indian mine workers, who rebel. Doña Maria escapes the workers' wrath, but her husband Don Manuel is killed. The workers go back to their homes, caring nothing about the riches of the mine, but when Doña Maria buries her husband, she discovers his hidden silver. She reopens the mine but cannily donates money to the church, treating the workers poorly but impressing the visiting clerics with her religious devotion.

World politics in the late eighteenth century make Spain's hold on Mexico tenuous. Doña Maria tires of her frugal lifestyle and yearns to use her wealth to join the Spanish nobility. Now she must move her silver, which she melts into ingots, across the Sierra Madre mountains to Mexico City and hires two former Spanish army soldiers to guard the convoy.

On the trek, one of the soldiers turns against her and demands that Doña Maria marry him; if not, he will accost her, confiscate her money, and give it to the workers. Astonishingly, she bullwhips the turncoat soldier into submission and has him hanged. She and the loyal soldier forgive the Indian mutineers, and she arrives in Mexico City where she becomes a celebrity. She transfers her wealth to the king's treasury where it is guarded by the nobility. She then disappears.[21]

Hearing Howard's story, Lacaud asks if the mine is still in operation. Howard says that it is, but it is owned by an American company that keeps all the money for itself and pays its employees only $40 a week.[22]

The next morning, the partners divvy up their goods and leave Lacaud to his own devices at the camp. Traveling conspicuously so as not to appear as if they are hiding anything, they enter a town where a government doctor is trying to dispense smallpox vaccine to the locals. Dobbs, Curtin, and Howard accept the vaccination as a gesture of support and head onward.

The men set up camp and are approached by a group of Indian farmers who ask help for a boy in the village who fell into a river. He was pulled out but cannot be revived. Howard goes with the men to the village where he uses artificial respiration to resuscitate the boy. The villagers regard Howard as a medicine man with healing powers. They ask him to stay, but he leaves to rejoin Dobbs and Curtin. Before long, however, he, Dobbs, and Curtin are intercepted by the father of the boy that Howard saved. He wants Howard to return to the village so they can repay their debt to him with a celebration. Dobbs wants to fight them, but the Indians insist. Howard goes off with the Indians and leaves his share of the gold in care of Dobbs and Curtin, saying he will rejoin them in Durango. The villagers fête Howard as a hero.

Lacking Howard's mediation, Curtin and Dobbs quarrel as they cross the Sierra Madres. Despite Curtin trying to keep calm, Dobbs becomes more and more paranoid and resentful. Finally, Dobbs declares to make off with Howard's share. Curtin objects, and the two men engage in a philosophical discussion about socialism.[23] Curtin resents people with power and wealth but he will not turn against his absent partner, Howard. Dobbs pulls a gun on Curtin, but Curtin disarms him. He cannot, however, bring himself to kill Dobbs.

As the two men travel, Dobbs broods and keeps needling Curtin. Curtin controls his temper and tries to stay awake for fear that Dobbs will make a move on him if he dozes. When Curtin finally drifts off, Dobbs reclaims his gun and forces Curtin to walk into the brush, where he shoots him. Now fully paranoid, Dobbs walks away but returns to the place where he shot Curtin and shoots him again as he lies on the ground.[24] Dobbs's rationale is that, if he was able to kill the enemy in the World War, and Curtin is the enemy, why not be able to kill him now? Dobbs eventually passes out from fatigue and, on awakening, goes to check on Curtin's body. Curtin is gone.

Dobbs cannot be distracted by Curtin's death. He leads his pack mules laden with everyone's gold dust toward Durango. Seeing a train pass by, he fantasizes a trip to England, then begins to fear that his crime will be discovered before he can flee the country. He is proud of overcoming Curtin and abandoning Howard.

Just outside of Durango, Dobbs and his burros are stopped by three bandits: Nacho, Miguel, and Pablo. Dobbs watches helplessly as the men unpack his gear. Dobbs reaches for his gun, which is packed away, but it is out of bullets. One of the banditos hits Dobbs in the head with a rock and Miguel, the leader, decapitates him. The outlaws steal Dobbs's boots and trousers and, finding the bags of gold dust, mistake it for sand that Dobbs was using to increase the market weight of his trapped furs. They empty it on the ground where it scatters in the wind.[25]

The three bandits try to sell their stolen burros in a mountain village, but the townspeople recognize the burros' brands as the stock that was sold to the three hunters. The village mayor questions the Mestizos while other villagers fan out to locate Dobbs, Curtin, and Howard. These villagers find Dobbs' headless body. Soldiers are summoned and take the bandits into custody but shoot them while they are "trying to escape."[26]

Curtin, near death, is discovered by a local man who brings him home and sends word to Howard to come help. Howard arrives and patches Curtain's wounds. Curtin swears revenge on Dobbs, but Howard magnanimously explains that $50,000 worth of gold would tempt any man to kill. They plan to find Dobbs and their stolen gold once Curtin can travel.[27]

Leaving Curtin to heal, Howard goes to Durango where the mayor tells him the story of Dobbs's murder. Of course, the gold has been lost. Howard brings the burros and what's left of their supplies back to tell Curtin, who is stunned. Then Howard begins laughing at the irony of it all.[28] They search the saddlebags and find two untouched pouches of gold dust.[29] At first, they ponder opening a store together, but Howard decides to go back to the native village and become their shaman. He invites Curtin to join him, and Curtin considers it.[30]

Synopsis of the Film:

A destitute American, Fred C. Dobbs (Humphrey Bogart), wanders through the streets of Tampico, Mexico. It is 1925. Clearly down on what little luck he has ever known (he has just lost a lottery), he is about to reach for a discarded cigarette in the street, but a Mexican kid grabs it first. Then he spots a well-dressed American (John Huston) in a white suit and receives from him a tostón (fifty pesos), which he uses to buy a meal. As he finishes his meal, an aggressive Mexican boy (Robert Blake) pesters him to buy a lottery ticket. He tosses his drink in the kid's face, but the kid persists, insisting, "I always have the winner." To make him go away, Dobbs buys 1/20 of a ticket for a number whose digits add up to a lucky thirteen.

Dobbs meets another American, Curtin (Tim Holt), on a park bench and together they bemoan the lack of work. Later, Dobbs again meets the white-suited American who hands him another tostón. Dobbs uses it to get a haircut and shave.[31] On leaving the barber shop, he again runs into the white-suited American who chastises him for picking on him a third time, hands him two tostóns, and tells him to make his own way from now on.

Outside a barroom at night, Dobbs panhandles another American, Pat McCormick (Barton MacLane), who offers him construction work if he wants it. Dobbs accepts the offer and, later that night, he and Curtin ship out to a jungle location. They work in blistering heat with the rest of the rigging crew, but when they return to Tampico weeks later, McCormick stiffs everyone for the pay.

With barely enough left for cheap accommodations, Dobbs and Curtin sleep at a flophouse where they meet Howard, an old prospector who talks fast and seems to know all about finding gold. Dobbs swears that if he found gold he'd never be greedy, but Howard says, "I know what gold does to men's souls" and that he "never knew a prospector who died rich."

One day Dobbs and Curtin spot McCormick on the street. He is escorting a woman and looking prosperous. They confront him about their back pay and he leads them into a bar where he tries sweet-talking them out of his debt. He strikes first, but they beat him and take from his wallet only what they are owed.[32] They return to the flophouse and try to entice Howard to teach them prospecting. The Mexican boy shows up. Dobbs is about to kick him away again, but he announces that Dobbs has won 200 pesos as his share of the lottery. Newly enriched, Dobbs, Curtin, and Howard agree to pool their resources and prospect for gold.

On the train from Tampico to Durango, they are attacked by the bandit Gold Hat (Alfonso Bedoya) and his hoards, but federales on the train repel them. At Durango, the trio buy burros and supplies and head off deep into the wilderness "where the mountains stick up through the clouds" pretending to be hunters to deflect the curiosity of anyone they may encounter. En route, Curtin and Dobbs are amazed that the considerably older Howard has more stamina than they do. The trek is grueling, and Dobbs wants to give up. Howard berates him and says that they have been walking on gold all along, but that the supply itself is farther up the mountain.

Prospecting for gold is not easy. The men build a sluice to bring water to wash the sand from the gold dust, they haul buckets of water and ore, and slowly amass thousands of dollars of gold dust that still must be refined. As the gold dust piles up, Dobbs wants to divide it so each man can hide his stash from the others. Howard warns them, "I know what kind of ideas even supposedly decent people get when gold is at stake." This begins to come true when Dobbs is digging alone in the mine and there is a cave-in. Curtin hears it and starts to rescue him but hesitates for a moment, then goes in.

The allure of riches inspires the three men to fantasize around the campfire. Curtin wants to get land and raise crops; Howard wants simply to live; Dobbs wants short-term pleasures of the flesh. Although the men sleep watchfully together after each day's long toil, each becomes wary when another leaves the camp to "check the burros," fearing that one of them may be searching for where their partners have hidden their "goods" (they dare not use the word *gold*).

Buying supplies in Durango, Curtin is befriended by a nosy man named Jim Cody (Bruce Bennett) who sees through Curtin's hunter façade. As the men talk cautiously, there are gunshots; federales have captured two bandits, made them dig their own graves, let them smoke a last cigarette, and summarily executed them.

Humphrey Bogart was his mother's favorite model for her baby food portraits. Contrary to popular belief, he was not the model for Gerber baby food. *Wiki Commons.*

ABOVE: Humphrey Bogart, Bette Davis, and Leslie Howard in *The Petrified Forest*, the role that brought Bogart from Broadway to Hollywood, but only after Howard lobbied Jack Warner. *Wiki Commons.* BELOW: Bogart as Roy Earle in *High Sierra*. John Huston's screenplay won the picture its green light, and it was here where he and Bogart met and bonded—over drinks, naturally. *Wiki Commons.*

Bogie and Bird. *The Maltese Falcon*, of course. *Wiki Commons.*

"The Battling Bogarts"—Humphrey Bogart and his wife Mayo Methot—with their dogs during a rare domestic truce. Life *magazine by uncredited Warner Bros. photographer, Wiki Commons.*

John Huston in uniform during his service in the US Signal Corps' motion picture unit during World War II. His documentaries remain riveting today, including one that was suppressed for decades. National Board of Review *magazine, February 1946; Wiki Commons.*

ABOVE: (L-R) Bruce Bennett (back to camera), Tim Holt, Humphrey Bogart, and Walter Huston in *The Treasure of the Sierra Madre*. *Wiki Commons*. BELOW: Mug shot of B. Traven after he was arrested in England in 1923 under the name "Ret Marut." *British Authorities, London, 1923, Wiki Commons*.

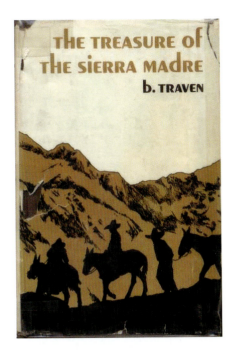 

ABOVE LEFT: Book Cover, *The Treasure of the Sierra Madre*. ABOVE RIGHT: *Der Ziegelbrenner*, "Brickbuilder," 1921 radical pamphlet published by Ret Marut. *Wiki Commons*. BELOW: Authenticated signature of B. Traven ("Hal Croves") in a published edition of *The Bridge in the Jungle*. Photo by the author; courtesy of Pancho Kohner.

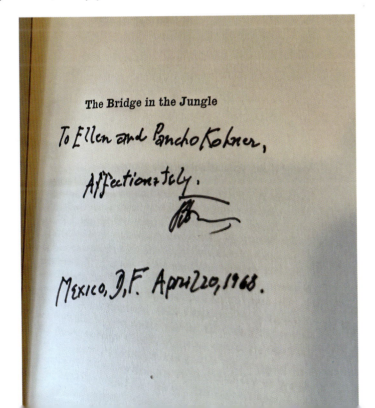

The Bogarts: Humphrey, Betty, Stephen, and Leslie, 1956. Corpus Christi Caller-Times-AP; *Wiki Commons.*

ABOVE: The Committee for the First Amendment heads to Washington, DC, to witness the HUAC hearings in October 1957. Pictured are Marsha Hunt, Shepperd Strudwick, Paul Henreid, Jane Wyatt, Sterling Hayden, Geraldine Brooks, Lauren Bacall, Danny Kaye, Humphrey Bogart, Richard Conte, and Evelyn Keyes. Several of them were later blacklisted. Los Angeles Daily News, *Wiki Commons*. BELOW: B. Traven's (Ret Marut's) stepdaughter Malú Montes de Oca and her husband Timothy Heyman in a photo taken May 2, 2019, by Amrei-Marie. *Wiki Commons*.

Humphrey Bogart and Lauren Bacall aboard his boat, the *Santana*, during the production of *Key Largo*. *Wiki Commons.*

Bogart and Bacall perform on Cecil B. DeMille's *Lux Radio Theatre. Wiki Commons.*

ABOVE: Bogart finally won his Oscar® in 1952 for *The African Queen*. Other winners backstage: Bette Davis, George Sanders, Karl Malden (Best Supporting, *A Streetcar Named Desire*), and Greer Garson (presenter). Davis and Sanders were apparently added to the photo for star power because they were not nominees. *Wiki Commons*. BELOW: Humphrey Bogart and Jennifer Jones in John Huston and Truman Capote's delightfully screwy *Beat the Devil*. *Spinoziano, Wiki Commons*.

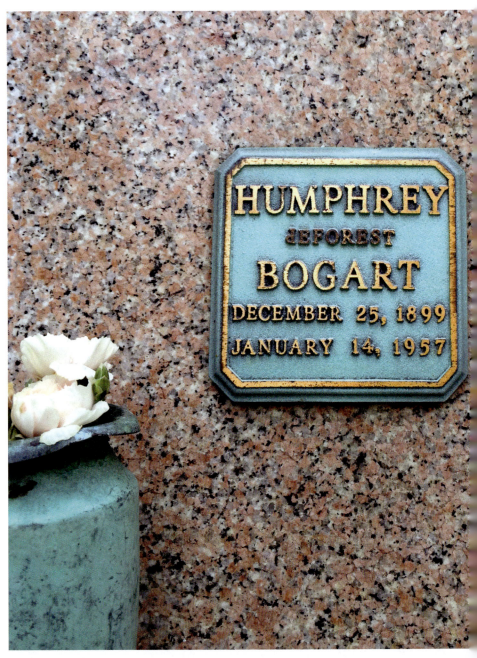

Humphrey Bogart died January 14, 1957, and was interred at Forest Lawn cemetery in Glendale, California. This is his grave marker. *Wiki Commons*.

ABOVE: Humphrey Bogart (left) and John Huston spend time away from the movies on Bogart's boat, *Santana*. Photofest. BELOW: Bogart (left) and Bacall (center) confer with Huston on the somber set of *Key Largo*. Photofest.

ABOVE: (L-R) John Huston, Walter Huston, Humphrey Bogart, and cinematographer Arthur Edeson during the elder Huston's visit to the set of *The Maltese Falcon*. *Photofest*. BELOW: Humphrey Bogart panhandles spare change from an American tourist (John Huston) in *The Treasure of the Sierra Madre*. It was Hal Croves who suggested Huston play the part after seeing him hand out spare change to Mexicans during a location scout. *Photofest*.

ABOVE: Truman Capote wrote, and John Huston may or may not have cowritten, *Beat the Devil*. *Photofest*. BELOW: (L-R) Lupita Tovar, B. Traven, and Paul Kohner. Traven had a yearslong crush on Tovar, who was married to agent Paul Kohner. Toward the end of his life, Traven didn't care who knew who he was, including Tovar and Kohner's son, Pancho. *Pancho Kohner © Pancho Kohner.*

ABOVE: Pancho Kohner directing John Huston as Sleigh, based on Walter Huston's Howard in *The Bridge in the Jungle*, B. Traven's sequel to *The Treasure of the Sierra Madre*. *Pancho Kohner © Pancho Kohner.* BELOW: John Huston as Sleigh in *The Bridge in the Jungle*. *Pancho Kohner © Pancho Kohner.*

Cody surreptitiously follows Curtin back to the campsite and extorts the partners to allow him to dig for his own gold while they dig for theirs. If they refuse, he will go back to Durango and file a claim on his own—unless, of course, he jokes, they decide to kill him. He goes off to allow the three men to vote, but when they approach Cody with their guns drawn, ready to kill him, Cody points out that bandits are approaching from below. It's Gold Hat. All four men must now stick together to fight off Gold Hat and his gang. In the attack, Cody is killed and the federales show up to chase away the remaining bandits without noticing that the miners are there. This solves the Cody problem but in so doing has revealed the men's changing morality. They find a letter on Cody's body. It's from his wife begging him to give up his hopeless prospecting and come back to Texas to help her raise their daughter. Howard and Curtin want to give some of their gold to Cody's wife, but Dobbs, who has begun acting possessively, refuses to commit.

Other strangers arrive at their camp: four Mexican villagers who beg Howard to save the life of a child who has fallen into water and cannot wake up. Howard goes to their village and brings the boy around, returning afterward to the gold strike. Shortly, the villagers return and demand that he come back with them to their village to be honored. He reluctantly agrees, asking Dobbs and Curtin to hold onto his share of the goods and he'll meet them later.

Without Howard to mediate, Dobbs and Curtin argue bitterly. Dobbs goes over the edge and, one night, shoots Curtin and takes his gold. Unsure whether he has finished the job, he returns to where Curtin fell but discovers that Curtin was only wounded and has crawled away. Dobbs sets off for Durango and Curtin makes it to the Mexican village where they bring him to Howard for treatment.

Now on his own and near death in the arid land, Dobbs is ambushed by Gold Hat and his gang at a waterhole. The bandits kill him, take his burros and supplies, and thoughtlessly scatter the bags of gold, thinking it is sand. When Gold Hat tries to sell the burros in Durango, the animals' brands incriminate him, and he and his compadres are executed by federales.

Howard and Curtin arrive in Durango during a windstorm. First, they are told that Dobbs has been killed. Then they see that the bags containing their gold have been opened and their contents scattered with the swirling dust. There is nothing the men can do but laugh at the irony. Howard decides to return to the village to become their shaman. Curtin will sell their belongings and go to Texas to find Cody's widow. The mountain has reclaimed its own.

Assaying *Treasure*

Despite the success professionally and artistically in John Huston's career of *The Maltese Falcon*, it is *The Treasure of the Sierra Madre* that brought him his only Academy Award®[33] and therefore deserves closer scrutiny. This will involve an analysis of the transition from book to screen and the politics of making a dark film in an industry built on escapism.

Hollywood has never been comfortable with downbeat endings. For decades, people went to the movies for entertainment—to be taken somewhere else mentally for two hours plus cartoon, newsreel, short subject, previews of coming attractions and, on special occasions, dish night. Hard-hitting dramas had to end happily, or at least be emotionally satisfying. Prestige pictures were extolled for enrichment and awards; they were "good for you," like spinach. Such films were also only one or two out of the thirty or forty each studio released every year.

After World War II, Americans started to become more aware of the responsibilities that came with victory. When Johnny came marching home, he arrived with his eyes open. He had seen death on the battlefield and somehow the escapist fare screened at the local bijou seemed anemic. Lightweight fare had generated record-setting profits during the war, but the postwar box office started to falter. The films of the transitional years 1946 and 1947 show the studios grasping for clues as to what these newly mature viewers wanted to see.

The founding moguls were stubborn. They were strongly pro-America and they didn't want to see their adopted country criticized from within by dissenters pointing cameras at its postwar problems. And even if they felt adventurous and wanted to dramatize society's ills, their hands were tied by the Production Code that forbade many of the elements that attracted socially conscious filmmakers: race, sex, language, discrimination, and drugs, the mere mention of which would deny a picture a Code seal.

John Huston was a man who chafed at constraints. Although he could have a light touch, he seldom ventured into light subjects. After his World War II experiences, in particular, his filmography contains an astonishing number of what have come to be regarded as classics that make political or social points.

The Treasure of the Sierra Madre was the first of these. Studio head Jack L. Warner, whose parsimony was legendary, and cautious production chief Hal Wallis, deferred their concern for the bottom line once they sensed Huston's excitement over the material. Even though they approved of *Treasure*, they would waver during production as they groused about delays, budget overruns, and disputes over how their stars looked. But that was why Huston insisted on shooting on location, hundreds of miles from Burbank.

Ironically, Warner Bros. had been a bastion of social relevance at the dawn of the sound era: *Little Caesar* (1931), *Public Enemy* (1931), *I Am a Fugitive from a Chain Gang* (1932), *Wild Boys of the Road* (1933), and *Baby Face* (1933) were only a handful of their releases to deal with crime, punishment, and sexual exploitation, One film, the legendary *Convention City* (1933), a veritable chronicle of debauchery, was credited with single-handedly bringing about enforcement of the Production Code.[34] But that was before Darryl F. Zanuck left the studio to form Twentieth Century-Fox, and his successor, Wallis, had less interest in social causes.

The Treasure of the Sierra Madre was Warner Bros.' return to relevance. The timing was perfect, the gumption was there, and its caution about the wages of greed was set a safe twenty-five years in the past. Its star, Humphrey Bogart, had just signed a new contract that made him the highest-paid actor in movies. John Huston was a studio wunderkind with *The Maltese Falcon*, hard-hitting documentaries he'd just made for the Army, and the dramatic film *Across the Pacific* having cleaned up at the box office.[35, 36] Warner considered prestige films to be "good for the industry" provided their budgets were controlled.

Warner was still conflicted. Bogart had just become a romantic leading man with *Casablanca* (1943), and here he was reverting to the kind of irredeemable tough guy he had played for twelve years before he met Rick Blaine. He was so proud of embarking on Fred C. Dobbs that he told critic Archer Winsten, when the two men met outside of New York's "21" restaurant, "Wait till you see me in my next picture, I play the worst shit you ever saw!"*

One concern for the studio was that, other than nonspeaking Mexican extras, there were no women in the story and the sole romance was between Dobbs and gold. There were exciting gunfights between the prospectors and the bandits, but the star died at the end and everybody's hard-won gains were literally gone with the wind.

What made *The Treasure of the Sierra Madre* resonate at the time, and makes it continue to do so, is its uncompromising integrity. It remains faithful throughout to the stated notion of the corrosive power of wealth, and every storytelling device is summoned in support of that theme. More subtle are the subjects of the exploitation of one culture by another, and

---

* A. M. Sperber and Eric Lax, *Bogart*, New York: William Morrow and Company, 1997.

the acceptance of ad-hoc justice in which government federales are little different from vigilantes. Much of its resonance stems from B. Traven's avowed socialist views, both moral and economic, and is reflected in the character constructions of Dobbs, Curtin, and Howard.

Dobbs is the hardened capitalist who, as Eric Lax points out, paradoxically cannot recognize a break when it presents itself (he rebuffs the boy selling lottery tickets, and he misses the gold dust at his own feet) but happily exploits those who can.[37] Howard is the old man with knowledge and the wisdom to respect the vicissitudes of Fate; he represents the institutional memory of the system that others attempt to manipulate.[38] And Curtin is labor, willing to side with management when there is a common threat (outlaws, war), but who becomes its victim when profits are involved. Curtin is also capable of corruption, hesitating when Dobbs is buried by a cave-in, or agreeing to kill Cody (in other words, their competition). For that matter, even Howard capitulates in Cody's death sentence. The ending, in which everybody collides with his fate (one dies, two gain enlightenment), demonstrates the futility of struggle. It is important that Dobbs is undone by his own greed and not by either Curtin or Howard; it is also not coincidental that not only does gold bring about his undoing, but it arrives from a man symbolically named Gold Hat.

Fate unites Dobbs and Gold Hat in another way that is not mentioned in the novel but is introduced into the screenplay by Huston and Traven. In the book, Dobbs dies at the hands of unnamed bandits, but this lacked power; on the screen the struggle between matched heroes and villains is the stuff of drama. Huston and Traven hit upon combining the book's three bandit encounters—the train siege, the "stinkin' badges" shootout at the camp, and Dobbs's death—into a single ongoing relationship between Dobbs and Gold Hat.[39] Later, when Gold Hat and his cronies are executed by federales, Huston adds the touch that Gold Hat wants to be shot wearing his gold hat. He is executed off-screen, and the wind blows his hat in front of the camera. This is not in the script, nor are the executions. In the script, villagers surround the bandits and tie them up. The fatal burnishes are Huston's.

Present in the novel but not in the film is criticism of outside commercial interests that exploit the native Mexicans, and the unholy alliance of the Catholic Church that not only enables this oppression but also benefits from it. Likewise missing is Traven's commentary about how the earlier Conquistadors and oil companies imprisoned, tortured, and otherwise crushed the indigenous people over the centuries in order to reap the region's oil, gold, and other natural resources. Downplayed in the film is that Dobbs and Curtin are unemployed oil workers driven to the streets by the oil companies who cut salaries and pit workers against each other in the manipulated job market.[40] Even if Hollywood hadn't just gone through divisive union activities prior to the war, there is no way this would have made it into a mainstream motion picture.[41]

These changes are key to Huston's adaptation of Traven's novel. In a word, he depoliticized it. Gone are stretches bemoaning the evils of capitalism and the moral superiority of communism and socialism. Just as Traven's views made him a target (whether real or imagined) in Europe, so Huston—while he may have been sympathetic—chose to focus on the drama and pruned the political underpinnings. Not only did much of this thinking never make it into the screenplay, much of what did was removed.

Huston's sympathy for the people of Mexico is evident in the way he has cinematographer Ted McCord photograph them. In the extended sequence in which Howard brings a drowned boy back to life, one particularly beatific woman is shown. She is not an actress, and she barely emotes, but Huston intercuts between her and the lad, and Max Steiner adds ethereal music underpinning the emotion.[42]

Often wrongly criticized for so-called objective filmmaking and shooting with long takes, Huston has a fondness for medium close-ups. As in *The Maltese Falcon* and his later work he follows his actors as they move, one crossing the other while the camera is passed like a baton, keeping them sequentially in the frame. While he ordinarily favors shooting up at people, in *Treasure* he has a penchant for shooting Bogart from slightly above, as if to diminish him. He shoots Walter Huston from slightly below, giving him credibility, and Holt from eye level, reinforcing visually their relative moral positions.[43]

As for landscapes—most of which look barren or entangled in brush, vines, or cacti—they were as harsh on the actors and crew as they are on the characters. Whether on location in Mexico or in the California Sierras doubling for Mexico, Huston and cinematographer Ted McCord compose disarmingly beautiful postcard vistas that increasingly defer to claustrophobic coverage. This starts off as a tale of men versus their environment and becomes a contest of men versus men.

The physically challenging setting, despite Huston's decision to shoot it in the cooler but more meteorologically volatile rainy season, is relentless (regardless of its proximity to a vacation spa). With the windstorms created by offscreen aircraft propellers, it's chokingly oppressive. It wouldn't be surprising if the outdoor scenes were purposely overexposed or printed lighter to make them appear blindingly hostile. The climate helps the audience identify with an exhausted Dobbs who begs to leave all their equipment behind and head back to Tampico until Howard does his dance and alerts his companions to their strike.

Cody, the interloper (played by Bruce Bennett), who was named Lacaud in the novel, is played for contrast. In the novel, he lives, but in the film, he is killed offscreen in the bandit attack, after which the trio of prospectors find a letter he had been carrying. The letter is from his wife and reveals that his attempt to force himself on the three main characters is born, not of greed, as they had surmised, but out of desperation to save his family back in Texas. As James Naremore points out in his annotated edition of the screenplay, in any other film, reading the letter would be a moment of drama and perhaps sentiment. As done here, it is an indictment of the three men who were just about to execute Cody.⁴⁴ Even Howard is tainted for agreeing to take part. As he had warned the others, gold does that to a man.

Howard waxed philosophical in a speech cut from the script. Waiting for the bandits to attack them at their campsite, the men are torn between trying to kill as many of them as possible and discussing how to bargain for their own lives. Curtin suggests offering them their goods (code for "gold") and guns in exchange for mercy. Dobbs doubts they know what mercy is. Howard answers Dobbs that they wouldn't know mercy because they had never been shown any. "If our people in the States had lived in poverty under all sorts of tyrannies for hundreds of years, they'd have bred a race of bandits, too." He likens it to foreign countries taking oil, silver, and copper from these indigenous people's land. This speech passionately explains Traven's protective attitude toward the original peoples of Mexico. Perhaps it was included in the script to gain Traven's favor, but it never made it to the screen.⁴⁵

Watching Dobbs with the hindsight of having seen Bogart as the crumbling Captain Queeg in 1954's *The Caine Mutiny*, one can compare the actor's two demonstrations of mounting paranoia. Both are developed gradually, but the latter is more sudden, taking place in court when his captain's authority is attacked and neither he nor his ball bearings can hide his emotional crisis. Dobbs's psychological collapse comes entirely from within and is more gradual. Bit by bit his dreams become material, his impatience and distrust increase, and he projects upon his two partners what he believes he would do in their place. By the time the men have mined their riches, in the book he is ready to restore the mountain; in the film he questions why this is necessary, and the more spiritual Howard explains it to him. There is no single turning point at which Dobbs begins to crack, as opposed to Queeg's more explosive breakdown on the witness stand.

Given Bogart's intensity and Walter Huston's scene-stealing crustiness, Holt, as Curtin, becomes an observer and occasional facilitator. When, for example, Curtin starts to lift a large desert rock in order to kill a gila monster that has crawled beneath it, Dobbs thinks that he is after his stash, for that is where, unbeknownst to Curtin, he has hidden it. Curtin dares Dobbs to stick his hand under the rock, telling him that there is, in fact, a gila monster there and will not let go of his hand should it bite. Does Dobbs trust Curtin or not? On location Huston, ever the prankster, arranged with a prop man to hide a snap trap under the rock to snare Bogart's hand when he reached under. As Dobbs does not reach there in the film, it must have been a rehearsal gag and Bogart fell for it, foolishly trusting Huston. Because the viewer knows Curtin is innocent, Dobbs' threatening action sells the moment without requiring much from Holt's acting.

Max Steiner's musical score has at times drawn criticism for sounding too lush, but it is entirely appropriate to reflect the changing psychology of the three characters. At times its full orchestration speaks to the grandiose ambitions of the three men while, at other times, it recedes into barely audible underscoring to indicate the men's fragile mental states. Steiner alternates Mexican themes with brassy Anglo tunes that contrast the clash of two cultures. Then there is the hymn-like scoring behind Howard's reviving of the drowned child in the Indian village. It hovers behind the action, quietly creating tension, then diminishes once the child is saved. There is no triumphant blaring forth, only the perfunctory ending that underplays the triumph of a spared life. The actors sell the scene, not the musicians. Throughout, Steiner supports the film rather than dominating it, although he is not above hitting a fanfare to button a scene and cue a transition.

The Treasure of the Sierra Madre is an existential film. Fate turns the corner before the men do. Not only do they wind up with nothing for their efforts, but the very object of their desire is reclaimed by the mountain from which they took it. It has all been for nought, and what lesson has been learned? Choose saner partners? Carry more defensive weapons? Forget about the stinking badges? Never count on luck? Between Howard and Curtin, Howard is the winner; he becomes the village prophet and will be cared for until he dies. Curtin will go to Texas to tell Cody's widow what happened (no doubt leaving out mention of his own complicity) and will perhaps settle down with her to grow crops as he once fantasized. Both men's dreams have been met, but it is an open question (depending on how cynical one is) whether their fulfillment will be permanent. It is this feeling of unsettlement that subtly undercuts the apparent end of the story. This is what makes for greatness. Both the novel and the film resonate with those who read and view it because each contains enough details to imagine what might happen afterward.

They say that the difference between plot and story is that the plot is what happens, but the story is what the work is about. *The Treasure of the Sierra Madre* is about more than gold and greed, as readers and audiences have been discovering for nigh unto a century.

CHAPTER 8

Key Largo, HUAC, and Betrayal

While *The Treasure of the Sierra Madre* was in postproduction in Hollywood, another kind of production was underway in Washington, DC. On October 20, 1947, the House Un-American Activities Committee (HUAC) under chairman J. Parnell Thomas, opened hearings into suspected Communist influence in motion pictures. The hearings were part of a Republican-led attempt to undo the progressive policies of President Franklin Roosevelt's New Deal, as well as get electoral publicity by attacking the movies. Over the course of two weeks, ending on October 30, in time for Halloween, some thirty witnesses were called before the committee to offer their opinions. Those who did so voluntarily were called "friendly witnesses" while those to whom subpoenas were issued were called "unfriendly witnesses." By one means or another, some seventy-nine people had been asked to attend before Chairman Thomas declared, "at the present time the committee has a special staff making an extensive study of Communist propaganda in various motion pictures."[1] In other words, he gave up the public portion of the proceedings and moved the inquisition behind closed doors.

One of the friendly witnesses had been Jack L. Warner.

First, some backstory. Jack Warner arrived at HUAC in a precarious position. A staunch capitalist, during World War II, he and his brother

Harry had been personally urged by President Roosevelt to produce a film of the memoir by Joseph E. Davies, the US Ambassador to Russia. Titled *Mission to Moscow*, it was designed to encourage Americans to support "our glorious Russian allies" in the fight against fascism. Scripted by Howard Koch, directed by Michael Curtiz, and starring Walter Huston as Davies, it was released May 22, 1943, to negative reviews and occasional anti-Communist protests. Warner chafed at making a pro-Soviet film, but FDR's request was a command, and when he testified before HUAC on October 27, 1947, the mogul was still embarrassed to have acceded. Among his widely quoted remarks was that he and his brothers would "be happy to subscribe generously to a pest-removal fund . . . to ship to Russia the people who don't like our American system of government and prefer the communistic system to ours."

Some of Warner's bitterness stemmed from the brutal ongoing unionizing efforts by film crews. The studios had raked it in during World War II as audiences sought escapism, including morale-building war movies. By V-J Day over ninety million people were buying tickets every week, and most of their money flowed straight from the till to the studios because the film companies owned most of the theaters. As during the Depression, budgets and wages had been held down during the war, not only out of patriotic thriftiness but also because materials were needed for the military, and the War Department got first dibs.

Union organizing resumed after the war. So did studio resistance. On October 7, 1945, labor riots broke out in front of the Warner Bros. studios in Burbank and a strike was called that continued until October 25. The next year, on September 28, even more violent clashes took place at both MGM and Warner Bros. Warner, as did the other moguls, insisted that the unrest was caused by Communists. He was proud of the billboard he had erected at the Barham Boulevard main gate that read "Combining Good Citizenship with Good Picture Making." After Warner's hired goons opened fire on the rioters, studio contract writer Julius Epstein joked, "Combining good citizenship with good marksmanship."

When Warner testified before HUAC that Monday he could not have helped but notice familiar faces watching from the back of the Caucus Room of the old House Office Building. Among the reporters and congressional personnel were John Huston, Humphrey Bogart, Lauren Bacall, and more than a dozen others who had flown to Washington, DC, to protest the hearings. Calling themselves the Committee for the First Amendment, they were organized by actress Myrna Loy, screenwriter Philip Dunne, and directors John Huston and William Wyler.[2] CFA assembled a large group of film people to show their support of the men who had been subpoenaed. They bought newspaper space to announce their existence and to state that they were opposed to communism but supported free speech. The fact that Communists also had free speech in America was lost on most people. Many CFA members made a radio broadcast on ABC on October 27 called "Hollywood Fights Back" in which they took HUAC to task for violating the First Amendment's protection of freedom of association.[3]

The Committee for the First Amendment did not fly directly back to Los Angeles. On Wednesday, October 29, they traveled to Philadelphia where Bogart gave a radio interview reminding listeners that this fair city was the birthplace of the Constitution and the Bill of Rights. "This has nothing to do with communism," he stated. "It's none of my business who's a Communist and who isn't. The reason I am flying to Washington is because I am an outraged and angry citizen who feels that my civil liberties are being taken away from me and that the Bill of Rights is being abused and we feel that nobody in this country has any right to kick around the Constitution of the United States, not even the Un-American Activities Committee."

In New York on the 30th they held court at "21" and were pleased to learn that Chairman Thomas had suddenly ended the hearings without calling the rest of his witnesses, either friendly or unfriendly. Public opinion was running fifty-fifty on the Thomas Committee's search for pinkos in Hollywood, for which no hard evidence was presented but where slander flew freely. The CFA continued their tour west by stopping in Indianapolis,

Cincinnati, Peoria, and Chicago. Along the way, they were surprised to read editorials in which their quotes were invented, and they were being criticized for citing the Constitution. At issue was the disruptive behavior of the Hollywood Ten, which is what the unfriendly witnesses were being called, and which arguably turned the press against them and their supporters.

On that account, Ring Lardner Jr., one of the Ten, said with some perspective, "It would have been much more dignified to simply appear before the Committee and say, 'You have no right under the Constitution to ask these questions and therefore I'm not going to answer them.' Instead of that, we got some dubious advice from our legal counsel. They said, in effect, 'We think an American jury might like to acquit you, but they have to take the Judge's word for all the legal and Constitutional issues. The only way they can acquit you would be on a question of fact. Therefore we think you should say you were trying to answer the question in your own way.' Well, each of us did that in one way or another, and we would have got a lot more support from our liberal friends if we had simply taken the more dignified approach. But it was kind of far-fetched to argue that we were trying to answer the question which we said they had no right to ask. However, I'm still proud of what we did do. I don't regret it for a moment."[4]

On November 2, members of the CFA made another "Hollywood Fights Back" broadcast over ABC radio. This time Bogart was one of the leading voices. "We sat in the committee room and heard it happen," he said. "We saw American citizens denied the right to speak by elected representatives of the people. We saw police take citizens from the stand like criminals. We saw the gavel of a committee chairman cutting off the words of free Americans. The sound of that gavel, Mr. Thomas, rings across America because every time your gavel struck, it hit the First Amendment to the Constitution of the United States."[5]

John Huston, who was a CFA organizer as well as a member, did not approve of the behavior of the unfriendly witnesses and agreed they did more damage to the cause than good: "It was a sorry performance," he lamented. "You felt your skin crawl and your stomach turn. I disapproved of what was being done to the Ten, but I also disapproved of their response. They had lost a chance to defend a most important principle."[6]

Bogart and Bacall left California to return east to New York on November 10. There they did a little publicity for Bogart's new film, *Dark Passage*, and relaxed. While in the city, Bogart met with "someone high up in the Hearst organization" (Bacall's words) and made clear the reasons for their protests. Meanwhile, the papers, especially those run by Hearst, for whom columnist Westbrook Pegler carried the right-wing torch, refused to let up their criticism of the Hollywood contingent for, in their view, supporting communism. As the biggest star on the trip, Bogart drew the most fire. Through the third week of November, he was under quiet pressure from studio executive Steve Trilling and some of the publicists to back off his statements.

Unknown to Bogart and most rank-and-file industry people, on November 24 and 25 representatives of all the film companies met in secret at New York's Waldorf-Astoria Hotel to decide how Hollywood would react to the hearings. Albert Warner represented the studio among forty-seven others ranging from CEOs to functionaries. At what became known as "the Waldorf conference," it was made clear that Wall Street, which provided the studios' finances, wanted matters settled, and so did the international markets who were refusing to show movies made by Communists, real or alleged. Midway through the first day, reports reached the confab that Congress had voted contempt citations against the Hollywood Ten. Hearing this, as well as learning of antisemitic comments made on the floor of Congress by Mississippi Democratic congressman John Rankin, the moguls panicked and, by the next day, had created the blacklist.[7]

The Waldorf conference ended on Tuesday, November 25, with Eric Johnston, President of the Motion Picture Association of America, reading a statement that became known as the Waldorf peace pact. It stated that anyone charged with being a Red would be dismissed. Two of the Ten—Alvah Bessie and Albert Maltz—worked at Warner Bros.[8]

On December 1, the Bogarts boarded the Twentieth Century Limited for Chicago and changed trains for Los Angeles. Although Huston, who was finishing the screenplay for *Key Largo*, had wanted to go to New York to be with them, Jack Warner ordered him to return to the studio.

While the Bogarts were traveling, telegrams were exchanged with Warner Bros. personnel who were being pressured by right-wing forces to "do something" about the Bogarts' public appearance. Additional pressure was being applied to companies that had been approached to become involved with Bogart's new production company, Santana Productions, over such pending projects as *Knock on Any Door*. Investors wanted to insert clauses in their financing agreements guaranteeing that Bogart would distance himself from his colleagues on the Committee for the First Amendment.

Somewhere between New York and Chicago, a telegram was sent to the Bogarts containing language, some of which was reportedly ghostwritten by Jack L. Warner himself, that Bogart was to read to reporters. In it, he would recant his trip to the hearings. On December 2, at a press conference when he was doing publicity for *Dark Passage*, Bogart read, and Bacall agreed, that, "the trip was ill-advised, even foolish, I am very ready to admit. At the time it seemed like the right thing to do."

Bogart's mea culpa continued. "I have absolutely no use for communism nor for anyone who serves that philosophy. I am an American, and very likely, like a good many of you, sometimes a foolish and impetuous American." Later he admitted, "We went in green, and they beat our brains out."[9] For several months into 1948 Bogart continued to apologize for his naïveté and insisted he'd been used.

Shortly after this, Katharine Hepburn, who had not gone on the trip but was a CFA member (although she said she had never given money to them), made her own announcement. She had substituted for a friend by making a speech at a Henry Wallace rally and didn't know what she was getting into.[10]

Bogart's act did not go unnoted by his friends, who reflected indirectly on his behavior. Edward G. Robinson, who had survived the screen gangland wars with him, wrote in his memoir, *All My Yesterdays*, "For all his outward toughness, insolence, braggadocio, and contempt (and those were always part of the character he played, though they were not entirely within Bogie) there came through a kind of sadness, loneliness, and heartbreak (all of which *were* very much part of Bogie the man). I always felt sorry for him—sorry that he imposed upon himself the façade of the character with which he had become identified."[11] Another friend, Jules Buck, said, "I don't think it ever went away. He could have been more."[12]

According to Karina Longworth in *Slate* magazine, after the subpoenas hit the fan, Ira Gershwin hosted another meeting of the CFA at his home, and it was close to empty. Said Abe Polonsky (who was also subpoenaed by HUAC but was never called), Bogart attended and got in Danny Kaye's face, yelled, "You fuckers sold me out," and stormed out.[13]

Over the years, Bacall developed a story that she provided whenever people quizzed her on their acquiescence, saying that they did not realize that they were being used, to some degree, by the Unfriendly Ten. Writing in her memoirs thirty years later, she avoided entirely the fact of Bogart's mea culpa, but referred to it obliquely by writing, "The Committee had had that much effect, and Bogie was furious that he'd been convinced of the necessity of any kind of explanation. He took no oath, swore to nothing, just made his stand clear—and did he resent it! I don't know now whether the trip to Washington ultimately helped anyone." She observed that Hollywood "should be courageous but . . . is surprisingly timid and easily intimidated," avoiding further comment on herself and Bogart.[14] "Bogie was a man of principle," she said, "and because he was a man of principle, he never felt it was right for him to go back on anything he said. Perhaps he thought that the studio could put so much pressure on him that he wouldn't be able to work, or that he would not be able to take care of me. But he never felt good about having made that statement." Added Richard

Brooks, who worked with him his next film, *Key Largo*, "Bogie was never the same again."¹⁵

Joe Hyams tells it differently in *Bogie: The Humphrey Bogart Story*, his affectionate biography written with the participation and approval of Lauren Bacall. "It was typical of Bogart," he wrote of the apology, "that once the mistake was made, he was willing to admit it." The mistake, to Hyams, was not Bogart's saying he'd been duped, but for siding with the Ten. "The one thing he could never forgive was a lie," Bacall added. "He said if you tell a lie your character has been damaged. If you lose character, you have nothing."¹⁶

As for Huston, he was shocked when he learned of Bogart's reversal: "I talked to him about it when he came back out [to Los Angeles]. He said he thought that we had made a mistake. I regard as a mistake how he did this. He should have stuck to his guns." Forty years later, Huston was still stung, telling Bogart biographer A. M. Sperber, "I felt Bogie was out of line. But he was only the first of quite a number." That said, Huston, although he was one of the CFA's four organizers, apparently issued no public statement, exculpatory or otherwise.

But he did give an answer, albeit obliquely. Actress Marsha Hunt, who had been on the flight to Washington, was threatened with blacklisting when her name appeared in *Red Channels* in June 1950.* Summoned to a meeting with Roy Brewer, head of the largest industry union, the IATSE (International Alliance of Theatrical Stage Employees), she was told she could clear her name by signing a letter of recantation. She refused. "He then said," she recalled, "'if one of the three people who had the idea [of the Washington trip] were to tell you that he now believed it was originally thought of by Communists, would you believe then?'" She said yes.

---

* *Red Channels* was a compendium of 151 high-profile celebrities and the supposedly subversive organizations to which they belonged or to whom they once sent a donation. It was compiled by right-wing former FBI agents and was consulted by employers throughout the broadcast industry.

A meeting was arranged to meet that person in the Beverly Hills Hotel lobby. "I sat and sat near the columns in the lobby watching the elevator," she continued, "and finally it opened and out came John Huston. He came toward me, sat beside me, and, looking clearly away from me, just in about two sentences said how they hadn't realized it at the time but in fact the flight to Washington really had been planned by Communists." Hunt admitted that she was stunned into silence by what she'd heard, adding, "A giant had just crumbled before my eyes."[17] She was blacklisted from films until 1971 and died in 2022 at age 104.

As for Jack Warner's venomous "pest control" testimony during the hearings, to be generous, it was very likely written by one of his staffers, given how Warner struggled to read it before the committee as if he was seeing it for the first time. It almost immediately became an embarrassment; Huston recalled that he and Warner, who generally got along, discussed his toadying acquiescence, and Warner asked, already knowing the answer, "That makes me a squealer, doesn't it?" Huston coldly responded, "Yes it does."[18]

Key Largo was the next adventure for Huston and Bogart. Months earlier, on July 25, 1947, at the urging of producer Jerry Wald, Warner Bros. had bought the film rights to Maxwell Anderson's play *Key Largo* and placed it on the production chart. Wald pitched it as a combination of *To Have and Have Not* and *The Petrified Forest*, both of which had drawn notice for Bogart. Anderson's drama opened on stage in 1939 as a free-verse stage play. Starring Paul Muni and directed by Guthrie McClintic, the work featured an extraordinary cast that included José Ferrer, Uta Hagen, Karl Malden, James Gregory, and William Challee. It started with a prologue on a hill in Spain with Loyalist forces, moved to a wharf in Key Largo, Florida, and ended inside the basement of a home near the wharf.

It is a confined but explosive drama. King McCloud (Paul Muni), like many American idealists, had volunteered to fight with the Loyalists during the Spanish Civil War (July 1936–April 1939). When he and his fellow fighters get word that Franco's forces are advancing on their position, he decides that resistance is futile and abandons his men, who all perish. One of them is his friend Victor D'Alcala (José Ferrer).

The play finds Victor's father, Wheeler (Harold Johnsrud), and his daughter, Alegre (Uta Hagen), outside their home in Key Largo, Florida. The wharf has been commandeered by the gangster Murillo (Frederic Tozere) and his four henchmen who set up a gambling parlor with the protection of Sheriff Gash (Ralph Theodore). Mr. Wheeler was blinded in a previous war in which he fought. Murillo has designs on Alegre. His goons have murdered a customer who got wise to their crooked roulette wheel, and they dumped his weighted body in the ocean. Mr. Wheeler and Alegre make a deal with two Seminole Indians (William Challee and Averell Harris) who have escaped a chain gang: they will sneak onto the wharf after dark and free the body, hoping it will float to the surface and draw attention that will summon honest police to get rid of the gamblers.

King McCloud arrives with a guilty conscience. He has been visiting the families of his former comrades with stories of how bravely they died. His last stop is Victor's home where his tale of Victor's bravery wins attention and admiration from his widow, Alegre. By now King's story is that he deserted Victor and the other men but quickly returned, only to find all of them dead. He was then captured by Franco's men and, to survive, served with them until the truce.

Murillo quickly sees that King is a coward and proves it by handing him a gun and daring him to shoot, which King cannot do. Wheeler wants King to leave but Alegre has become attracted to him and gives him Victor's empty room. Murillo, who plans to steal Alegre's virtue, demands to switch rooms with King.

The murdered man's body turns up and the Sheriff arrives, not to investigate, but to demand that Murillo find a scapegoat to pin the killing on. Murillo blames it on King. To save King's life, Alegre and Wheeler blame the two escaped Seminoles, who are then taken and, not long after, are killed "escaping." When King realizes how much Alegre is attracted to him, he grabs a gun and forces Murillo to confess. One of Murillo's henchman shoots King, who kills Murillo. King dies but has reclaimed his honor.

To say the least, the film that emerged from the stage play was vastly different:

Just after the end of the Second World War, former major Frank McCloud (Humphrey Bogart) arrives at the Hotel Largo in Key Largo, Florida to pay a call on the family of George Temple, a man who served under him in the Italian campaign and was killed in battle. George's widow, Nora (Lauren Bacall), runs the hotel with George's father, James Temple (Lionel Barrymore). Even though the hotel is closed for the season, Temple has rented it to a group from Milwaukee who came to Florida to fish: chatty Richard "Curly" Hoff (Thomas Gomez), nasty Edward "Toots" Bass (HarryLewis), inscrutable Ralph Feeney (William Haade), sleepy-eyed Angel (Dan Seymour), and a boozed-out blonde, Gaye Dawn (Claire Trevor). The sixth member of their cabal is holed up in his room.

Sheriff Ben Wade (Monte Blue) and his deputy, Clyde Sawyer (John Rodney) swing by to ask Mr. Temple if he's seen the Osceola brothers, two local Seminole Indians who have escaped from jail with only a month left on their sentences. They have not. Nora receives word of an approaching hurricane. She, Frank, and Mr. Temple reminisce about George, and Frank tells them of George's bravery in battle.[19]

As the storm approaches, several Seminole Indians, including the fugitive Osceola brothers, arrive looking for shelter in the hotel but are blocked by the tourists, who reveal themselves as members of Johnny Rocco's gang. Curly draws a gun and takes Frank and the Temples hostage. He and his men have also captured Deputy Sawyer.

Now Johnny Rocco (Edward G. Robinson) makes his entrance. He has been soaking in a bathtub to beat the heat and humidity. Rocco is a Capone-like mobster who was exiled to Cuba but has secretly returned to the United States to lay groundwork to reclaim his power. The skipper (Alberto Morin) of the boat on which Rocco will return to Cuba arrives in a panic and says he needs to move the craft away from the reef because of the increasingly rough waters. Rocco makes him leave it where it is.

Mr. Temple mouths off to Rocco, who ignores him as he sets his sights on Nora. Mr. Temple gets so angry at filth like Rocco that he tries to stand from his wheelchair and falls to the floor. Frank knows about Rocco and fills in the Temples on the criminal's history. When Rocco threatens to shoot him, Frank uses logic to talk him out of it: he'd have to kill too many witnesses. Rocco accepts the numbers.

Gaye enters and wants a drink but on Rocco's orders no one dares give her one. Rocco and Frank continue to verbally joust; Frank gets the better of Rocco intellectually and Mr. Temple adds to the insults, promoting Rocco to give Frank a gun and dares him to use it against him. Frank declines, equivocating, "one Rocco more or less won't matter." Deputy Sawyer, however, scoops up the gun and fires it at Rocco. It was a trap; the gun was empty. Rocco shoots Sawyer and kills him. Nevertheless, everyone in the room calls Frank a coward.

Rocco's men dump Sawyer's body at sea and return to the hotel just as the power fails and the phone and lights go out. Rocco's henchmen bring a suitcase to the main room; this contains the "deal" that Rocco has come to pull off. Gaye wants a drink and Rocco promises one if she will sing her old nightclub song, "Moanin' Low." She does, but Rocco refuses, further humiliating her. Frank gives her a drink and Rocco slaps him. Again, he does not react, but now Nora realizes it's part of a strategy to keep them all alive.

The storm gets worse. Rocco paces like the proverbial caged animal, casting his shadow on all the others who fall silent. Twisting the blade, Mr. Temple tells how a past storm took the lives of 800 people. Rocco starts to lose it and shoots at Frank with the empty gun. The Indians huddle outside, pleading to be allowed inside as Temple has allowed in the past.

The storm lets up. Mr. Temple invites Frank to come and live with him and Nora. Rocco's men discover that the escape ship has fled, and Rocco leans on Frank, who knows his way around boats, to sail them to Cuba. Frank resists, but before this can be settled, the sheriff arrives looking for Sawyer. Nobody dares say anything. When the sheriff leaves, his cruiser headlights find Sawyer's body that the storm-tossed surf has washed ashore. Rocco tells the Sheriff that the Osceola brothers killed Sawyer. Wade goes off and kills the Osceolas while trying to take them in.

Rocco's contact, Ziggy (Marc Lawrence), arrives with his gang and has a gala reunion with Rocco. He has come to buy the suitcase, which is full of counterfeit money. Nora, Mr. Temple, and Gaye counsel Frank not to agree to sail them to Cuba. Frank, holding George's medal, ponders the dilemma when "your head says one thing and your whole life says another." Ziggy leaves. Rocco and his thugs prepare to leave for Cuba with Frank at the helm. Gaye surreptitiously steals Rocco's loaded gun and slips it to Frank.

At sea aboard the hotel's boat, the *Santana*, Frank gets rid of the gang one by one:[20] he swerves and throws Ralph overboard; he shoots Toots (who shoots and wounds him) and kills Curly. A frightened Rocco shoots Angel and tries bargaining with Frank, offering to share the loot with him to let him go. Instead, Frank shoots Rocco dead and heads back to the hotel, radioing ahead that he is returning.

Gaye agrees to go with the Sheriff to identify Rocco, and Mr. Temple is ashamed that he betrayed the Osceola brothers and allowed the Sheriff to kill them. (The surviving Indians do not forgive Temple for his betrayal of the Osceolas and for his hand in shutting them all out in the storm.) As the dawn breaks, Nora opens the windows and lets the sunshine in.

Getting *Key Largo* from stage to screen involved more than adding action elements. The first step was persuading John Huston to direct it. Huston wanted nothing to do with the play. He found it dated and confined, and Anderson's blank verse impenetrable. Richard Brooks, assigned by the studio to work with Huston on the adaptation, felt otherwise, no doubt because he would earn $8,000 for the job. Huston told Brooks, who had dreams of directing, that if he could find a way to make the film work, he might change his mind, advising him to "challenge the lie until it becomes the truth."[21] The first change Brooks made was to drop the background of the Spanish Civil War, which had largely been forgotten in the wake of World War II, and make it a contemporary story that he pitched as "Little Caesar in Cuba." This twist intrigued Huston, who saw Rocco's gangsters as a precursor to the modern-day right-wingers who had taken over the United States government. "The high hopes and idealism of the Roosevelt years were slipping away," he said, "and the underworld—as represented by Edward G. Robinson and his hoods—was once again on the move, taking advantage of social apathy. We made this the theme of the film."[22] Bogart's Frank McCloud makes this point forcefully by dryly praising Rocco as an empire builder. Rocco takes it as a compliment until the coin drops and he realizes the sarcasm. For his part, Huston was referring to the Red-baiters, although the Red baiters probably thought he was digging at Communists.

Robinson's presence in the film signaled another change. The story goes that Huston had originally wanted Charles Boyer to play Johnny Rocco, a decision that even now seems impractical and must have sounded worse at the time. Huston then suggested Robinson. Robinson at first balked at taking another gangster role after trying for years to escape them, but the $12,500 a week salary eased his resistance. Moreover, in the days following his breakthrough as Little Caesar, he got billing over Bogart. Now Bogart was on top, the result of Jack Warner having screened *The Treasure of the Sierra Madre* and notified his sales department to go all out selling and promoting it. Any billing conflict was solved by giving Bogart first billing in the titles and Robinson second billing but higher on the screen. That way Bogart could say he had first billing and Robinson could say he had top billing.

Robinson's casting, however, was not assured, even with his history at Warner Bros. His politics had been brought into question during the HUAC hearings, and he would go on to have a full-page listing in *Red Channels*.[23] Despite his stardom and track record, Robinson had to assure

Warner that he was not a Communist, and he lived under that cloud until 1955 when the arch-conservative filmmaker Cecil B. DeMille wanted to cast him in *The Ten Commandments* (1956). Once Robinson assured DeMille that he wasn't a Red, he was cleared all over town.[24]

During the *Key Largo* shoot, Bogart deferred to Robinson, making sure that everyone was present on the set before Robinson was called. As for Huston, he jettisoned the character's planned entrance walking down a flight of stairs and introduced him, instead, smoking a cigar and soaking in a bathtub looking "like a crustacean with its shell off," an unforgettable image that has represented the film and Robinson ever since.

Other key roles were taken by wheelchair-bound (arthritis) Lionel Barrymore on loan from MGM, Lauren Bacall, and Claire Trevor, who cut her fee to be able to work with Huston and to star again with Bogart (they had appeared together in *Dead End* in 1937).

In November 1947 Huston and Brooks flew to the actual Key Largo, an island in the upper Florida Keys archipelago, sixty miles from Miami. Brooks reported that Huston was still simmering following the HUAC shambles. Staying at the one hotel in town, Huston asked about the storm basement where Anderson had set much of his play. The hotel owner told him that homes in the area don't have basements because if you dig down two feet you hit water. This did nothing to improve Huston's respect for Anderson and firmed his resolve to change as much as possible. The final straw was learning that Anderson was a political reactionary who hated FDR. Huston, an FDR supporter, devised a way to get even.

Before production could begin, the script had to be passed by the Production Code whose Joseph I. Breen examined it for moral and political transgressions. On November 5, 1947, Finlay McDermid, Warner Bros.'s liaison with the Breen censorship office, sent a provisional 121-page script to Breen for Code inspection. One week later, Breen wrote to Jack L. Warner that the script was unacceptable under the provisions of the Code. He pointed out several violations, among them McCloud's killing of the gangsters, the corrupt sheriff who is bribed to cover up the murder of the deputy and then kills the two Osceola brothers, the portrayal of Hazel (the character later renamed Gaye) as a kept woman, the drinking, and the "very general low flavor of this story" whose characters all operate outside the law.

The negotiation continued by correspondence through January 14, 1948, until the Code approved everything that Brooks and Huston had not only written but rewritten. Among the changes, both major and minute, are:

- The name Murello was first changed to Lazar to avoid sounding like the actual mobster Lucky Luciano. It finally became Rocco;
- Gaye (formerly Hazel), although an alcoholic, would be shown drunk only once or twice. She must also not be portrayed as a "kept woman" so it was established that she insisted on coming along even though no one wanted her there;
- The words *jerks*, *louse*, *lousy*, *Lord*, *God*, and *gangster* should be eliminated;
- Don't flaunt guns;
- Reduce the brutality;
- The action of Murello putting his mouth next to Nora's (Alegre's) mouth should be changed;
- References to a "shipment" should not imply drugs (it becomes counterfeit money);
- Omit mention of McCloud's divorce;
- Murello's killing of Angel is unacceptably brutal;
- Submit the lyrics of the song ("Moanin' Low") for approval;
- It must be clear that there is an effort made to kill McCloud before he starts to shoot; he cannot shoot first;[25]

This list of changes was neither more nor less extensive than notes given to other major films of the era, particularly those that reflected the mature post–World War II sensibility. Huston and Brooks were obligated to adhere to the Code while struggling to make their work dramatically valid. Viewing the existing film will show what they did and didn't obey, and on April 5, 1948, *Key Largo* was awarded Code seal #12932.

Before filming commenced, Huston rehearsed it for three weeks starting December 15 at the studio, in whose soundstage the bulk of the picture would be completed. Shooting itself began in January 1948 with second unit work in Florida. It was civilized; Bacall poured tea every afternoon, and Barrymore stayed in character as a grumbling old man. They were in production when *The Treasure of the Sierra Madre* opened theatrically and began garnering ecstatic reviews. Huston took note of two notices that were written by James Agee; he correctly sensed that the young man had more in him than film criticism. Reports are that, during the production period, Lionel Barrymore, rather than Huston, became the father figure among the ensemble.

Robinson and Bogart played off each other like old friends with a backstory who respected each other's talent, and Huston gave them free reign. When it came to Claire Trevor, however, he was more devious. Her character is an alcoholic entertainer whom Rocco demeans by forcing her to sing for a drink, then, in the end, denies her. The script called for Trevor to sing the song "Moanin' Low" by Ralph Rainger and Howard Dietz. This concerned her because she was not a singer and kept asking Huston for the chance to rehearse. He put her off until the moment he wanted to film her performance and demanded that she get into costume and do it without practice. This was, of course, just what he wanted for her character, and she resented it—until she won the Academy Award for best supporting performance. It was a contrivance, but it demonstrates Huston's perceptiveness as a director as well as his cruelty as a man.

There was a different kind of game in play between Huston and Bogart. Frank McCloud, at the end, summons courage to fight Rocco and his men; he redeems himself and stays alive, albeit wounded. This is in contradiction to the actor's folding to studio pressure after the Washington junket. (Whether Frank is truly a coward during Rocco's taunts or is wisely biding his time is not clear either in performance or editorially.) Letting the film's Frank McCloud live while the play's King McCloud died in an absolving sacrifice is more than a Hollywood ending. It's a reminder that people who have disappointed others can earn redemption while they are still alive and can make amends. This must have been a constant reminder to Bogart during the shoot, and surely Huston didn't let him forget it. He dared not try the same abuse on the less experienced Bacall, however, who had likewise withered in the political heat. She was still a novice in both acting and Hollywood politics and benefitted from her husband's discrete coaching. By the time Huston published his autobiography in 1980, the matter was not worth mentioning.

Eventually it was time for Huston to not only get even with Anderson's politics but at the same time antagonize Lionel Barrymore, who shared them. Remembered Bacall, "There was a scene in which Eddie Robinson was attacking Franklin Roosevelt and Lionel Barrymore had to defend him. Well, Lionel Barrymore—whom I adored—*hated* Roosevelt. And most of us, of course, loved him. Lionel had to defend Roosevelt so strongly that he had to get up—he was in a wheelchair then—he had to get up out of the wheelchair and go after Robinson, and then fall. John loved to watch his face when he had to say that Roosevelt was a great man! John enjoyed situations like that."[26]

Bacall appears to have misremembered the incident here and in her memoir, as a viewing of the film reveals. The scene in question made no mention of FDR, but contains Barrymore's excoriation of Rocco and his brethren, and how the nation just rid themselves of his type. Perhaps Huston directed Barrymore to have in mind that he was defending Roosevelt, but the motivation is invisible in the existing scene.

The studio set designers built the hotel interior and façade on sound stages, including views of the encroaching hurricane seen out the fake windows. The dockside and water scenes were captured on the studio's ranch and backlot. The remarkable settings are a testament to studio craftsmanship. Historian Chris Whitely reports that the exterior storm scenes are stock footage reused from the studio's 1948 picture *Night Unto Night*.

Huston changes his shooting as the film progresses and cinematographer Karl Freund's camera becomes increasingly mobile as the dramatic tensions rise. From fairly flat staging at the beginning, as interpersonal plotlines intersect, so do the people, and—as Huston characteristically does—the camera follows one actor, is picked up by another actor who walks in front, and then settles on a third. It's more ballet than blocking. This has always been Huston's gift as a director: breaking up dialogue with movement. Freund, who innovated the German Expressionist school of photography in the late 1910s, uses his skill to find depth in the darkness after the hotel has lost power. Huston dwells on Robinson's face, filling the screen with it to enhance his menace. For his part, Robinson crafts his performance adding subtlety within his bravado. At five-foot-five, Robinson was significantly shorter than Bogart and is photographed that way, yet whenever his character becomes threatening, he is photographed from below, making him tower over the others.

For all his initial reticence in making the film, Huston is generous with each player, slowly building, then breaking, then restoring Nora's interest in Frank; mitigating Barrymore's trademark crustiness; allowing Claire Trevor an extraordinary complexity as Rocco's decrepit moll; and even according sympathetic screen time to the local Indians, including their 108-year-old matriarch. Watching *Key Largo*, which was shot largely in sequence, is like watching a man become increasingly interested in his own work.

Key Largo was produced at a cost of $1.8 million and returned $4.4 million in worldwide rentals.[27] Ordinarily this would be celebrated, but the definition of profits was changing as the film entered the marketplace in July 1948. Warner's net profit for 1947 was just over $22 million but, the next year, profits fell to $12 million.[28, 29] The year after, they were $10 million. Theatre attendance in general was down. Then came television.

The final element was a blow from which Hollywood never recovered. After twenty-seven years of legal wrangling, in 1948 the United States Department of Justice brought a massive lawsuit, *United States v. Paramount et al*, 334 US 131, against the "big five" studios (Paramount, Metro-Goldwyn-Mayer, Twentieth Century-Fox, RKO, and Warner Bros.) as well as the "little three" (Universal, Columbia, and United Artists), charging vertical integration, collusion, and restraint of trade.[30] Citing the Sherman Anti-Trust Act, the government sought to break apart the entrenched system in which the studios produced, distributed, and exhibited their own films in their own theatres. Although these conditions existed practically from the emergence of the studio system in the 1920s, this suit had begun in 1938 but was delayed by the war.

The studios dreaded government intervention in their monopoly, not the least because of their famously Byzantine bookkeeping. (The running gag was that "in Hollywood, even the books have books.") The case was argued before the US Supreme Court from February 9 to 11, 1948, and resulted, on May 3, 1948, in directing a Consent Decree that spun off theaters from their parent studios. Mandated to take effect by 1951, its effect on the studios was to slow the flow of cash and force them to fight for bookings based on the merit of each film rather than by "block booking" an entire season's slate, good or bad. Owning fewer theatres than the other studios, Warner Bros. was in better shape than MGM or Paramount, both of whom had substantial theatre holdings to divest.[31, 32]

The Consent Decree had a profound impact on the studios. Without ensured playdates for their product, the income slowed down. Lucrative actor and director contracts were cut back or abrogated. Budgets were reduced.

At the same time, the new rules immediately opened the marketplace to independent producers, distributors, and exhibitors, all of whom would play a key role in the production and success of Huston's and Bogart's next film, *The African Queen*.

CHAPTER 9

The African Queen

With the enforced breakup of the studio system under the 1948 Paramount Consent Decree, independent producers finally had competitive entree to the movie marketplace. None of these producers was more independent or competitive than Sam Spiegel. He was also, in the words of fellow producer Gottfried Reinhardt, a congenital crook. He was a conniver and a charmer who could, as one foe said, "slit your throat and convince you it was necessary." Billy Wilder labeled him a modern-day Robin Hood who stole from the rich and stole from the poor. He was a deadly negotiator, a serial cheater with both money and women, and there was ample proof from creditors that he never signed any piece of paper that contained the words "pay to the order of." And yet his producing credits include some of the most acclaimed films of all time, among them *On the Waterfront*, *The Bridge on the River Kwai*, *Lawrence of Arabia*, *Suddenly, Last Summer*, *The Chase*, and as is the happy case here, *The African Queen*.

Spiegel's origins are as vague as his finances. He was probably born in Jaroslaw in 1901 in what eventually became Poland and attended the University of Vienna where, ironically, he studied economics. In 1927 he left his wife and child (according to one unconfirmed account) and arrived in New York on the SS *Mauritania*, then made his way to San Francisco where he was briefly imprisoned for impersonating an Egyptian official.[1] He traveled down the west coast to Hollywood, then to Berlin to produce films for Universal's office there. When Hitler rose to power in 1933, Spiegel fled to Mexico and finally back to America in 1935. In that year he produced (with Boris Morros and Samuel Rheiner) the portmanteau film, *Tales of Manhattan*, under the name S. P. Eagle, a spelling he would continue to use through *The African Queen*.[2]

It's unclear whether Spiegel created the stereotype of the brash, womanizing, cigar-chewing Hollywood producer or adopted it after seeing other producers' success with it. It suited him. It fed his reputation as "the velvet octopus," which is what he became in the back seat of a taxi or limousine when a starlet sat beside him.

Some filmmakers approved of his ways because they benefitted the film they were making. Said Elia Kazan, "The only guy who was at all helpful as a producer was Sam Spiegel with *On the Waterfront*. He's one of the few who even knows what he's doing."[3] Supposedly he spoke nine languages, never told the same story twice about how he escaped Hitler's ovens, and was so resourceful that, again, Kazan marveled, repeating a legend, "if he were dropped, stark naked and without funds, into the heart of a capital city, by the next morning he'd be fashionably dressed and living at ease in a *grand luxe* hotel."[4] Burnishing the image of producer, he developed the habit of calling people "baby" (as in "it's a great picture, baby"), probably for the same reason John Huston called people "kid"—it saved both of them the trouble of remembering names.

It makes sense, then, that Spiegel and Huston would work together. Both men could bewitch others into doing their bidding, both men enjoyed life away from movies as much as they enjoyed life making them, and both always seemed to land on their feet (though just often on somebody else's feet).

When Huston was finishing *Key Largo* in 1948, and with the wind of *The Treasure of the Sierra Madre* behind him, he chose to partner with Spiegel in Horizon Pictures on one condition: that Spiegel find the financing. Somehow he did, and the men set off to make *We Were Strangers* as Huston's first independent film after his Warner Bros. contract ended. Scripted from Robert Sylvester's novella *Rough Sketch* by Huston and Peter Viertel, it starred Jennifer Jones and John Garfield in a story about Cuban revolutionaries who try to assassinate that country's president. Research for the script brought Huston to Cuba and a meeting with Ernest Hemingway. The two alpha males regarded each other with suspicion at first sight. In his memoir, Huston chronicles an adventure aboard a boat where the men matched sharpshooting at a floating log (Hemingway kept hitting it until Huston decided to stop fooling around and take aim, he wrote), an iguana hunt, and finally a boxing match that Huston, a former fighter, forfeited after learning it would endanger Hemingway's health. In the end, the men became friends.

We Were Strangers was an inauspicious debut for Horizon Pictures. It did not do well at the box office, and many critics treated it poorly, criticizing its vaguely Marxist themes in the wake of the nation's ongoing concerns over communism. Huston noted that Jennifer Jones seemed insecure in her craft and required very specific direction, even how to sit down, but that, once she was told in detail what was required of her, she made the movements her own.[5]

Huston followed *We Were Strangers* with *The Asphalt Jungle*, a uncompromising heist story adapted by Huston and the prolific Ben Maddow from W. R. Burnett's 1949 novel. Often wrongly cited as Marilyn Monroe's first film (she had made eight previous appearances, including in the Marx Brothers' *Love Happy*), it could be said that it was the first time on screen that she was memorable. Meanwhile Huston guided Sterling Hayden, Louis Calhern, Jean Hagen, Sam Jaffe, and James Whitmore to what became a noir classic and a hit for MGM.[6]

His next MGM outing was *The Red Badge of Courage*, a faithful and poetic screen adaptation of Stephen Crane's civil war novel about an army deserter who redeems himself in battle. Starring Audie Murphy, the most decorated American soldier of World War II and a deeply troubled man in his personal life, the odyssey of the film was captured by *New Yorker* writer Lilian Ross in her 1952 book *Picture*, considered the first full-length examination of Hollywood filmmaking.[7] Her book became a classic but the film never achieved public acceptance. This continued Huston's accidental tradition of alternating commercial hits and misses. By any accounting, his next film would be a smash. And it was.

C. S. Forester's 1935 novel *The African Queen* was a road picture set on the water. It follows the combative relationship between the rough-hewn skipper Charlie Allnutt and the proper churchgoing Rose Sayer as they are drawn into an act of heroism in Africa in the early days of World War I. The well-read Huston was aware of the book, and it is possible that he spoke to Warner Bros. about making it there; in fact, in 1946 the company did acquire the rights as a vehicle for Bette Davis. Their interest lasted one year and one script, which the studio's Finlay McDermid sent to the Breen Office for vetting. On April 16, 1947, Breen informed Jack Warner himself, not McDermid, that "this basic story seems to comply with the basic requirements of the Production Code." Despite this, Breen followed with three single-spaced pages of alerts, most of which had to do with words spoken in the Cockney accent in which the film was originally planned. Language excisions, written in argot, included *Gawd*, *bleedin'*, *'ot as 'ell*, *'ymn singin' Methodis*, *Lor' love a duck*, *'ell, on our be'inds*, and *Lor'*. Inasmuch as the pair would change from adversaries to lovers in the course of their adventure (the book was more vivid than the eventual film), Breen warned that Charlie and Rosie should never be shown less than fully clothed, even while swimming, and to check with the First Presbyterian Church of Hollywood to ensure no offense to the religious community.

In an effort to defuse any question of sexual contact between the two middle-aged characters, Breen wrote that it should be made perfectly clear in the action that Allnutt is only thinking of boozing and taking it easy rather than seeking a romantic partner. (But not too much booze because that is also prohibited.)

The film's African setting inspired the censor to warn reflexively against any portrayal of natives in any degree of nudity, and he noted, "Page 20: We recommend that Allnutt's line be amended to read 'My two native fellers. . . .' Negroes seem to resent the appellation 'black.'"[8]

There is no indication in the Production Code files whether Warner Bros. made these changes before dropping the project. What is known is that they tried to offload the property to another company, and no one wanted it, with or without Bette Davis. For a while it floated past RKO as a vehicle for Elsa Lanchester and her husband Charles Laughton, who could have easily embraced Allnutt's Cockney persona and made quite another, but no less interesting, film. The property also (according to Huston) made a stop at Columbia where they didn't know how to cast it, either, and passed. For a time, Twentieth Century-Fox considered the project but bowed out because of the high cost of shooting on location.[9]

After *The African Queen* had not found any port in the development storm, Huston and Spiegel came calling with their Horizon Pictures. Warners wanted $50,000 for the package. Huston debated whether he should direct another film first for a payday to get the money for Horizon, but Spiegel went to Sound Services, Inc., a company that provided recording equipment. Somehow, he talked them into putting up the acquisition fee (perhaps, opined Huston, by promising to use their equipment and providing a screen credit) and Horizon was in business.[10]

Casting began before there was a script. Huston, of course, wanted Bogart to play the grizzled, drunken chief of the tiny Congo vessel. He knew it was outside his friend's comfort zone as an actor (though not as a sailor), but he knew the actor would rise to the occasion if prodded enough and told him, "The hero is a lowlife, and you are the biggest lowlife in town and therefore most suitable for the part." Rather than risk having Bogart attempt Cockney, Huston made Allnutt Canadian, which still made him an enemy of Germany.

What of Rosie? It was Spiegel's idea to send the Forester book to Katharine Hepburn, who immediately accepted, even though she had doubts about Spiegel's finances and the script. To overcome the first, she had her father wire $10,000 to the bank in case she needed funds to return from Africa to the States. As for the second, that would have to wait.

For someone known for her opinions and judgmental nature, Hepburn seemed to admire Spiegel. "He is a real impresario," she wrote, "in the true sense of the word. He got the ball rolling on *The African Queen* in spite of no money, no nothing. . . . He has a sharp mind. And a deep well of energy. I liked him. He loves his work and he loves life."[11]

Spiegel budgeted the film at $1 million[12] and obtained production funding from the Walter F. Heller Company of Chicago, John and James Woolf's Romulus Films, distributor United Artists, and international territorial presales promises based on the lure of Bogart, Hepburn, and Huston. Agents Michael Baird and Alvin Manuel facilitated the deal with Romulus, who had initially wanted the film made with British actors John McCallum and Googie Withers but yielded to Spiegel's and Huston's choices.[13]

Bogart was to be paid $125,000 deferred and 30 percent of the profits, and Hepburn would be paid $65,000 up front, $65,000 deferred, and 10 percent of the profits.

Huston asked James Agee, who had so warmly reviewed *The Treasure of the Sierra Madre*, to try his hand at helping him adapt *The African Queen*. As Huston describes their process, "we got up early in the morning to play a couple sets of tennis, have breakfast, and then go to work, work through until lunchtime, lay off for a couple of hours, and then work again for two or three hours, and another two or three sets of tennis, dinner. And after dinner we'd work. Jim was forever bringing more pages. He was doing an enormous amount of work, and I didn't see how he could manage to turn so much work out. And then I discovered that he was working at night and getting very little sleep."[14] The two men finished *a* script, but not *the* script, in that the ending (as shall be shown) was very much still under discussion when the crew left for Africa. In his memoirs, Huston says that he discussed the ending with Forester and that he and Spiegel preferred a neater ending than the one the author had provided.[15]

With production imminent, Huston embarked on a reckie to Africa to search for locations. He brought with him writers Peter Viertel and John Collier, hoping that, among the three of them, a new ending would present itself.[16] Agee did not go with him. A heavy drinker (though not while writing with Huston) and smoker, Agree had a heart attack, which took him off the film. "I remember after he'd had his heart attack," Huston continues, "we were alone in a room; it was two or three days after the heart attack and Jim said, 'give me a cigarette.' And I said, 'no, Jim, it wouldn't be fair to the doctor.' He thought about that and nodded, 'Right.'"[17] Agee died May 16, 1965, at age forty-five. His unfinished autobiographical novel, *A Death in the Family* (1957), which was completed posthumously by editor David McDowell, would win the 1958 Pulitzer Prize.[18]

Huston's and Agee's adaptation begins in August 1914 in German East Africa where British Protestant missionaries Samuel Sayer (Robert Morley) and his sister, thirty-three-year-old Rose (Katharine Hepburn was forty-three at the time) are spreading Christianity among the natives. Their supplies are delivered by the *African Queen*, a thirty-foot steam-powered boat skippered by Canadian Charlie Allnutt (Humphrey Bogart). Allnutt is a genial drunk blissfully untroubled by social graces whom the Sayers tolerate with studied politeness (Samuel) and patrician condescension (Rose).

On one trip, Charlie warns the Sayers that war has broken out between Britain and the Germans who occupy the territory. Rather than evacuate, the missionaries choose to stay in Kungdu, believing that the Germans will exempt their mission from harm. The Hun does not; in fact, after Charlie departs, soldiers invade the village, kidnap the villagers into military service, and burn everything. Samuel is beaten and loses his mind from the trauma, and then from fever. When Charlie returns after the attack, he and Rose bury Samuel. Charlie persuades Rose to escape with him aboard the African Queen.

For all his apparent coarseness, Charlie is a skilled sailor and strategist. He explains that the British cannot attack the occupying Germans because the Kaiser has the *Königin Luise*, a gunboat, guarding the lake that the British Navy would have to use as access. Rose takes Britain's inability to attack as a challenge for the two of them to use the explosives that Allnutt has on board to blow up the *Luise*. Charlie reluctantly agrees, even though Rose's superior attitude irritates him.

The *African Queen* is not the most reliable of vessels, but Charlie knows how to keep her moving. Rose is a different story. Although Charlie teaches her how to use the tiller to guide the boat, he cannot breakthrough her haughtiness. Making it worse, one night Charlie ties one on only to awaken to the sloshing sound of Rose emptying his precious cache of liquor into the river.

The two navigate a gentle set of rapids and slip past a German encampment at Shona where they are fired upon. This damages the boat's boiler. Charlie fixes it in time to steer clear, but this maneuvers them into a more dangerous set of rapids. They survive these rapids and are so exuberant that they embrace. This sudden affection surprises them both, for it is clear that they have become attracted to one another despite their vastly disparate stations. After this, Rose no longer refers to him as "Mr. Allnutt," but as "Charlie," and he now calls her "Rosie."

A third, far more deadly rapids warps the *African Queen*'s propeller shaft. Charlie and Rose fix it by forging a new blade and diving into the river to bolt it to the assembly. They chug along until the river becomes swampy and the boat becomes mired in plant growth. When Charlie and Rose can no longer use poles to push the *Queen* along, he dives in the shallow water to tow it. When he emerges, he is covered with leeches. He is terribly shaken, and Rosie comes to his aid to remove them. Realizing they are still stuck,

Charlie reluctantly slips back into the water to pull the *Queen* out of the tangles knowing that he will again be set upon by leeches. Afterward, he falls ill with fever and Rosie prays for their relief, completely unaware that they are mere yards from the lake. Soon a rain comes, the river rises, and the *African Queen* floats free on its own.

Now Charlie and Rose set their sights on blowing up the German gunboat. Charlie fashions two torpedoes out of compressed air cannisters, explosives, ammunition, and an inventive percussion trigger. They mount them on the bow of the boat and steam out onto the lake. A storm blows up, however, and the *Queen* sinks. Charlie and Rose lose sight of each other in the choppy water.

Here the book and the movie diverge. Forester's ending is more measured: After Rosie and Charlie are separated in the storm, they are brought aboard the *Luise*. The captain decides that it would be uncivilized to hang them, so he flies a flag of truce and turns them over to the British. By this time, the British troops have arrived and ignore the truce, heading off on their own to sink the *Luise*. The British Naval commander tells Rosie and Charlie to go to see the British Consul and urges Charlie to enlist in the South African Army. Charlie and Rosie decide they shall get married. "So they left the Lakes and began the long journey to Matadi and marriage," Forester writes. "Whether or not they lived happily ever after is not easily decided."

The new ending contrived by Huston and his collaborators helped make *The African Queen* a classic:

Charlie is pulled from the water and captured by the Germans. He resolves to being executed as a spy on orders of the captain (Peter Bull) and doesn't care what happens to him since Rosie is lost. Then Rosie turns up. She is also sentenced to hanging as a spy. As the nooses are placed around their necks, Charlie asks the captain to marry them. Rosie is moved by this proposal and lovingly consents. The captain performs the ceremony, ending with, "By the authority vested in me by Kaiser Wilhelm the Second I pronounce you man and wife. Proceed with the execution." Rosie and

Charlie are about to be hanged when the wreck of the *African Queen* floats up with its torpedoes exposed and rams the *Luise* broadside, destroying her. Rosie and Charlie swim off together toward Kenya. Whether or not they lived happily ever after is not easily decided with this ending, either, but movie audiences since 1951 have happily presumed that they do.

The brilliance of the Agee-Huston screenplay for *The African Queen* is that everything that happens in it feels inevitable. This is deceptive; in fact, it required significant changes from Forester's elongated novel, including cutting extraneous material, changing the style to something more comic, and enriching the characterizations. The book, which is told from Rose's point of view, begins with her brother Samuel's death after the attack by Von Hanneken's German troops, which is not shown. Then Allnutt appears and helps bury the Reverend and takes Rose to safety. The film introduces Allnutt first, then shows the attack on the village, then has Allnutt return to bury Samuel and rescue Rose. The change does more than provide star Bogart with an entrance. It allows for the development of the Sayers' situation as contrast for what will follow.

The use of vocatives is also instructive. The book seldom if ever uses them; with only Rose and Allnutt on the boat, there is never any question of who is talking to whom. The film, however, is strewn with them, and the contrast—Rose is condescending, Charlie is mocking—is obvious. It's "Mister Allnutt" this and "Mister Allnutt" that. Allnutt even chides Rose for her constant use of "Mister Allnutt" by reminding her that there are only two of them on the boat. After they survive the second rapids, her disdain falls away completely as they kiss and begin to fall in love.[19] Marking this, after the rapids she calls him "Charlie" and he calls her "Rosie." Among the joys in watching the film is seeing two consummate pros change gradually but consistently.

It took several days for Hepburn to feel comfortable playing Rose, whom she initially saw as icy and cruel. Huston resolved it with one piece of direction. In the book, the battle of wills begins when, first, Rose empties

Allnutt's liquor reserve into the river and, second, grows deeper when she gives the garrulous Allnutt the "silent treatment" that her brother used to give her when she annoyed him. Huston and his writers use her silence to allow Allnutt a sarcastic monologue at her that she deflects with equanimity, finally reminding him of his promise to blow up the *Luise*. Underscoring the sequence, every time Allnutt raises his voice, the jungle animals react with noise in the background.

Rose's inner conflict between her religious modesty and her female desires plays to a greater extent in the novel, particularly as she throws off her brother's puritanical yoke and finds herself drawn to Allnutt. After they shoot the rapids, of course, their relationship changes. Here the book becomes almost lurid: "He looked down at Rose beside him, her sweet bosom close to him. He, too, was glowing with life and inspired by the awesome beauty of the place . . . Rose was conscious of kisses, of her racing pulse and her swimming head. She was conscious of hands which pulled at her clothing . . . Rose was made for love."[20] No wonder the Production Code threw a fit when they saw the new script. Before the company went to Africa, the Code office signaled that it was not pleased with what they read. For that matter, neither was Huston. When Gladys Hill, Spiegel's assistant, sent the then-current version to Jack Vizzard of the Code office on March 26, 1951, Vizzard's boss, Joseph Breen, sent back three-and-a-half pages of notes on April 2. Some repeated his concerns from when the project had been at Warner Bros. in 1947, but many were new. The Big Complaint started on page 108. This referred to Charlie's and Rosie's embrace after surviving the rapids, a sequence which Breen called "an immoral relationship which is treated quite as a matter of course, with not the faintest voice for morality or indication of compensating moral values." For this reason, he declared, the script could not be approved as written. He then repeated some of the earlier cautions given to Warner Bros. such as avoiding any form of nudity (especially in the "natives"), that nobody be caricatured (primarily the minister), no peeling off of clothing, no fade-out suggesting a sexual union, and deleting various *damn*s and *Lord*s. Breen also objected to what would have become one of the film's most memorable moments: Charlie Allnutt's stomach growling in the tea scene.[21] On October 19, after the picture wrapped, Spiegel told Hill to wire Breen (which went out on October 22) "Have made all changes suggested by your office" and requested a code [seal] number "subject your final approval of picture stop thanks and affectionate regards, Spiegel."[22]

The finished film bears out who won (at least insofar as borborygmi). It's a testament to how a director and skilled actors could keep the spirit of the Code without being inhibited by its letter.

The location scout brought Huston, Spiegel, Guy Hamilton, and art director Wilfred Shingelton to Nairobi, Kenya where Huston's gun and rifle collection were promptly confiscated by the Kenyan authorities who forbade game hunting. Hunting had been the reason Huston had agreed to do the picture. After flying over Kenya, Uganda, and Lake Victoria, Huston declared that Kenya was too open for the confined jungles his picture needed. He settled on the Ruiki River in what was then the Belgian Congo; then go to Butiaba, Uganda, and finish at Uganda's Murchison Falls.

When it came time for the actors to go on location, Bacall accompanied her husband. She planned a six month stay, leaving their two-year-old son, Stephen, in Los Angeles in the care of his nurse, Alice Hartley. The reason was pragmatic as well as romantic: Bogart's first three marriages had fallen apart because he was separated from his wives, and neither "Bogie" nor "Betty" wanted it to happen again. As for Huston, he had just married Enrica Sonia "Ricki" Soma who, five months later on July 8, 1951, would give birth to their daughter, Anjelica. Tragically, while seeing the Bogarts off at the Los Angeles airport, nurse Hartley suffered a stroke in the terminal and later died. Bacall's mother raced from New York to take over caring for infant Stephen.[23]

Much has been written about the adventure of *The African Queen*, including by Katharine Hepburn in her 1987 memoir, *The Making of the African Queen: Or How I Went to Africa With Bogart, Bacall and Huston and Almost Lost My Mind*. The legend has grown over the years, embellished by Peter Viertel in his 1953 roman à clef *White Hunter, Black Heart*, that Huston went to Africa to shoot two things: *The African Queen* and an elephant. He did the former and not the latter, although the story persists that he did. "I always take exception to people who take it too literally," Huston's daughter Anjelica told journalist Steve Rose in a discussion of Viertel's book. "I think, for the purposes of novelization, you have to pump up the volume a bit." Nevertheless, she said that the gun room in their family home in Ireland, though it had some stuffed animal heads, was devoid of a pachyderm.[24]

Hepburn's concern, other than money, remained the script. When they were in London in April 1951 before departing for Africa, she kept trying to confer with Huston, but all he would do was placate her with a frustrating, "Is that so dear. Interesting." Said Hepburn, "He put one constantly on the defensive." Nobody else seemed to have problems with the script, which Huston and Viertel were constantly rewriting in London and then on location in Africa. She voiced her concerns to Bogart, who shrugged, "Well, we're here, we liked it, we'll do it. Working with John is always a bit, well, you know, like this. They'll find the money. They have to."[25]

On May 13, as everyone was arriving at the camp that had been built for their location stay in the Congo, Huston announced triumphantly, "Well, I've found it. We have almost every kind of disease, and almost every known kind of serpent." They had to work quickly before an onslaught of bad weather and a procession of soldier ants (a.k.a. army ants). They did not succeed at either. To guard against army ants, crews dug trenches around their accommodations and filled them with kerosene, which they set alight when the insects attacked. Then it was time to move on.

The hardships mounted. Bogart took to calling Huston "the monster." Both men knew it was a friendly jab, but jab it was. "I think that was largely because I'd take him off to places to make films where he had no desire to be," the filmmaker explained. "Bogie loved his own hearth and to drink his Scotch and soda in the luxury of his own study or drawing room. And he'd find himself in the badlands of Mexico or the dark heart of Africa and didn't know why except that he'd said 'yes' in some unstable moment."[26] The two men maintained their health by drinking Scotch and eating only canned food. Their alcohol levels were said to be so high that any mosquito that might have dared to bite either of them would drop dead.

"Bogie's lack of sweating seemed to me a very unhealthy sign," Hepburn noted. "I anticipated his early collapse in the jungle, for I had heard that he drank quite a bit. What the hell. I'd already been with him ten days. He did drink quite a bit, but it had no effect on him, as far as I could see, either for better or worse. He and Huston would be a great team. They drank more than plenty."[27]

"They had to clear the jungle in order to build a camp for the entire company," recalled Bacall, "and we all lived in these huts that were made out of bamboo and palm. There were leaves with mother earth for the floor. It was fascinating. I mean, it was wonderful. And John would come to the location in a car, and all the little native boys would stand along the edge because we were freaks, obviously, to them, and they would hang onto their private parts there. They had no clothes on, you know, and one hand would be [down] there and the other hand would be waving and John was sitting in the car like the King of England with the royal wave."[28]

For Hepburn, who on every occasion mentioned that her father was a urologist, finding comfort facilities would be a problem throughout the shoot. It would be for Bacall, as well, but Bacall didn't go on record about the difficulties. Finally, Huston had the crew construct a portable loo for Hepburn's exclusive use. It was reverently towed along the river with the

African Queen and the crew barge so it could be at her beck and call—except for the time it got hung up on overhanging trees just when she needed it. The male crew, of course, could just use the river or the bushes. Huston, Hepburn reported, had his own outhouse that she never saw him use. "[That] would explain a great deal," she concluded.[29]

Food was a problem, primarily a meat shortage. In Biondo, the Congo, Huston contracted with a local hunter to bag game for the catering table. The man was highly successful as there was always meat on the menu. According to Bacall, however, it was not advisable to ask what kind of meat it was.[30] One of their dishes included something the hunter called "long pig" but when they asked him for more details, he was evasive. Several days later they found out why when soldiers arrived to take the man away. It seems that villagers had been disappearing from local settlements and the hunter was being held responsible. This story has circulated for years. Guy Hamilton, an assistant director on the film, has called it "absolute bullshit" but it has yet to be proved.[31] Or disproved.

While Huston would come to regard shooting *The African Queen* as an adventure he would gladly repeat, the most famous behind-the-scenes story belongs to Katharine Hepburn. The actress was having trouble getting a bead on her character of "Rosie," the preacher's spinster sister. After several days' shooting during which Huston felt she hadn't quite captured the role, the independent Hepburn asked her director for help. Huston told her to adopt a "society smile" and act like Mrs. Roosevelt. Ever after, the strong-willed Hepburn said that was "the best goddamned piece of direction I ever got."[32]

Huston and Bogart were in such synchronicity after decades of friendship and working together that there are no anecdotes of whether Bogart needed direction of the specificity that Hepburn appreciated. On a more personal note, Bacall told Huston biographer Lawrence Grobel that Huston once asked Bogart, "You seem to have your life so together. . . . How do you manage to do all that and not get bored?"[33]

Hepburn reported that Bogart, although cordial and professional, seemed distant during the shoot. Perhaps this was because Charlie Allnutt was more challenging than his previous roles: a mixture of vulgarity, charm, and vulnerability. This was no easy blend, given Bogart's innate resistance to being dominated by a woman, even if the woman was Katharine Hepburn. Of all the hardships they encountered on the hot, humid, and remote African locations, his only vehement objection was to having live leeches attached to his body in the infamous scene in which he frees the *African Queen* from entanglement by towing her through the infested waters. Huston contrived to have producer John Woolf tell Bogart that it would violate his contract if he refused, but the actor dug in his heels. Finally, they used rubber leeches. Huston told Dick Cavett a different story in his 1972 appearance. All of the leeches, he said, were real. "They weren't out of the African swamps, however, they were chemically pure leeches imported from London. He hated them just as English leeches; he had that reaction quite naturally."[34]

Spiegel was constantly pressuring Huston to hurry and finish, and although he detested the discomfort of Africa, he endured visiting the location to press his point. This resulted in fisticuffs between the two determined men, Huston fighting for his schedule and Spiegel possessed of the belief that unpleasantness leads to successful films. When Hepburn fell ill with dysentery—so ill that she lost twenty pounds and had to excuse herself between takes to use the facilities—Spiegel wired Huston to keep her out for fifty-six hours. After a fifty-six-hour delay, the insurance would kick in. Comparing Hepburn's appearance in the scenes shot in Africa with those filmed later in London, one sees profound differences.

"Some people got really ill," Huston reported years later. "Katie stood up quite well. Bogie did. I did. I think we were three of the elect out of the whole group. Almost everybody else became—Katie got a little ill, but she recovered."[35]

The weather played a part in the way Huston and Bogart got along. When rain canceled shooting, Huston would hie off to the wilds to go hunting. Bogart, by contrast, was a homebody to whom Africa was an inconvenience and he wanted to get it over with. Bacall put it as "John was fantasy, Bogie reality," and it explains why the two men's relationship centered primarily on work.

African shooting ended on July 17, 1951, with interiors and process photography completed thereafter in London. The revised ending and closeups were shot in Shepperton's tank with the camera angled to avoid catching the tops of nearby buildings. The tank was also used so the actors wouldn't be sickened by immersing themselves in the contaminated African river water.

Postproduction was as dramatic as the film itself. Spiegel leaned on Huston to rush the editing so he could make the cut-off date for year-end Academy Award eligibility. The Technicolor printing process was more complex than other color processes, but once a first acceptable print was struck, the producer carried it himself on a plane to America. The plane to Boston was buffeted by a storm over the Atlantic, and then there was a two-day delay in Customs before he could fly the final leg to Los Angeles and arrive just in time. The reviews, needless to say, were ecstatic.

The only issue that dragged on for months was Sam Spiegel's failure to pay his bills. As the profits rolled in, Horizon Pictures was sued by agents Michael Baird and Alvin Manuel for their unpaid ten percent profit participation plus seven percent interest.[36] Horizon's financial woes would continue well into the release of the film when, in 1953, Shamark Enterprises attached film rentals that United Artists owed Horizon. Shamark's Jack Broder held that Horizon owed him $120,000 in commissions for his help in financing other films.[37] The December before, light was shed on Spiegel's financial maneuverings when he and his wife Lynn filed for divorce, including making public everybody's salaries on *The African Queen*. In 1955, Spiegel turned the tables and sued United Artists for $61,859 in overdue profit participation.[38]

In the days when campaigning for Oscars was permitted by the Academy, Bogart hired a publicist to encourage a best actor nomination, and it worked, although he pretended modesty. "The honest way to find the best actor would be to let everybody play Hamlet and let the best man win," he told the press. "Of course, you'd get some pretty funny Hamlets that way."[39] Hepburn was also nominated for her lead performance, Huston for directing, and Agee and Huston for their screenplay. Viertel and Collier went uncredited.

Humphrey Bogart won his only Academy Award on March 20, 1952. Greer Garson presented it to him, and when his name was announced as the winner, Lauren Bacall let out a scream heard by the whole audience in the Pantages Theatre. Accepting the statuette, and perhaps mindful of what happened the last time he made a political speech, he graciously offered, "It's a very long way from the heart of the Belgian Congo to the stage of the Pantages Theatre, and I'm very glad to say that it's a little nicer here than it was there. I just want to pay a slight, as a matter of fact a very big tribute to Mr. John Huston and Miss Katharine Hepburn, because they helped me to be where I am now. Thank you very much."[40]

The African Queen did so well for its financing company, Romulus Films, that the Woolf brothers who owned it enticed Huston to make *Moulin Rouge* for them in 1952. Bogart managed to squeeze in two films (*Deadline U.S.A.*, 1952 and *Battle Circus*, 1953) and a TV guest appearance (*The Jack Benny Program*, 1953) before rejoining Huston for a film which to this day defies categorization.

CHAPTER 10

Beat the Devil

eat the Devil (1953) has been called a "shaggy dog film" in that it rambles before eventually coming to an end without coming to a point. Over the years it's become a cult movie, which is what they call a film that appeals to a devoted coterie, none of whom are the originally intended audience. Danny Peary, who wrote about it his 1983 book *Cult Movies 2*, concludes that it is "An in-joke between those who made this 'lark' (Huston's term) and those who accept it in the spirit in which it was made."[1]

The fact is, *Beat the Devil* was born in compromise, planned in arrogance, filmed in panic, and released in desperation. The script never did come together, the leading man nearly got killed, the director was playing it by ear, and the distributor lost faith as soon as it got a look at the early results. This is hardly the way experienced filmmakers like to work, yet they were professional enough to pull it off, however misshapen the results might have wound up.

Here's the plot: Ravello, Italy is roughly 1600 kilometers from the protectorate of British East Africa (today Kenya) and this is where Billy Dannreuther (Humphrey Bogart) has persuaded a quartet of rogues—Peterson (Robert Morley), Julius O'Hara (Peter Lorre), Major Jack Ross (Ivor Barnard), and Revello (Marco Tulli)—that there is land containing valuable uranium deposits, and they are in a race to buy it. It is possible that the psychotic Ross has murdered Paul Van Meer, a British colonial officer who got wise to them early on. Billy has had business reversals that cost him his Italian villa, and this explains his eagerness to become involved with the crooks and lead them to the land. Billy has brought along his lovely wife Maria (Gina Lollobrigida).

While waiting for the Nyanga freighter that will take them from Italy to Africa, the Dannreuthers meet two other passengers, Gwendolyn and Harry Chelm (Jennifer Jones and Edward Underdown). Harry is a stuffy British twit and Gwendolyn is his ebullient wife who also happens to be a charming compulsive liar.

The ship is delayed, which bothers Peterson who fears that someone else will buy his coveted ore-rich land. He is suspicious of Harry who boasts of his fortune and governmental connections. Harry's ultra-Britishness makes him attractive to Maria Dannreuther, an Anglophile. This does not bother Billy because he is confident in his marriage and amused that Gwendolyn is more attracted to him than he is to her. While thinking that she and Billy are alone (not knowing O'Hara is watching) she mentions the uranium in East Africa. O'Hara reports her indiscretion to Peterson who fears that the Chelmses are competition.

Peterson and Billy decide to fly to Africa to preempt the Chelmses and the boat, but the car in which they are being driven by Billy's chauffeur (Aldo Silvani) breaks down. Billy, Peterson, and the chauffeur push it along a mountain road to make it start but it gets away from them and plummets over a cliff along with their luggage and the cash that Peterson was going to use to buy the land. Word reaches O'Hara, Ross, Ravello, and Gina back at the hotel that Billy and Peterson are dead (the chauffeur isn't mentioned). Wanting to continue with the scheme but needing money to replace Peterson's stash, Ravello tries to enlist Harry Chelm. Peterson and Billy show up alive, surprising the others, but the uranium cat is now out of the bag.

Finally able to board the Nyanga whose captain (Saro Urzi) is a drunk and whose purser (Mario Perrone) is a wiseacre, everyone in the group grows to distrust everyone else. Ross breaks into Harry's cabin and nicks a metal dispatch case that Peterson believes contains helpful information. Instead, they find only mundane business papers. Peterson wires a source in England for information on the Chelmses; a return wire informs him Harry is merely a hotelier and has only airs, not fortune or connections. Harry becomes so irritated at Peterson's obvious scheming that he swears to turn them in the moment they make land. Peterson orders Ross to kill him one night while they are cruising to Africa. Billy heads off Major Ross's assassination attempt, saving Harry. Harry rightly accuses Ross of attempted murder but Gwendolyn, for some reason, insists that Harry is mentally unstable and has invented the story. Harry is outraged at her duplicity and the captain locks him in his cabin where no one can get at him.

The ship's oil pump breaks and the captain tells the passengers, whom he doesn't like, to get to the lifeboats. Billy heads to Harry's cabin to free him from his handcuffs but discovers that Harry has already fled overboard and has left a note that he is swimming to shore to turn everyone over to the authorities.

Billy, Maria, Gwendolyn, Peterson, O'Hara, Ravello, and Major abandon the ship and row to northern Africa where they are immediately confronted by a party of Arab horsemen who bring them to Ahmed (Manuel Serrano), the local judge. Ahmed suspects them of spying or providing weapons to their local enemy. Peterson expected to be tortured, but Billy suddenly makes a break to escape and is captured.

While the others wait in a cell, Billy relaxes with Ahmed, who has pictures of Rita Hayworth plastered on his walls.[2] Somehow Billy has charmed his way out of custody. He lies that he knows Hayworth and can make an introduction. Together the men scheme to make Peterson pay money which they will split, and for Ahmed to send the foursome back to Italy unharmed.

Back in Italy, Peterson and his partners are questioned by Jack Clayton (Bernard Lee) of Scotland Yard about the death of Van Meer.[3] He is almost persuaded by Peterson's explanation when Gwendolyn, telling the truth for the first time, implicates him and the other three. Peterson, O'Hara, Ross, and Ravello are quickly hauled off in cuffs when a telegram arrives for Gwendolyn. It's from Harry who says that he swam ashore safely and made his way to East Africa where he bought the uranium-bearing land, so now they are rich. All Billy can do is laugh.

At once a tale of high intrigue and a spoof of one, *Beat the Devil* was based on a book by Huston's friend and Irish neighbor Claud Cockburn who wrote under the name James Helvick. Huston was finishing *Moulin Rouge* in 1951 when he leaned on Bogart's company, Santana Productions, to license Cockburn's book and hire the author to write a first draft screenplay. Cockburn was having financial problems and Huston contrived to pay him with Bogart's money. Unfortunately, Cockburn's script turned out to be unacceptable, so Huston next asked Tony Veiller, with whom he had just worked on *Moulin Rouge* and earlier on *The Killers* (1946) to try an adaptation. He partnered Veiller with Peter Viertel. This took some guts on both men's part because Viertel had just shown Huston the manuscript of *White Hunter, Black Heart*, his roman à clef about the making of *The African Queen* in which the Huston character, John Wilson, comes off as a charming and obsessed conniver. Admiring Viertel's gall, Huston was game and hired him.

Bogart's Santana Productions began with his own $400,000[4] investment to cover the salaries of himself, Huston, Veiller, Viertel, the actors, and whoever would wind up playing the female leads. Producer Mark Hellinger and Robert Lord were partners.[5] Bogart took a cut in his own salary to help the budget.[6] He also called on the Woolf Brothers' Romulus Productions, who had made *The African Queen*, to do so again with *Beat the Devil*. Final funding came from United Artists, which would distribute. The total was around $1 million.

The Veiller-Viertel writing collaboration led nowhere and this should have sent signals. Viertel and Veiller had taken Cockburn's story seriously while Huston regarded it as a satire. (Critics and audiences have had the same problem ever since.) Yet the patchy script was all that Santana had to send to the Breen office for censorship, so off it went. As expected, the censor held that the script's cadre of thoroughly unsavory (if charming) characters was unfit for the screen. As that was the point of the entire film, it was back to square one.

Casting progressed while the script was being eviscerated. Huston quickly lined up Robert Morley, fresh from *The African Queen*, and Peter Lorre, to play half of the quartet of conmen at the center of the scheme. The others were Ivor Bernard and Marco Tulli. It wasn't lost on even the most casual observer that Morley and Lorre were homages to Sidney Greenstreet and Lorre himself in *The Maltese Falcon*. To play Bogart's tempestuous wife, Maria Dannreuther, as well as to enhance the film's European commercial appeal, Gina Lollobrigida was enticed to make her first American film. The only major role uncast was that of Gwendolyn Chelm, the charming compulsive liar who woos Bogart's Billy Dannreuther.

As it happened, producer David O. Selznick was looking for a film to star his wife, Jennifer Jones, and was trying to get Huston to direct one for him. It was no secret in Hollywood that anyone wishing to work with the talented Jones had to deal with her husband's obsessive meddling, which he managed to do even when someone else was the producer. The actress Huston wanted to play the conniving woman at the romantic center of the story was Jean Simmons. When Simmons was unavailable, Huston thought Lauren Bacall would work and went over Bogart's head asking her to consider it. This prompted Bogart to write a mock complaint to Huston charging him with plotting to hire his wife. It mattered not; Bacall was already obligated to Twentieth Century-Fox for *How to Marry a Millionaire*. Huston thereupon told Selznick he would use Jennifer Jones.

The script delays were causing havoc with Bogart's commitment to Warner Bros., to whom he owed a picture that was slated to roll in January 1953, and he had to be done with *Beat the Devil* by then. When it looked as though that wouldn't happen, Bogart had to plead his case to Jack Warner to delay their film. To everyone's surprise, Warner agreed.

A further delay was that Huston, having enjoyed working with Katharine Hepburn on *The African Queen*, had promised her that he would direct her next film.[7] This would make him unavailable for *Beat the Devil*. Rather than approach the mercurial Hepburn on his own, Huston wangled a third party to grant him release by explaining that he would make more money directing Bogart than directing her and could use the fee to settle his debts.[8] She consented. Then everyone left for Italy.

Here Selznick, ever protective of his wife, suggested that Huston and Bogart hire a young writer named Truman Capote to join them on location in Ravello at $1,500 a week. Capote did just that, working with Huston to write ahead of the picture, which is a Hollywood term for composing the next day's scene the night before and, in some cases, sitting right there doing it on the set. It was these pages that Huston adjusted when Capote delivered them, later taking cowriting credit. Sometimes the actors even made up their own lines.

Thirty years later, Lawrence Grobel interviewed both Huston and Capote at length for two separate books.[9] When asked point blank if Huston actually wrote *Beat the Devil*, Capote answered frankly, "Oh, John has never really written a screenplay," continuing, "he never wrote a word of *Beat the Devil*. It was all mine. I wrote every day it was being made. I was always just one day ahead, sometimes I was down there in the morning distributing the script to the cameraman and the poor actors." Pressed on the subject after both Capote's and Huston's deaths, Grobel reported, "Capote said that he wrote the script and John liked to drink. Now, I approached John about that. I said, 'Truman says that he—' and John looked at me and just said, 'We did it together.' You take it as his word or not. You need somebody in charge. In John's case, he was always in charge. Capote, whatever he did, John would always go back and work on it. I feel that it depends on how one looks upon collaboration. When you're sitting with Huston and he's coming up with ideas, and you're the hired writer on it, you're going to be writing down some of those ideas."[10]

Capote was a workhorse. He even delivered the goods when he was laid up in hospital during production with an impacted wisdom tooth. Despite being under a doctor's care, he delivered six pages the morning after his surgery.

Ensconced in Ravello, Italy during production, Capote and Huston shared a room. This created a situation for Capote, who was openly gay, and Huston, who was aggressively straight (and even at times homophobic). "I knew him and know him extremely well," Capote recalled. "Everybody thought we were having an affair, including Humphrey Bogart, who lived next door to us, and he spread it everywhere—the sounds that he could hear in the room at night between me and Huston, Huston had finally gone 'that way,' etc. And Huston played straight into it because he thought it was very funny. Half of the crew were scarcely speaking to him; they were so appalled. It was a very funny situation. I enjoyed it, I thought it was quite funny, I didn't mind it a bit."[11]

Bogart also learned that, gay or not, Capote was not to be trifled with. "They got along famously until one night," Huston said. First Bogart and Capote held an arm-wrestling contest which Capote won three times in a row, and when Bogart picked fisticuffs with the diminutive writer, he got roundly defeated when Capote tripped him, and the star fell on his ass. "I forget what the occasion was," Huston continued, "but they began to wrestle. Truman, who's a little bulldog, pinned Bogie's shoulders to the floor. Bogart pretended it hadn't happened."[12]

This was the great contradiction in Bogart's persona: although he played tough guys on the screen, he was not one in real life.[13] Huston, however, was the real thing, and Bogart seemed to defer to him, despite the occasional inconvenience that Huston's filming methods presented. Huston, despite his courtly manner, was a supreme manipulator and it's reasonable that he used Bogart more to his own advantage than to Bogart's. It was a kind of codependent relationship.

"I think they were friends mostly," Danny Peary says, "but I think he was abusive and probably controlling. Bogart trusted Huston. Huston could write and direct and Bogart didn't do either of those things. Bogart put himself in the hands of directors he trusted. And he probably trusted Huston."[14]

They made a good team, but each man seemed to know what he was worth both singly and together. A case in point involved a dinner party that Lauren Bacall threw at their home for eight friends, one of whom was Huston. When it was time to move into the dining room, Huston had neither showed nor phoned, and she was livid. Bogart told her, "Look, you've got to learn to take people as they are. John is fun—better company than most—but not too reliable at times. Social events aren't that important to him. Enjoy him for what he is. He's not going to change." Nevertheless, at an event at the Beverly Hills Hotel a little later, Bogart told Huston that Betty was sore and please make amends. Huston put his arms around Bacall, cooed "Hello, honey," and laid on an apology so thick that Bacall couldn't be sure if he meant it or was joshing her. But she never again invited him to a sit-down dinner.[15]

Before *Beat the Devil* started, there was an accident that nearly canceled the whole film. As Huston relayed to interviewer Elwy Yost,

> We were quite unprepared. The script was in a desperate way, not good, and just circumstances had conspired to put us in a spot. I did propose to Bogie, by the way, that we forget the whole thing. I saw a way to get out of it without it costing anybody any large sum of money, as it was a bogus company. I felt responsible because I had originally introduced the idea of doing this book and I said, 'Bogie, you know, we can get out of this and save our skins,' and Bogie said. 'John, it's only money' and Bogie was not an easy man with a buck, so that took me back on my hocks and we proceeded to make the picture.

But on the way down to Ravello we were being driven from Rome and had to go through Naples. The road separated; the one to the left was to the Madonna casino and to the right was to Naples, and the driver didn't know which way to go and went right through a stone wall in between the two, an island in the middle. It was quite an impact. We went right through this three-foot stone wall, and I looked and Bogie was in the back seat. I had seen it coming and so I had a chance to brace, and Bogie was just coming up like Lazarus. All his front teeth have been knocked out.

In addition, Bogart had bitten through his tongue. "And as one does," Huston continued, "I laughed. I couldn't help but laugh. He swore at me, and that was the way we started *Beat the Devil*."[16] Bogart had his tongue stitched together and his dental bridge (not teeth) replaced, and a week later—with makeup covering his bruised lip—he was shooting. There has been speculation that Peter Sellers, well before his international fame as Inspector Clouseau, dubbed some of Bogart's lines when Bogart's injury slurred his speech.[17]

Perhaps because of Bacall's absence, Bogart became gloomy during filming. He treated his depression with alcohol, and only Huston was able to control him. Not that Huston was on the wagon himself. Capote recalled smelling smoke coming from the room and pushed open the door to find the director passed out drunk on the floor with an electric space heater about to set the wall afire. Roused from his stupor, Huston could only mumble that he liked the smell of smoke. As for Bogart, was he an alcoholic or just a heavy social drinker? Huston thought the latter. "He had no pretentions," he said. "He loved having a good time, loved acting the fool and getting into scrapes. He was never quite as drunk as he pretended to be—he was not an alcoholic or anything. On his holidays, he loved to hit the corners." [18]

After ten weeks of shooting in Italy, the company moved to London for postproduction. Huston abandoned most of the editing to associate producer Jack Clayton who explained that Huston was a visual artist who had little patience for putting the pieces together. While in London, Huston also tried to rekindle his romance with Olivia de Havilland.

Bogart and the Woolf Brothers were concerned that the film would never make its cost back, and they were right. It was released in London on November 24, 1953, and in New York on March 12, 1954. Many US critics didn't get it, and no wonder; the film was cut by four minutes for its US release with a narration added by Bogart's character who told the story in flashback. The full version went into European release by Romulus and the cut was handled in the US by United Artists. It grossed $1.1 million in the United States and Canada and £115,926 in the United Kingdom.[19, 20] By any reasonable measure, the film barely broke even, if at all. United Artists gave its rights back to Santana Productions in 1957, after which Columbia Pictures purchased the property and handled it through their arthouse division, Royal Films.[21]

In his Bogart biography, Joe Hyams writes of a lunch with the actor in which Bogart showed him a sheath of letters Huston had forwarded to him from customers and exhibitors praising the film, which he called "the thing." These were to counter a newspaper advertisement taken out by disappointed theater owners apologizing to audiences who had paid to see *Beat the Devil*. "The exhibitors are behind us all the way," Huston had written Bogart, "I'm afraid too far behind, say $1,000,000." This meant that the film should have taken in $1 million more than it did. "What burns me up," Bogart told Hyams, "is we risked a great deal of money to make this picture. I put in about $400,000 of my own money, and I don't think there's an exhibitor in the business who would risk five cents of his money in a film." Bogart's aim was to get Hyams, a journalist, to write his complaints in a story, and "see if you can get the quotes exact for a change." Countered Hyams, "If I quoted you exactly no one would print it." After the story ran, Bogart called Hyams to report that he had been fending off calls from upset exhibitors all morning. But then he said. "It was a good piece, kid. Looks like we told them off, huh?"[22]

Beat the Devil is unquestionably an acquired taste. It has all the elements and double-crosses of a caper film, but they are spread between scenes that have little to do with advancing the plot, although they do enrich the characters. The humor emerges in the form of wisecracks that generally come out of whatever mouth is available at the time.[23] Although there is much to admire in watching the interplay, the film doesn't seem to know whether it is going for laughs, thrills, or to inspire an essay contest. Inevitably, over the years it acquired cult status.[24] It also entered public domain in 1982 when Royal Films apparently failed to renew its copyright. There it resided for decades on poor VHS and DVD copies until August 2016 when an uncut version was restored in 4K by Sony Pictures in collaboration with Martin Scorsese's The Film Foundation. The new version rearranged scenes, removed Bogart's voice-over, added excised footage, and extended the running time from 89 to 93 minutes. (Some versions have been reported at 100 minutes.)

Is *Beat the Devil* a satire for the ages or a squalid misfire? Should it win points for trying something bold? Or did it truly succeed, if only for a select audience? Does "you had to be there" work with a million-dollar budget?

"It took three or four years for it to begin to catch on," Huston told interviewer Dick Cavett, "and then it slowly grew into that, into a cult."[25]

Sometimes one can learn more from a failed film by a great director than from a successful one. The scenes in *Beat the Devil* are well-written, acted with flair, and directed with elan. But they don't fit together. In one moment, the film winks at the audience (Gwendolyn's incessant fabrications and Billy's indulgent tolerating of them), and in another it is tense (the player piano continuing while the murderous major stalks Harry). Gina Lollobrigida, Italian through and through, plays a would-be Anglophile while Edward Underdown as Harry Chelm, English to his core, is a bigger fraud than any of the real crooks. Peter Lorre makes a better Kaspar Gutman than Robert Morley does and gets off the best line in the picture: "Time. Time. What is time? Swiss manufacture it. French hoard it. Italians squander it. Americans say it is money. Hindus say it does not exist. Do you know what I say? I say time is a crook." Above all, Bogart—who in real life could burst any bubble—is almost completely passive as Dannreuther. He watches the others tie themselves in knots of conspiracies and betrayals while remaining as the audience's surrogate and wasted in that passive capacity. He is clearly middle-aged, has had perhaps a little college, and his character undergoes no consequential change despite his experiences. His one heroic act is saving Harry from being murdered by the Major, but the scene is so casually constructed as to avoid the required tension. By the end of the film, Billy has achieved nothing; he is just as broke as when he started. He still has his wife but he lost the uranium deal, and the bad guys are out of the picture.

In this sense, *Beat the Devil* is the ultimate Huston film: everyone in it (except Harry) has his or her dreams shaken or shattered, "just like the film itself," says Peary. "This film started out to be one thing and turned into another."[26] When it failed, Bogart moved forward, partnering Santana Productions with Columbia Pictures. He died before *Beat the Devil* had its apotheosis.

Typically, Huston blew it off. He went straight into his dream project, *Moby Dick*, and for the rest of his career almost habitually alternated flops with hits, regaining his muse and fame toward the end.[27]

Beat the Devil was to be the last time Huston and Bogart worked together. In 1955, producer Walter Mirisch asked Huston to join William Wyler and Billy Wilder in a deal at a new company called Allied Artists. Huston told Mirisch that he wanted to do Rudyard Kipling's *The Man Who Would Be King* with Bogart and Clark Gable. An excited Allied Artists bought the book for him, but when Bogart died the deal fell apart. Then Gable died after acting for Huston in *The Misfits*. Subsequently, Huston tried to set it up with Richard Burton and Peter O'Toole (he was neighbors with O'Toole in Ireland) but that failed to come about. AA had held onto the rights and, in 1975, Huston was finally able to direct the film with Sean Connery and Michael Caine. It stands as one of the best movies that any of them ever made.

CHAPTER 11

Life After Death

Humphrey Bogart made seven films following *Beat the Devil*, including some of his best: *The Caine Mutiny*, *Sabrina*, *We're No Angels*, and *The Desperate Hours*. As he was making *The Harder They Fall* in 1956, he developed laryngeal cancer, and the diagnosis was made known to everyone in his circle except him. The stories of friends visiting him during his homebound decline are heart-rending, but all of them stress his bravery. Richard Brooks told of how he balked at spending time with a sickly Bogart, and Bogart, seeing his expression, challenged him, "What's the matter, can't you take it?"

"In those final days," John Huston recalled to interviewer Regis Philbin, "he proved to be as tough as any character he ever played. It was one hour a day when they received guests. This was observed right up till he was too weak to even be lifted down the stairs, so he used to crowd himself into this dumbwaiter and come down to the first floor. He was then put into a chair and wheeled into the drawing room and have drinks and talk. And that's the last picture I have of Bogie."[1]

In her book, Katharine Hepburn recounted Spencer Tracy's farewell to his old friend from *Up the River*, made at the beginning of their careers. "There was no bunk about Bogie. And on that last day, when Spencer patted him on the shoulder and said, 'Goodnight, Bogie,' Bogie turned his eyes to Spence very quietly and with a sweet smile covered Spence's hand with his own and said, 'Goodbye, Spence.' Spence's heart stood still. He understood."[2]

Humphrey Deforest Bogart died the next morning, January 11, 1957. Lauren Bacall asked Tracy to deliver the eulogy, but the great actor declined, fearing that he would not be able to speak without breaking down. Bacall then turned to John Huston who spoke at his friend's service. "No one who sat in his presence during those final weeks will ever forget," Huston said in his soft, honey voice. "It was a unique display of sheer animal courage ... one quickened to the grandeur of it, expanded and felt strangely elated, proud to be there, proud to be his friend, the friend of such a brave man.... We have no reason to feel any sorrow for him, only for ourselves for having lost him."[3]

"He always said that when he died, he wanted no mourning for him," his widow wrote a decade after his death. "He believed those who mourned for the dead were really mourning for themselves. He wanted friends to drink a private toast and have a laugh. And that is what they did."[4] As his coffin was closed, Bacall placed with him the gold whistle he had once given her, the one he'd had inscribed with, "If you want anything, just whistle."

A year after he died, Bogart was already at risk of being forgotten. New stars such as Marlon Brando, Paul Newman, Lee Remmick, Geraldine Page, Joanne Woodward, and Tony Curtis were emerging. None of them yet had the weight or command of Bogie (it was said that he could dominate a scene simply by entering it), but they were alive and he wasn't. His films were not yet widely available on television, and this was decades before home video. Repertory and art cinemas were more interested in Bergman, Antonioni, Fellini, Truffaut, Godard, and Kurosawa than they were in Hawks, Walsh, or Curtiz, all of whom had directed Bogart. Revivals of golden age Hollywood movies were rare. As a result, Bogart's old movies, like other out-of-release product, languished in studio storage archives, oftentimes fading and decomposing as the volatile chemistry of nitrate film did its destructive job. Old movies had little worth in the era of Cinema-Scope, Cinerama, 3D, and stereophonic sound.

Then came television and suddenly Hollywood's past had value. In 1956, through a complex sales deal, Jack Warner sold his company's entire pre-December 1949 library to Associated Artists Productions for $21 million.[5] AAP was a television syndicator and sold packages of old movies to local TV stations that were hungry for product, ironically using a "block booking" philosophy in which the broadcaster had to take every title or get none of them. In 1958, AAP was acquired by United Artists. Years later Ted Turner bought the library and, when Turner was purchased by Warner Bros., the library came back home.

In the meantime, the Brattle Theatre in Cambridge, Massachusetts, which in 1953 had given up stage plays and installed a rear-projection system to show movies, booked a series of Bogart films. This was an economic decision; old movies were such a nuisance for a distributor to handle that they could be bought for a flat rate of $25 or $50 a week rather than a traditional percentage of the gate. The Brattle, run by Bryant Halliday and Cy Harvey, selected some of Bogart's best (*Casablanca, Treasure of the Sierra Madre, The Maltese Falcon*, etc.). The series happened to coincide with the final exam reading week for nearby Harvard University and the students, with time on their hands, flocked to the tiny Brattle, and the Bogart cult was born.

Of course, *Casablanca* was the one that most people remember seeing there. Over the years, audiences would recite the dialogue along with the film (this was decades before audiences tossed toast at the screen during *The Rocky Horror Picture Show*). They would even rise along with Rick's patrons to sing "The Marseillaise." The Brattle continued to play Bogart festivals for decades until television, home video, and the fading interests of younger filmgoers rendered them obsolete. (The author sadly recalls attending a fiftieth anniversary screening of *Casablanca* at the Brattle when the audience not only failed to rise for "The Marseillaise," they couldn't even be bothered to yell *vive la France!* at its conclusion. This was a shock. I thought we'd always have Paris. *C'est tellement triste.*)

Beat the Devil joined the cult in 1964, which is an anomaly in that its older characters traditionally should have no appeal to young, hip audiences. "It's an old person's film," says Danny Peary, who wrote about it in *Cult Movies 2*. "The lead characters are middle-aged and there are no kids in it. They're all past their prime, everybody. Maybe not Gina Lollobrigida. And maybe we're not supposed to think Jennifer Jones has passed her prime, but her peak was years before, I think. It's funny that it became a cult film. I don't think it's for eighteen-year-olds on a date or even people in their twenties. It's really not for them."[6]

How would Bogart feel about being the focus of a cult? This was, after all, a man who enjoyed deflating the egos of pompous people, and no one risks pomposity more than someone who inspires a cult. "I think he'd be astonished and amused," offered John Huston. "Oh, he'd love it, but he'd also be amused by it."[7]

John Huston extended his filmography by twenty-nine titles following *Beat the Devil*, recapturing and extending the high reputation he had earned at the beginning of his directing career. Among them were *Moby Dick* (1956), *The Misfits* (1961), *Freud* (1962), *The Night of the Iguana* (1964), *Fat City* (1972), *The Man Who Would Be King* (1975), *Wise Blood* (1979), *Under the Volcano* (1984), *Prizzi's Honor* (1985), and *The Dead* (1987). He occasionally returned to acting, memorably in *Chinatown* (1974) and *The Wind and the Lion* (1975), and the long-delayed *The Other Side of the Wind* (2018) and in other films, such as Noah in *The Bible: In the Beginning*, less so. One of his most unusual roles was in the little-known sequel to *The Treasure of the Sierra Madre* titled *The Bridge in the Jungle* (see Appendix 6) in which he starred as the character based on Howard, the prospector his father Walter had played in the original film.

Huston's decline was prolonged. Author Lawrence Grobel was writing the family history that became *The Hustons* when John was in and out of hospitals. "He hated the hospital," Grobel says. "He hated to be bored. He would go there, and we would talk. Then the doctor would come and pound his back to get the phlegm up. Then sometimes when he was staying at Burgess Meredith's house, or another house, or in West Hollywood, he had a coughing spasm, where I didn't know if I should pound his back like the doctors do or leave him alone. I didn't want to kill him. 'I don't know if I could talk anymore,' he would go. I said, 'Don't worry, John, don't worry. I'm just going to sit here with you until I know you're feeling okay.' We did, we sat there for five, ten minutes, and then we'd start talking again. It was a respectful relationship I had. I think he knew it was important what I was doing, because he was giving me the last two years of his life. It's a rare thing for someone to spend that time if he thinks he's wasting his time. Who knows what he would have thought of the book?"[8] *The Hustons* was published two years after John's death.

Huston died on August 28, 1987, while on location for *Mr. North* which his son Danny was directing from a screenplay written by Huston and Janet Roach (the two had previously written *Prizzi's Honor*). The cast of that film included Anthony Edwards, Anjelica Huston, Mary Stuart Masterson, Virginia Madsen, Tammy Grimes, Harry Dean Stanton, Robert Mitchum, and Lauren Bacall, all of whom signed on out of affection for John and to help Danny start his filmmaking career. Huston's death came on a rainy day in the humid New England summer with his companion, Maricela Hernandez, holding his hands in hers. Asked to summarize Huston's life, Lauren Bacall said, simply, "he was *about* something."

Huston's varied filmography, including those he made with Bogart, have a curious trajectory. The majority of them are about dreamers whose hopes are dashed, either by fate or some inner flaw that dooms them, in which case they realign their goals or embrace the tragedy of their lot.[9] The half-dozen Huston-Bogart collaborations show the development of this continuing theme. In *The Maltese Falcon*, Sam Spade solves the mystery but loses his lover, Brigid O'Shaugnessy. In *Across the Pacific*, he succeeds in his mission to thwart the Japanese attack, but at the cost of the life of the father of Alberta Marlow, the women to whom he has become attracted.

It is with *The Treasure of the Sierra Madre* that fate takes the upper hand and disappoints each of the three prospectors to various degrees, only the surviving two of whom gain perspective on their lot. The cleansing of the Frank McCourt character in *Key Largo* mitigates Huston's penchant for victory in defeat, even if Frank returns to shore as a wounded hero. The real losers here are Sheriff Wade and Mr. Temple who share the guilt for their part in killing the innocent Osceola brothers.

Charlie and Rosie triumph in *The African Queen*, and perhaps this is why the film wildly succeeded: audiences love winners. Its lessons were not learned for *Beat the Devil* with its litany of miscreants who, in the end, have nothing to show for their enterprise. Moreover, while Billy Dannreuther gains nothing from assisting the uranium speculators, it should be remembered that, before the story starts, he has already lost his car and his villa. On the other hand, he does get to keep Gina Lollobrigida.

Bogart today has become a curiosity, a man both of his times and ahead of them. Fortunately, he is remembered only for his best films, those that can legitimately be called "Bogart movies" and don't have to be named. Huston continued to be reevaluated by film scholars who cannot agree whether he was an auteur or "merely" a craftsman, as if any single label can define the man. An ongoing issue is how involved he was in writing his scripts; that is, whether he faced the terror of the blank page or came in after somebody else did a first draft. What ought to matter is the finished film and, in that regard, there is no questioning the man's achievements.

As for Bogart, he is still celebrated in images, websites, and documentaries. He is a figure from the past who remains relevant in the present. His cynicism is as timely today as when he embodied it both on and off the screen during his heyday as one of the greatest stars Hollywood ever produced. The six films that he and Huston made together broke molds and showed the way for maturity, boldness, and moral complexity that are needed today more than ever in a world that has reverted to black and white as the prevailing moral choices.

Appendices

The research for this book led down many avenues, all of which were relevant but some of which did not fit cleanly into the Bogart-Huston narrative. The reader is encouraged to gather greater understanding of earlier chapters with the appendices that follow:

Appendix 1   Henry Blanke: A Filmmaker's Secret Weapon
Appendix 2   Walter Huston Appreciation
Appendix 3   The Gold Standard
Appendix 4   The Elusive B. Traven
Appendix 5   John Huston, B. Traven, and the Mexican Connection
Appendix 6   *The Bridge in the Jungle*
Appendix 7   Dashiell Hammett and Sam Spade
Appendix 8   The Rat Pack

Appendices

APPENDIX 1

Henry Blanke:
A Filmmaker's Secret Weapon

When the public thinks of producers from Hollywood's Golden Age, they are apt to name, at best, David O. Selznick, Samuel Goldwyn, or perhaps Cecil B. DeMille. Even at Warner Bros., where producers were routinely called "supervisors" so as not to eclipse Jack Warner's primacy, one is more apt to think of Hal B. Wallis. But the quieter Henry Blanke (BLANK-ee or BLAHNK-uh) was the most valued producer on the Warner Bros. lot and the most desired by anybody who got to make a picture there. His stewardship of over eighty pictures, from the scandalous *Convention City* (1933) to *Hell is for Heroes* (1962), with credits along the way such as *The Fountainhead* (1949), *Young at Heart* (1954), and *The Nun's Story* (1959) show his range and, more importantly, his discretion in handling controversial subjects. His shepherding of *The Maltese Falcon* and *The Treasure of the Sierra Madre* brings him into the Huston and Bogart orbit. In the first, he encouraged a first-time director to use his judgment to make his film his own way. In the second, he used his influence and his wiles to keep budget and schedule pressure off of the filmmaker even during World War II.

In the days of the studio system, producers were responsible for the day-to-day guidance of a production. Unlike today when a producer is frequently someone with a business card who knows someone who has money or access, a studio producer in the best sense would scout for screen-worthy projects from the outside or wrangle for key assignments within the studio, file daily progress reports, soothe ruffled egos, and guide artists to a common goal. It involved taste, diplomacy, and trust.[1] Blanke had all three. He even got along with Ayn Rand (*The Fountainhead*, 1949).[2]

He was born Heinze Blanke on December 30, 1901, in Berlin-Steglitz, Germany. His father, Wilhelm Blanke, was a noted painter. Shortly after Heinze's birth, the family moved to Vienna where he grew up. Too young to fight in World War I, Blanke won employment after the war at Berlin's UFA studios as a production assistant and cutter but was fired for participating in a workers' strike. He became assistant to Ernst Lubitsch and, when Lubitsch was hired by Warner Bros. in 1923, emigrated with him to the company's Hollywood studio and worked on the company's silent films. He returned to Germany to become an assistant director to Fritz Lang on Lang's masterwork, *Metropolis* (1927), and was rehired there by Warner Bros. to supervise their German productions. In 1932 he returned stateside to Warners to head the studio's foreign department. When Darryl F. Zanuck left Warners in 1933 and Hal Wallis was appointed head of production, Blanke and Sam Bischoff became the studio's primary producers.

In 1938, Blanke was working on *Jezebel*, which William Wyler was directing. When Wyler needed help on the second half of the picture, Blanke asked his friend John Huston, who was then a studio contract writer, to consult with him (Huston eventually received cowriting credit). It was there that Blanke became aware of Huston's formidable talent and charismatic personality. The men grew so close that Huston would later write, "that's how I fell in love with him. From that moment on, Blanke was my champion and mentor."[3] It was Blanke who pushed for Huston to get his directorial wings on *The Maltese Falcon*, and it was he who deflected the memos from production chief Wallis who complained about pace, photography, and any number of creative elements so Huston would be free to make the film his way. He also served as buffer between Wallis and any number of other directors. Whether the astute Wallis ever caught on or was happy to let Blanke suffer any fallout remains a mystery.

When Huston was starting *The Maltese Falcon*, Blanke encouraged him to direct each scene as if it was the most important one in the picture. The advice proved to be solid, and when Huston won the Oscar for directing *The Treasure of the Sierra Madre*, he held the statuette aloft and announced to the Academy members, "If this were hollow and had a drink in it, I'd toast Henry Blanke."

Blanke's career at Warner Bros, spanned twenty-five years and some of their most important pictures including *A Midsummer Night's Dream*, *The Green Pastures*, *The Life of Emile Zola*, *The Adventures of Robin Hood*, *Old Acquaintance*, and, of course, *The Maltese Falcon* and *The Treasure of the Sierra Madre*. Blanke and his wife Ursula were cofounders of the European Film Fund (along with Paul Kohner, Ernst Lubitsch, Billy Wilder, William Wyler, Joe Pasternak, Henry Koster, and many more expatriates) whose mission was to rescue German Jews and others fleeing Hitler, and to financially support them until they got a foothold in America so they would not be a burden on their new country.

Astonishingly, despite producing dozens of acclaimed films, Blanke was never given an Oscar, not even an honorary one, nor the Irving G. Thalberg Memorial Award.

APPENDIX 2

Walter Huston Appreciation

Walter Huston was one of the finest actors of his generation who appeared in over four dozen films but is remembered most fondly as Howard in his son John's *The Treasure of the Sierra Madre*. It was a role unlike all his others, which included Mr. Scratch in *The Devil and Daniel Webster*, the disillusioned businessman in *Dodsworth*, and Abraham Lincoln in D. W. Griffith's eponymic biographical drama. The fact that he played the old prospector in *Treasure* almost unrecognizably as a toothless fast talker hid the patrician elegance for which he had hitherto been known. Walter was, of course, the father of John Huston and the grandfather of Anjelica Huston, and there is some passing fascination in the oft-noted fact that both he and his granddaughter were directed to Oscars by the same family member.

The Huston dynasty was not intentional. It was that happy confluence of talent, desire, and opportunity. Ultimately, Walter begat John, and John begat Angelica (actress), Danny (actor, director), Tony (writer), and Allegra (writer).

Walter was a Vaudevillian, civil engineer, and practitioner of that mountebank profession known as acting. Before the movies grabbed him, he was a prolific stage performer and once estimated, "I've played every role except the ice in *Uncle Tom's Cabin*." Notably, on screen, he was Abraham Lincoln for D. W. Griffith in the master's first talkie in 1930. That same year, he interviewed Griffith on screen for a prologue to a sound-added reissue of *The Birth of a Nation*. Abraham Lincoln was already his seventh film after his debut in 1929 at the end of the silent era. His stage skill and talent made him a popular performer in the early days of talkies (eight films in 1932 alone), and, over the years, his range was astonishing: the hypocritical evangelist opposite Joan Crawford in *Rain*, the stalwart banker in Frank Capra's *American Madness*, the disillusioned businessman in *Dodsworth*, Doc Holiday in *The Outlaw*, Mr. Scratch in *All That Money Can Buy* (a.k.a. *The Devil and Daniel Webster*), the Cohan paterfamilias in *Yankee Doodle Dandy*, and Ambassador Joseph E. Davies in the controversial propaganda effort, *Mission to Moscow*. His Broadway credits are equally varied, ranging from Eugene O'Neill's *Desire Under the Elms* to *Dodsworth* to a famously disastrous production of *Othello* to immortality as Pieter Stuyvesant in 1938's *Knickerbocker Holiday*, in which he introduced the classic "September Song" with lyrics by Maxwell Anderson and music by Kurt Weill.

As noted, Walter played a cameo role in John's debut feature, *The Maltese Falcon*, as Captain Jacoby who delivers the paper-wrapped black bird to Sam Spade before succumbing to wounds received by gunsel Wilmer Cook. He and John considered it a "good luck" appearance. But if he is remembered best for *The Treasure of the Sierra Madre*, the paths Walter Huston took getting there should be traced. His story begins in Toronto, Canada on April 6, 1884, when he was born to Elizabeth and Robert Houghston. The name, changed for show business purposes to the more easily remembered *Huston*, continues to cause confusion between the Americans and the British, the first of whom pronounce it *Hewston* and the latter of whom say *Hooston*.[1]

One of four children, Walter left school at the age of sixteen when his early success in local vaudeville shows inspired him to act for a living. His mother, surprisingly, agreed with his quitting formal education (his grades encouraged him to make that decision) but insisted he learn a profession as a day job to meet the bills that acting was less certain to pay.

Thus did Walter become an office clerk, a role for which he was thoroughly unsuited. It did not last long.

Nan (Ninetta) Sunderland became Huston's third wife in 1931 but was already his mistress in 1928 when they costarred in the George M. Cohan-Ring Lardner show, *Elmer the Great*. Huston was married at the time to Bayonne Whipple (real name: Fanny Elmina Rose) who, upon hearing of her husband's affair, confronted Sunderland backstage at the Lyceum Theatre to no apparent effect. The play closed in October 1928, but the Huston-Whipple marriage lasted until October 1931, after which Huston took Sunderland as his wife. It was a match made on Broadway; after *Elmer* closed, the Hustons had success in 1934 with *Dodsworth*, adapted by Sidney Howard from the Sinclair Lewis novel about a businessman tempted to leave his wife while they take a European trip. Mrs. Huston played Edith Cortright, Samuel Dodsworth's "other woman." Huston was asked to play the role when Samuel Goldwyn bought the film rights, but Nan was disappointed when she was not brought to Hollywood as Edith; Mary Astor won the job. She did appear as Desdemona opposite her husband's Othello in his fabled 1937 stage failure, but as his star ascended, hers decayed. As the marriage progressed, she devoted herself to being Huston's wife and he divided his time among her, movies, and a succession of mistresses. When *The Treasure of the Sierra Madre* became reality in 1946, the marriage was effectively over, but neither partner sought to end it. By the time Walter traveled to Mexico to play Howard, Nan was in Chicago's Passavant Hospital after her bouts of depression led to becoming an inpatient, and then to enduring electroconvulsive therapy. The joy that had once suffused them as a couple while they were performing together had passed.

What brought Huston to Howard? Nepotism. Said Walter, "John said he saw my part as an old man who talked fast and throws away his lines, a hard-bitten old prospector used to spending weeks and months in solitude. I told John that was the way I understood the old coot, too."[2] What's remarkable about his performance is that the stereotype of such an old man would have led the audience to dismiss not only his integrity but his sanity; certainly that's what Dobbs planned to do until he and Curtin discovered during their mountainous trek that Howard was heartier than they were. Had Huston played Howard like Gabby Hayes, he would have failed; his winning decency in the role replaced braggadocio with credibility.

During the shoot, father and son reportedly acted like conspiratorial playmates. When the scene arrived in which Howard berates Dobbs and Curtin for missing the riches they were treading on with their very feet, he told John to keep the camera running while he tried something. On film he dances a jig before his befuddled companions. He later explained to his son that the jig had been taught to him for his character Ephraim Cabot by playwright Eugene O'Neill when they were rehearsing *Desire Under the Elms* in 1924.

A veteran scene-stealer, Walter had a willing enabler in John, and the duo was so formidable that Humphrey Bogart famously griped, "One Huston is bad enough, but two are murder." And yet Walter knew he had to hold his own against Bogart, whose descent into madness was the showier performance. Balancing expertly on the border between being that "old coot" and being the moral center of the story, Howard, it might be argued, is the master manipulator, for he not only insulates himself from the inevitable conflict that he correctly foresees between Dobbs and Curtin, but he also gets to live among the Indians for the rest of his days. In that respect, when he brings the young village boy back to consciousness in the story, it almost exonerates him for agreeing to take part in assassinating Cody at the campsite.

What emerges with repeated viewings of *Treasure* is that Howard is the most powerful and complex of the three prospectors. For all the fulminating Dobbs does and however passive Curtin is, it's Howard who knows the lay of the moral landscape. Looking at it in reverse, one might say that it is Howard who seduces Dobbs and Curtin into prospecting for gold, not the other way around. What works against this is that, at the time, neither

Curtin nor Dobbs has two dimes to rub together, so to what end would Howard pontificate? Nevertheless, he is so eager to share his experience that, when fortune does arrive, Dobbs and Curtin are ready to go. So what if Howard winds up broke at the end? His village retirement community is, in a sense, the indigenous people who live on the land yet want nothing beyond what they see. It is Walter Huston's charismatic performance that permits this view, not text in the book or screenplay. In a world where gold turns a man's head and blinds him to what is happening to him, who needs to be led down a road that is already glowing with riches at the far end?

Walter Huston was never without work following his Oscar win for *Treasure*. He made no further Broadway appearances (and reportedly turned down *Death of a Salesman*, sensing it would be a hit but not wanting to be locked into a long run). He did appear in three films, none of which approached the quality of *Treasure*: *Summer Holiday* (1948), *The Great Sinner* (1949), and *The Furies* (1950). After finishing *The Furies*, his agent Paul Kohner told him that Fox wanted him to make *Mr. 880*, a Robert Riskin script about a counterfeiter who produced only dollar bills. He accepted and prepared to start shooting on April 10, 1950. In California for costume tests during the first week of April, he celebrated his birthday on the fifth and retired to his hotel room where he felt he was passing a kidney stone. Instead, the pain was coming from an aortic aneurysm. He died on April 7.

John was heard sobbing loudly at the funeral with his wife, Ricki Soma, at his side to comfort him. Later he told the press, "He was a great person and a great actor. He died peacefully and without struggle. I have never seen so quiet a death. He died as modestly as he had lived. When the time came, he just died."[3]

Some people noted that the last words he spoke on film in *The Furies*, a western twist on *King Lear*, was his death scene, "There'll never be another like me." Indeed.

APPENDIX 3

The Gold Standard

> And it's blow, boys, blow, for Californio!
> For there's plenty of gold,
> So I've been told,
> On the banks of the Sacramento!

This chorus from the traditional song, "The Banks of the Sacramento," is more on the side of optimism than reality.[1] It was inspired by an accidental discovery, on January 24, 1848, by a man named James Marshall who had been hired by another man, John Sutter, to supervise the construction of a sawmill on the American River at the base of the Sierra Nevada mountains. As Marshall glanced into the water flowing from the water wheel, the sun glistened off a shard of metal the size of a flower petal. Suspecting what it was, Marshall retrieved it and gave it a perfunctory test that confirmed its legitimacy. From then on, there was no way to keep the discovery of gold a secret. The Gold Rush was on.

Worldwide, there may be as little as 0.004 ounces of gold per ton of earth, yet that has never dissuaded countless prospectors from devoting years of their lives, and sometimes their lives themselves, to its acquisition.

Gold and other precious metals are weighed in troy ounces, one troy ounce being 31.103476 grams versus a regular ounce being 28.35 grams.

Gold is valuable because it's rare and difficult to mine. The time involved finding it and getting it can involve years, but because *The Treasure of the Sierra Madre* runs less than two hours, it's tempting to think that Dobbs, Curtin, and Howard stumbled on their lode relatively quickly. In the book it takes several grueling weeks just to find the vein and longer to process it.

Aurum, its Latin name, is abbreviated *Au* with an atomic weight of 79, placing it between platinum and mercury (laterally) on the periodic chart.[2] It is shiny and the color of, well, gold. It tends to be found alongside deposits of lead and copper, washed on the bottom of sandy streams, and in sea water. Historically, the search for gold motivated the age of discovery in the late 1400s when significant deposits were discovered in Central and South America, Mexico, and the Caribbean islands. The 1848 discovery at Sutter's Mill in California turned out to be one of the largest hauls in centuries, followed by discoveries in Alaska and the African Transvaal.[3]

Adventure stories, historic photographs, and legends characterize the gold prospectors as grizzled old men stooped over riverbeds, swirling sandy water in a pie tin hoping that some of the grains sparkle. This is only one aspect of the trade, but the principles of extracting it are consistent: placer, mining it from veins in the rock, and separating it from other ores.

Placer is the simplest process and is the one used in *Treasure*. Here the particles of gold are dispersed among gravel and sand and can be obtained by washing the mixture in water in ever-widening circles until the unwanted particles spill over the edge of the pan and the shiny gold is left behind. This is done in small batches. A more efficient way to do it is with the construction of a sluice, which is a kind of trough in which a constant stream of water washes a constantly replenished supply of sand to yield gold dust.

A more mechanized way is the use of high-pressured water stream against rock, washing away large quantities of gravel that is run through a sluice system.

The industrialized harvesting of gold depends on the discovery of veins of the mineral. Here gold must be separated from the metals traditionally found with it, copper and zinc; in fact, one third of the world's gold comes as a happy byproduct of zinc and copper mining. A sophisticated version of electrolysis is used to separate ions of copper from the kludge of other metals.[4] The process begins by crushing the rocks of ore that are removed from the vein, suspending them in water, and adding sodium cyanide or calcium cyanide alongside zinc to allow the gold to precipitate, or fall out of solution. Other rare earth metals may also be found this way.

Just as the vein the Sierra Madre was eventually exhausted, so are actual commercial gold reserves. The World Gold Council describes the "life cycle" of a gold operation as requiring one to ten years to explore and find new deposits (only ten percent of which are worth pursuing), and one to five years to plan, construct, and lay the legal foundation of land licenses and permits.[5] These details, however, can lead to a ten-to-thirty-year operation of extraction and refinement, much of which is guided by the market value of gold. (This may be code for controlling the market by "managing" the availability of gold.) The process now involves innovative mining techniques and safety requirements for the miners.

When the mine is exhausted or the ore becomes too expensive to remove, it may take between one and five years to close and restore the mine, as Howard, Dobbs, and Curtin felt compelled to do to the mountain where they found their riches. The mine owner or operator must then monitor the site for up to ten years to see to its environmental restoration.

Gold has applications beyond bling, dental work, and edible petals on French pastry (although its malleability allows it to be hammered into incredibly thin leaves). Although about half of today's gold is found in jewelry and coinage, it is also widely used in electronics, computers, and in medicine (gold injections to treat arthritis), and the space program (that gold record on Voyager I).

It is also the basis of some world economies as well as many individual economies. Gold is considered to be a stable investment in times of financial instability, particularly in times of a volatile stock market.[6] Gold prices tend to rise as the value of the US dollar falls, the major difference being that, unlike stock, gold doesn't pay dividends.[7] A more seductive allure is that, unlike a stock portfolio in which paper or digital records represent money, gold is gold; it has a physicality. This makes it attractive to a subgroup of investors who question the world economic system, a view that has been embraced by a segment of the population who challenge the legitimacy of the US Federal Reserve and other government and quasi-government institutions such as the Bilderberg group.[8]

The United States has been on the gold standard on and off since the 1870s in line with the economies of other industrial economies. When paper money was introduced, its value related to an equal amount of gold backing it up in the United States Treasury. After the second world war, however, a meeting at Bretton Woods replaced the gold standard with an exchange rate fixed by agreement of the nations attending the conference.[9] This changed in 1971 when the price of gold on the international market rose beyond what the Federal Reserve could redeem, and the US dollar—which had become the standard for many other world economies—began to float. In order to stabilize the value of dollars, the US made a deal with Saudi Arabia to base its price for petroleum on the dollar. Oil prices since then have had an enormous impact on US consumer prices.

Gold prices have varied over the years despite its relative stability. In June, 1915, for example, gold sold on the market for $591 per ounce. In 1920, following World War I, it had dropped to $315 per ounce. May 1934 boosted the value to $810 per ounce as the Great Depression started to ease, but its price dropped to $289 in 1970 when the Vietnam war drained America's coffers. May 1980 saw a huge spike to $2,400 per ounce when inflation struck and oil prices rose, making metal more secure than stocks. Gold crashed to $463 in 2001 when the economy improved and other investments became more attractive, but it spiked again in late 2024 to record highs of $2,600 per ounce when the USA credit rating was downgraded.

In 1924 when *The Treasure of the Sierra Madre* is set, gold was going for $24.67 an ounce. This means that, in order to have mined $25,000 worth of gold apiece, Dobbs, Howard, and Curtin (or, rather, their burros) would each have to have been carrying over eighty-four pounds of refined gold, not gold dust that Gold Hat didn't recognize as valuable.

APPENDIX 4

The Elusive B. Traven

For starters, his name is pronounced *tráhvin*, not *trāyvin*. Second, that's not his name anyway. Third, there's plenty of speculation what his name really is, or was, and it has grown since his death in 1969, or maybe he didn't die, maybe someone else did, or maybe he was two people. Or maybe not.

Not only is the author of *The Treasure of the Sierra Madre* and seventeen other published literary works (he may have written more under different names) supposedly unconfirmed, but even the people who worked with him on the film were never sure of his identity. "I think B. Traven's becoming one of those mysteries rather like Shakespeare," John Huston told documentary filmmaker Will Wyatt, who also wrote a book about him, in 1978, "and the more information we have about him now, the deeper the mystery becomes."[1]

The secret of Traven's identity lurks behind *The Treasure of the Sierra Madre*. As noted above, when the film was being produced, it was not a mystery, it was a nuisance that very nearly ended the picture before it began. That story is told in the chapter about the production of the film. The Traven story itself is more complex, and it was first articulated in a spellbinding account by John Huston while he was preparing to direct the picture. After he was discharged from the Army after World War II, he sent Traven, through their mutual agent, Paul Kohner, an early draft of his script. He was pleased when, on

September 2, 1946, Traven sent him a lengthy response with suggestions, typing B.T. as his signature. Huston answered on December 30 explaining his choices and accepting some of what Traven had offered.

On January 4, 1947, Traven replied. Some of the changes were major, some merely tweaks, but all show how a script and film are shaped by numerous inputs.

Traven began his notes by recommending a change of the stated date of the story. The film now begins February 14, 1925; the script begins in 1924; the book starts in 1920. Traven explained that the oil boom in 1920 was such that white men like Dobbs and Curtin would have easily found work and therefore would not be adrift unemployed in Tampico. He said that 1924 would be a better date if any date had to be given. He also quibbled, in the scenes in which Dobbs asks the white-suited man for change, that an American would ask, "will you lend a helping hand to a fellow" because anyone rich enough to be hit up by a ragged stranger would walk away from him.

A more serious criticism was how to arm Dobbs, Curtin, and Howard on board the train when it is attacked by bandits. Traven said that any American boarding a train armed would be in trouble; if they are to be armed, they should fetch weapons from their baggage.

He questioned Huston's placing Gold Hat in all three bandit encounters, preferring to have Dobbs killed at the end (so close to relief in nearby Durango) by several unidentified strangers, preferably teenagers. Older bandits, he said, would recognize the sand as pay dirt whereas youngsters would not know it was gold dust.

Huston's December 30 response displays his confidence. He said he was prepared to defer the matter of the film's date to when the Mexican authorities told him whether bandits tended to "knock over" trains in 1920 or later. He explained that he placed Gold Hat in all three attacks to show that Dobbs was pursued by Fate.

Still working through correspondence, Huston urged Traven to come to Hollywood so they could work together. Traven declined, saying that the

California climate would be bad for his health. Instead, he suggested that Huston visit him in Mexico. This overjoyed Huston, who had harbored a fascination with Mexican culture since his youth and was eager to return. Huston booked himself into the Hotel Barner in Mexico City and waited a week for Traven to keep his appointment. No Traven. Then one morning he awoke, sensing the presence of an intruder in his room.[2] "I woke up and someone was standing at the foot of my bed," the director continued. "It was a small man. I sat up in bed and said hello. He took out a card and gave it to me. Just shortly after daylight, this was. I read the card and it said 'Hal Croves, Translator, Acapulco and San Antonio.' After I read the card, he gave me a letter, and the letter was signed B. Traven. The letter said that he, Traven, was ill and that, in his stead, he was sending his intimate friend, Hal Croves."[3] Croves had exquisitely detailed knowledge of Traven's work, even speaking with the same phrasing Traven had used in his letters.

Huston kept his own counsel but had his suspicions. "Croves expressed the same thoughts that Traven had," Huston said, "and the thought crossed my mind that this could be Traven." He later permitted Croves to watch the shooting of the film and arranged for producer Henry Blanke to pay him a weekly stipend of $100. During this advisory period, Huston recalled, "He rarely opened his mouth, in fact. I would consult him occasionally, and I grew to consult him less and less because only rarely did he have an observation to make." When he did speak, Croves often used the pronoun "I" instead of "he" or "we" to refer to Traven. Huston recalls, "Occasionally someone would come up, some brash person, and ask him, directly and rudely, 'are you B. Traven?' When that happened in my presence, I'd flinch. I never asked him that question, by the way."[4]

When the film finished its Mexican location shooting, Croves disappeared, and Huston claimed never to have seen him again. But doing publicity for the film, he made the mistake of telling an interviewer that he thought Croves was Traven. When Croves learned of this, he was incensed and wrote, "John Huston, by being convinced, as he [said] himself, that I was Traven, and then paying me a lousy $100 a week, only shows publicly in how low an estimation he is holding Traven, the man, or the woman, as the case might be, whose story gave Mr. John Huston the chance of his lifetime."[5] He insisted thereafter that he would deny Huston permission to film any of his other novels.

Paul Kohner, who represented Traven, never met him either, although he did have letters. "All of my correspondence with Traven," he said, "is signed, at the beginning, just with a 'T.' Later on, 'B.T.'—typed, like the entire letter. Not signed by hand at any time."[6] Examination of several of his letters shows his signature as "B.Traven" without a space between the capital letters.

Kohner's relationship with Traven had begun through his wife, Lupita Tovar, the beloved "Mary Pickford of Mexico." Traven wrote her several fan letters and, at one point, surprisingly, requested that she come to a meeting in Acapulco where he lived. She and her husband traveled there and stayed in a hotel.

"He sent her a note via a little Mexican boy," Kohner recalled, "a native, to meet him at a certain place on the beach at five o'clock in the afternoon, I believe. It was already rather late. This was a very remote beach in Acapulco—and don't forget that, in those days, Acapulco wasn't the city that it is today. The friends with whom Lupie was staying in Mexico said, 'Listen, we'll not let you go there alone. We will go in the car and then you can go down to the beach and meet the man, and we will wait for you because we are worried; this beach is dangerous.' And so it happened, and he didn't show up. We waited for half an hour. She saw somebody sitting nearby. But she, of course, didn't do anything about it. The man didn't come, so she went back home. Next day came a very, very annoyed letter from Traven, insulted: 'You brought bodyguards to the meeting.' But it's very obvious he was there, or he wouldn't have been able to write this letter. 'Don't you trust me? What is the matter with you?'" In return, Kohner became annoyed at Traven and wrote him a letter accusing him of inventing Croves, and that, "he mustn't play that game with me. Anyway, I assure you that Croves was Traven and Traven was Croves. There's no doubt about that."[7] As a consequence of Traven's obsession with Tovar, Kohner became his agent.

Lupita Tovar tells a more elaborate version in her memoir.[8] The meeting, she writes, was arranged by contacting Traven through his Swiss publisher, and was effected when she and Paul visited Mexico after the war. As a Mexican movie star, Lupita was easily recognized in public. Traven instructed her to meet him at Caleta beach in the afternoon between 4:30 and 5:30 and to come alone, "or else I might get frightened, and I think I have so very much to tell you."[9] The actress dutifully drove there with director Alejandro Galindo and his brother, writer Marco Aurelio Galindo. "I went and sat on the beach alone with a copy of Traven's book," she writes. "There were three people in the water but no one else on the beach. Soon somebody was throwing pebbles at me from a distance—the scariest native you ever saw in your life." She ran back to her car, frightened, and the next day got another letter informing her that he waited for her at the beach but saw a lady "stunningly dressed in a white flowing bathrobe latest design and a very cute and becoming Hong Kong hat" but "knew it couldn't be you because I knew you wouldn't take three tough guys along" to protect her from him, who meant no harm.

Lupita and Paul returned to Los Angeles. Again, Paul corresponded with Traven, and this time they set a meeting in Mexico City. It was not to happen; a messenger arrived with a note telling Kohner that Traven was ill, but might he have a photograph of her? Kohner provided one but wrote a forceful note on the back chastising Traven for his behavior.

Traven and Lupita did meet years later when she was in Mexico burying her father and looking after her sisters. While there, she received a call from actress Delores del Rio who told her, "Lupita, come over for tea. Traven is here; he calls himself Hal Croves, but I know he's B. Traven." Lupita described him as a thin, tall man in white shoes. He spoke affectionately to her, but she discreetly did not call him by what she believed to be his real name. They met one last time, she reports. In 1968 her son Pancho was preparing to direct Traven's 1938 novel *The Bridge in the Jungle*. Lupita and Paul called on Traven with his then wife, Rosa Elena Luján. When she entered the room, he stood and said, in German, "Endlich!" (Finally). She responded by saying, "It wasn't my fault." By then he was old and frail.[10]

Regardless of both Kohners' earlier convictions, Traven has, at various times, been suspected of being the pseudonym for people from Jack London and Ambrose Bierce to a freed southern slave and Mexico's then-President Adolfo Lopez Mateos.

All right, then, but who was/were any or all of them along the way?

The name *Traven* first appears in the June 21, 1925, edition of the German newspaper *Vorwärts* with the serialization of a story titled *The Cotton-Pickers*.[11] The next year his novel *The Death Ship* is published in Germany by Büchergilde Gutenberg.[12] When his works are published in America, his American publisher, Bernard Smith, asks him for the usual personal information for the dust jacket and publicity. Traven tells Smith in strong language that there will be no photograph, that they are to say nothing about him, and that, if asked, they must say they don't know who he is.[13] (How he legally signed his contracts is a matter of conjecture, although he could have been working through a proxy. As for *Treasure of the Sierra Madre*, he signed the papers in the American Embassy in Mexico.)

In his documentary, *B. Traven: A Mystery Solved*, producer Will Wyatt has presenter Robert Robinson interview Mexican journalist Luis Spota who says he tracked Hal Croves to a bank in Acapulco and, using the questionable services of a friend who worked inside, accessed Croves's safe deposit box in July 1948. There he discovers that Croves uses the name B. Traven Torsvan and that his address is in care of M. L. Martinez,[14] Apdo 49, Acapulco, Gro [Guerreo], Mexico.

This is the same mailing address that Traven uses in his correspondence with agent Paul Kohner.

Spota learns that a Traven Torsvan runs a small café in Acapulco but, when he visits, he finds it devoid of patrons. Nevertheless, he sits down as a customer and soon a small man approaches and begins to make small talk with him. In the course of the conversation, Croves relates to Spota a tale about two men with machetes. As the man's narrative unfolds, Spota recognizes it as the plot one of Traven's short stories.

Using public records, Spota uncovers an identification card that was issued in Mexico in 1930, and finds that a Mexican passport was issued in Acapulco in 1942 to Traven Torsvan stating that he was born, not in Poland, but in Chicago, Illinois, USA on March 5, 1890. The documents also show that Torsvan emigrated from the United States to Mexico in 1914. When Spota goes back to the café and confronts Croves about this, Croves becomes angry. In July 1948 Spota's article about Traven/Torsvan appears in *Mañana* magazine. In a letter sent to the August 14 edition of the competing periodical *Hoy*, Croves denies everything.

Those who had contact with Croves, including John Huston, recalled that he had a slight European accent but were unable to specify it as German, Swedish, or another Scandinavian country. Why would an American have a foreign accent? Why would he write his first works in German and leave it to his publisher to translate them into English? (Or did he write them in English and have them first translated into German?) Moreover, Bernard Smith said that the German-to-English translations were terrible, and he had to rewrite them, adding quickly that he didn't change what Traven sent him as much as refine it. Those who read Traven's works in the original German attest to his skill as a writer. Why, then, would he present them to a publisher in English?

Three years later, in 1951, Torsvan, or Croves, receives Mexican citizenship and leaves for Paris. In late 1959 he returns from Paris with a wife, the former Rosa Elena Luján, who calls herself Traven's translator; he had first mentioned her in 1952, and she will be designated as the person to whom his publisher should send correspondence. (She will also come to manage his estate.) Papers filed at this point show Torsvan declaring that he was born May 3, 1890, in Chicago, Illinois. His wife Rosa Elena Luján states that she was born April 6, 1915, in Yucatán. This has been accepted as proof by many who have investigated the Traven mystery that Traven, Torsvan, and Croves are the same person.

Now comes Ret Marut. Supposedly born February 25, 1882, he surfaces in Germany in 1907 as an actor and playwright as well as a left-wing political activist.[15] He is the editor of his newspaper, *Der Ziegelbrenner*, which translates as "brickbuilder," an allusion to how he wants to construct a new society after the overthrow of the German government. Marut has several run-ins with the German authorities over his socialist beliefs and, in 1921, writes a friend that he is leaving the country and "[I] have ceased to exist." But not yet, because he winds up in London (via Rotterdam) in 1923. There he is threatened with deportation from England because he has no papers, and swears he is a US citizen who was born in San Francisco. Claiming San Francisco as his birthplace is a dodge in that birth and other important records were destroyed in the 1906 San Francisco earthquake and fire. (He will use a similar excuse in 1941 when Warner Bros. asks him for the contracts that he said he signed in Europe for the film rights to *Treasure* and he explains that they were destroyed in the World War II bombing of Europe.) According to photos taken by the British police, B. Traven also was arrested in 1923, leading people to believe that Traven is Marut. People who met both men have confirmed that they are the same person.

Some scholars who have researched the coincidences have come to believe that Croves, Torsvan, and Marut are the same person, but cannot decide if they are also Traven. Complicating the matter is the fact (coincidence?) that the name *Ret Marut* is an anagram of *ter traum*, which is German for "the dream." According to James Goldwasser, Marut's biographer, one of Marut's fellow anarchists, Erich Muhsam, read early B. Traven works and remarked on the similarity in writing style between Traven and Marut.[16] This connects with Huston's and others' observation that Croves spoke of Traven's works with intimate accuracy.

Meanwhile, by 1925, Traven is traced to Mexico where he takes part in a government expedition to Chiapas and chronicles the trip with photographs.[17] This is where he falls in love with the Mexican jungles and the people who dwell in them.

Significantly, 1925 is also the year in which the film (but not the book or script) *The Treasure of the Sierra Madre* is set. It is a time of economic inequality, with foreigners poaching the country's natural resources and aggressive government enforcement of the law by squads of federales who administer swift justice without bothering to use the judicial system. Traven also produces *The Death Ship*, an extraordinary feat if he is also on expeditions and still getting settled in a new country. Some people have opined that this is possible only if Traven is two people: one telling the stories and the other as his amanuensis. John Huston holds that, "I believe that Traven was two or more persons who worked in collaboration," as he tells Will Wyatt in 1978. "I still have my doubts that Croves and Traven were the same man." Although Huston said he had no further contact with Croves after *Treasure*, he also said that, on Croves's death on March 26, 1969, Croves's widow, Rosa, finally confirmed to him that Croves was Traven and Traven was Marut.[18] But he still wasn't persuaded, and wondered to Wyatt how Ret Marut could have left Germany in 1922 and three-and-a-half years later offered three novels to the world that did not deal with German social and political affairs, both of which were Marut's previously published calling.

The answer was uncovered in the Polish town of Swiebodzin by Wyatt for his documentary and, later, in the book he wrote that elaborates upon his odyssey. In the Swiebodzin town hall is a document that records the out-of-wedlock birth of Hermann Albert Otto Maximilian Feige to Adolf Feige and Hermine Wienecke Feige. Otto is one of seven children. But what led Wyatt to Swiebodzin?

When Marut was arrested in London in 1923 for lacking proper immigration papers, he gave his name as Otto Feige along with his actual birth information, apparently having no need or compulsion at the time to shield or invent any other identities. Wyatt located two of Feige's elderly siblings, a brother and a sister, who confirm Otto's identity from rare photographs of Croves and Traven. Moreover, they report that their father, Adolf, worked in a pottery factory and their mother, Hermine, worked in a cotton mill. The Polish word for a worker in a pottery factory that makes bricks is *Ziegelbrenner*, and Traven's first book was titled *The Cotton-Pickers*, alluding to his mother's mill profession. That, plus putting his mother's maiden name (Wienecke) on the arrest papers are connections that only the actual Otto Feige would know.

If even Lupita never confronted Traven by that name, how could she have been so sure in her book? Her son, Pancho, had additional contact with the enigmatic writer when he, Pancho, scripted, produced, and directed *The Bridge in the Jungle*. He met with the novelist and his wife, Luján, in 1938, by which time he had given up his charade and had no trouble answering to the name Traven. In other words, B. Traven became a lot of people in his life, but he started off as Hermann Albert Otto Maximilian Feige. Pancho Kohner says that the matter was so casual that nobody thought to mention it.

Why, then, would the man construct such a complex mystery if only to abandon it? Was he a staunch artist who believed that his work should speak for itself? Did he believe that the enigma of his identity would contribute to sales? There is no easy answer, particularly in a modern world where fame is both craved and transitory.

As Kohner left Traven and Luján, he presented the author with his copy of *The Bridge in the Jungle* and asked him for his autograph. Traven was agreeable, but his wife quickly seized the book and said that she would have her husband inscribe it and send it on. The book did arrive as promised, but Kohner was never fully sure whether the signature and inscription were Traven's or Luján's forgery. The handwriting looks like that of Traven and Croves as it appears on letters in Kohner's extensive files (see photographs).

Or maybe not.[19]

APPENDIX 5

John Huston, B. Traven, and the Mexican Connection

Both B. Traven and J. Huston loved Mexico. Traven first came to the country somewhere during June or July 1924. He had been deported from England for not being able to prove his identity and traveled by ship under the name Ret Marut, taking residence in Tampico, Tamaulipas where he began writing *The Death Ship*. It was published in 1926 in Germany by Büchergilde Gutenberg. That same year, as Traven Torsvan, he embarked on a scientific expedition to Chiapas. It was on this trek that he developed an affinity for, if not an infatuation with, the indigenous population.

Huston likewise developed a fondness for Mexico that began courtesy of money his father had given him to "see the world." While there in his twenties, he met a succession of interesting characters, many of whom had survived the revolution with assorted injuries. He eventually made the acquaintance of Colonel José Olimbrada. Through Olimbrada, Huston learned dressage and was given an honorary commission in the Mexican Army, a credential he exploited throughout his career. His Mexican experiences (which he recounted in his memoir) grew to include brothels, barrooms, poker games, a duel (not carried out; his mother showed up and intervened), and a taste for art.

An incident occurred on a mule train trek to Mexico City that Huston later used in *The Treasure of the Sierra Madre*. As he tells it, his group had pitched camp in the wilds and were approach by three Mexicans who asked for tobacco. The strangers were carrying guns. Huston's party gave the men cigarettes and food, and the men asked for ammunition. The boss of the mule train gave them some, but they wanted more. The situation grew tense; both sides adjusted their weapons, but soon the three men departed. That night, however, someone fired from the darkness into the campfire and shots were exchanged. The next night, another shot came into the camp; clearly Huston's party was being followed. The next day the mule train boss left a detail of armed men behind and, sure enough, they captured the banditos. In the melee, some escaped and some were wounded, but at least one man was turned over to the authorities in Chilpancingo. Huston surmised he was later hanged.[1]

Mexico had been in revolt from 1910 to 1920 but the passions and the scars were still evident when Huston first visited, when Traven arrived, and when they shot *The Treasure of the Sierra Madre*. It might be said that the seeds of revolt had been planted in 1848 when the United States and Mexico signed a treaty ending their war. American westward expansion had been ravenous in the nineteenth century, and the discovery of gold in the California territory exacerbated its lure. By the terms of the peace treaty with the United States, Mexico ceded fifty-five percent of its territory and retreated below an uneasy border that is still an area of contention.

In the early twentieth century, Mexico—its resources and its people— were being exploited by foreign interests, including American businesses. Its president by then was an ageing Porfirio Diaz who permitted these interests to operate, either directly or by ignoring it. In November 1910 landowner Francesco I. Madero challenged Diaz for the presidency. Diaz had him jailed. Nevertheless, Madero called for a rebellion—one of his supporters was the legendary revolutionary general Francisco "Pancho" Villa—which Diaz's federales were unable to crush. Diaz resigned in May 1911 and a tenuous peace was made while Madero took the office of the presidency in November of that year.

Almost immediately there was a peasant revolt demanding agrarian reform (land distribution) led by Emiliano Zapata. While that was in progress, Diaz's former generals staged a coup in 1913 and President Madero was forced to resign with Victoriano Huerta taking over (and killing his predecessors). Huerta lasted until 1914 when Venustiano Carranza became provisional president, then president in 1917. Carranza ruled until 1920 and managed to develop a constitution, then was forced from office. Between 1920 and 1940 Mexico was governed by a succession of revolutionary generals. When *Treasure* became a reality and was slated to start, President Miguel Alémán had taken over from Manuel Ávila Camacho in 1946. The revolution lasted officially from November 20, 1910 to December 1, 1920, but emotions and tensions do not read calendars.

Huston returned to Mexico in 1947 for his meeting with Traven but, as has been reported, was met instead by Croves. They reunited midyear when Huston began shooting *Treasure* and Croves was hired as Traven's representative to advise the production. After wrapping, they never saw each other again. In July 1947 journalist Luis Spota encountered Torsvan at the inn in Acapulco and pressed him for his true identity. Not only did Torsvan object to being called Traven, he said that he would commit suicide if Spota published a story about him. Spota told Torsvan that such a thing would be his own business and proceeded to publish his piece in the August issue of *Mañana*. Torsvan did not kill himself. The next year he left town and apparently did not return until 1957 after having (as Croves) married his translator Rosa Elena Luján in San Antonio. He remained in Mexico for the rest of his life with the exception of leaving for Germany in 1959 to attend the premiere of *The Death Ship*. He died in 1959 as Torsvan/Croves, later identified as B. Traven, who was in reality Ret Marut.

Traven was protective of indigenous Mexicans, and not as a matter of noblesse oblige. He worked beside them. He chronicled the exploitation of the southern Mexican Indians by government, church, and businesses (both domestic and foreign) in a series of what came to be called his "Jungle Novels," dramatizing the development of political awareness by the masses and, ultimately, their revolt. His books tell empowering stories of individuals, from soldiers to bureaucrats, whose eyes are opened to the suffering around them and turn against their bosses to help their own people.

The political enlightenment of Traven Torsvan began when he set out from Chiapas on the expedition that made him aware of his adopted country. Initially he seemed concerned with photographing the topography, but as he necessarily encountered the people dwelling on it, he opened his heart to them. The result was an extensive collection, some of which were published in *Land of Springtime*; many others are held by the Metropolitan Museum of Art in New York.

He learned that, in a country where the natives keep to themselves, change was imposed upon them when the European conquistadores enslaved them to mine ore and harvest mahogany and other resources. The money to be made did not trickle down, but was split between the land owners, mining companies, and governments. His six "Jungle Novels" tell the epic story of the events leading up to the November 20, 1910, revolution:

> *Government* (1931): A bureaucrat in a small village realizes that he can get away with stealing from his people, except they have nothing worth stealing. Instead, he lands a job as a labor agent where he can enslave his people to work in foreign-owned mahogany plantations.

The Carreta (1931): Andres Ugalde, a young peasant, becomes a cart driver for a wealthy family. When his father is sold to an organized hunting expedition to pay his debts, Andres takes his place.

March to the Monteria (1933): Peasants are impressed into service to *monterias* (organized hunting parties) that harvest the riches of the land.

Trozas (1936): Andres (from *The Carreta*) and Celso (an enslaved Indian) serve the *monterias* in harvesting mahogany as those who are forced into labor live in ever-worsening conditions. When the company is sold to the Montellano brothers who are more oppressive, all the workers leave, abandoning the Indians.

Rebellion of the Hanged (1936): It is 1910 and the first stirrings of rebellion against Porfirio Diaz are fomenting among the Indians. The first event is the workers' rebellion against the *monterias*.

General From the Jungle (1940): Juan Mendez becomes leader of a motley band of rebels fighting the government and manages to make headway to revolution.

While Traven Torsvan was being Hal Croves, John Huston was preparing to film *The Treasure of the Sierra Madre*. Their hotel encounter has already been discussed and, when the director and the proxy weren't working on the script, Huston, his wife Evelyn Keyes, and Croves went off marlin fishing. (This introduces a narrative asterisk: In every interview in which Huston tells of how he awoke in his hotel room to discover Croves at the foot of his bed, he makes no mention that his wife was with him, nor have interviews with Keyes placed her in Mexico with her husband.

Nevertheless, here they are together in this story.)[2] Huston reports that Croves hooked a massive marlin and, despite his earlier assurances that he was an expert fisherman, he was not, and lost the fish.

Huston, at times, could be as mysterious as Croves. Although gracious in repeating the story of his first meeting with Croves, he remained cautious about speculating on whether Croves was Traven, having been reprimanded for that single magazine article (although why someone in Huston's professional position with a major studio behind him should care—a studio that was grooming him as a major asset—is unknown). Surely, he never sought to film another Traven story even if Croves should change his mind. Perhaps he was concerned that his presence in Mexico might be jeopardized, but by whom? More likely Huston, an inveterate prankster and savvy showman, was simply playing the publicity game.

Huston did, indeed, retire to Mexico between pictures, although he lived for a time in Ireland. Those wishing to interview or visit him had to make the voyage to Puerto Vallarta, north of Las Caletas beach, on land leased to him in the 1970s and, later, transferred to the operator of the Vallarta Adventure tours.

Between John Huston and B. Traven, Mexico had two passionate advocates. The country provided each of them with adventure, escape, and inspiration.

APPENDIX 6

The Bridge in the Jungle

Hollywood being Hollywood, why didn't a film that was as honored as *The Treasure of the Sierra Madre* inspire imitators? It would be nice to think that this was because there was only one John Huston and Humphrey Bogart, but the answer is more logical: Traven didn't grant remake or sequel rights to Warner Bros. or anyone else.

And yet he wrote a sequel in 1938 called *The Bridge in the Jungle* that was filmed in 1970 by Pancho Kohner, the son of Traven's agent Paul Kohner. Difficult to see today, *The Bridge in the Jungle* concerns Gales, a crocodile hunter (Charles Robinson) who goes looking for the man who killed his father but gets lost in the Mexican jungle. He is rescued by Sleigh, a man who has come to live with the natives (and who is meant to be Howard from *Treasure* years later). Gales at first thinks that Sleigh is his father's killer, something that Sleigh denies but which nevertheless hangs in the air between the two men. Although Gales is accepted by the villagers, he and Sleigh develop a slightly antagonistic relationship until it emerges that Gales has heard that there might be silver to be mined. Sleigh rejects the idea, saying that silver requires rock and there's nothing around the village except water. On an antelope hunt with Sleigh, however, one of Gales's rounds pierces the ground and exposes surface oil deposits. He is eager to mine it but Sleigh warns him of the damage that it would do to the land and the people who live on it.

One of the villagers, Manuel (Javier Marc), returns from the oil fields where he is a rigger. He brings his wife, Elizabeth Chauvet, a fancy dress and gives their son, Carlito (Gilberto Ramos Atayde), a pair of expensive leather boots. During a village celebration, their son disappears. He fell off of the bridge across the river because the soles of his new boots were slippery. Men dive to retrieve Carlito's body, but nothing works until one of the elders lights a candle that has been blessed by a priest and sets it afloat on the water. Miraculously, the current carries it to the spot where divers find the boy's body. Unlike in *Treasure*, the boy has been submerged too long to be revived, so Sleigh keeps his distance. Gales cannot understand the spiritualism involved with the candle, and Sleigh tells him that the tribe will get over the boy's death in due course because this is the way of nature. It is the same reasoning he gave when he warned Gales away from exploiting the silver and the oil.

The Bridge in the Jungle reflects Traven's concern for the indigenous people and makes the point that the encroachment of civilization—be it oil drilling, silver mining, or even so much as the curse brought by new boots—is an unwelcome addition to the purity of their simple existence. While this may involve a measure of auctorial condescension, it makes sense when one considers the destruction of traditional civilizations in the name of "progress."

Pancho Kohner sought to film *The Bridge in the Jungle* and made a deal with David Picker of United Artists for a shared financing deal: UA would put up half the budget if Kohner could find the other half. He first tried a friend and fellow Traven devotee, who was supportive and proposed a partnership. Then, when they were in a meeting with the Syndicato, Mexico's chief labor union, Kohner's friend denounced him. It turned out that the friend had wanted to make the film years earlier but for some reason had never gotten around to asking B. Traven for the rights. Thus, on September 8, 1965, Hal Croves—identifying himself as B. Traven's legal representative—signed an option for the film rights to Kohner and Clasa Films Mundiales, S.A., the entity that Kohner found to cofinance the production. Traven would receive $50,000 upon exercising the option.

They established a budget of $283,000—minuscule by any calculation—to cover four weeks of location filming in Mexico. Kohner wrote the screenplay himself for what would be his first film. He encountered two others who had attempted the same task. One was Traven himself who presented Kohner with his 400-page adaptation that was wholly unsuitable for a film, period, let alone one of such a modest budget. Kohner also approached screenwriter Albert Maltz, one of the blacklisted "Hollywood Ten," to rewrite his tyro attempt. As Kohner writes in his memoir, Maltz answered the door and asked what Kohner was carrying. When Kohner told him it was his draft of *The Bridge in the Jungle*, Maltz shouted, "How did you get the rights to the book?" and "Where the hell did you get the nerve to write a screenplay?" slamming his door in young Kohner's face.[1]

Kohner got his share of financing from Edgar Bronfman's Sagittarius Productions. He asked John Huston, a long-time friend and client of his father, Paul, to play Sleigh. The intertextuality of this casting decision was immense: Huston would, in essence, take over the role his father had played in the film that he had directed more than a score of years earlier. For this task, John Huston would be paid $50,000.

This left $183,000 to make the film, that is, to deliver a 35mm color negative to United Artists. Kohner tells the full story in his memoir. It was to be his first film (he later directed other films and produced many more, including several starring Charles Bronson), and it would be shot under oppressive conditions in the jungles of Chiapas, Mexico. What was it like directing, not only John Huston, but the man who also won Academy Awards for writing and directing the original film?

"He was there to be an actor," Kohner recalls. "We had also known each other for years. He did, however, offer suggestions. For example, in the scene where he arrives in the village (with Gales folded over his horse), he was to go past a pounding pump. John suggested using a crane shot to follow them in. Well, we had a movie crane that was heavy and had a long, lightweight arm that raised, and we sent the crew into the forest to cut wood and start to build a scaffolding because we needed it very high. It took a lot of time, and we realized we could never get the crane up on top of it, so we just pushed the tower over onto the ground and I decided to bring them into the village with a cut. They would go past the camera in one shot, and we'd cut to the reverse as they go off. When John showed up, he saw what I had done and he didn't say anything, he just did it."[2]

The film was shot in sequence and Kohner modestly says that one can see his improvement as a filmmaker as the film progresses.

The Bridge in the Jungle was released by United Artists in October 1970 when it premiered at the San Francisco Film Festival and went into limited general release in January 1971. It appeared on VHS in the early days of home video and surfaces from time to time on streaming platforms.[3]

APPENDIX 7

Dashiell Hammett and Sam Spade

When novice writers ask for advice, the first thing they are usually told is, "write about what you know." When Dashiell Hammett[1] took up the pen, what he knew was detective work, and out of that experience he created Sam Spade in 1930's *The Maltese Falcon*. Largely ignored except by those who study the "hard boiled" fiction genre is that Hammett wrote only one full-length book and four short stories featuring Spade.[2] Nevertheless, the two men—one real and one imaginary—had much in common as well as much not in common. It may be interesting to compare the two, especially in light of how John Huston and Humphrey Bogart brought him to the screen.

Sam Spade was noble, but he was not pure. He was carrying on an affair with Iva Archer, the wife of his partner, Miles Archer, which placed his and Miles's secretary, Effie, uncomfortably in the middle. He also sleeps with Brigid O'Shaughnessy, and it's unclear whether he really does love her when he turns her over to the police at the end of the story or if he just told her he did to hurt her more. He has no qualms conniving with Kaspar Gutman to pin two murders on the gunsel, Wilmer, and he has his dead partner's name taken off the door before the man is even buried. At the same time, he wants to get to the truth even if it involves side-stepping the law, and he maintains a personal code of ethics despite wallowing in a world that lacks one. Muddying the moral waters, he feels he must avenge his partner's murder even though he was cuckolding him. He's the hero—in a sense, the only sane man in an insane world.

Dashiell Hammett, born Samuel Dashiell Hammett in 1894, had his own demons. His father was a failure in a succession of businesses, his mother was a nurse, and he had two siblings: an older sister, Aronia, and a younger brother, Richard. The family dwelled in Maryland where Dash, at age thirteen, quit school to help support his family. At age eighteen, when he was just old enough to get a license, he joined the Pinkerton's National Detective Agency. His eye for detail and focus on process made him a natural for the work he was hired to do, and he stayed with Pinkerton's until 1922 when, on assignment in a Butte Montana mining operation, he finally got fed up with the company's union busting and quit. He joined the US Army Ambulance Service in World War I and became a victim of the Spanish Flu that devastated world population. It left him with respiratory problems that led to tuberculosis.

Hammett was a self-taught writer, although he did take a journalism course that gave him the basics of composition. He began his career writing for the pulp magazine *Black Mask* and created the character of the Continental Op, a private investigator whom he never otherwise named, referencing the Continental Trust Building in Baltimore where the Pinkerton office was located when he worked there. He debuted in the October 1923 issue of *Black Mask*.

Continental Op was a detective devoid of glamor but who embodied the skills that Hammett had developed while working as one. Hammett is credited with developing the modern "hard boiled" detective genre whose style broke away from European-fashioned writing and spoke the way real people talk on the street. He wrote lean, stark, often violent prose that could be read with attitude and felt in the gut. Owing to the job he had to do—and no doubt embodying residual guilt from his Pinkerton years—Continental Op was not above deception in performing his job. These situational ethics were a new twist in crime fiction.

Pulp writing in this era brought in a penny a word, and to supplement his income (and support an estranged family), Hammett wrote advertising copy for a jeweler. When *Black Mask* gained a new editor, Joseph Thompson Shaw, in 1926, Shaw advised Hammett to write novels (which could be serialized before being compiled as books). Hammett did just that, writing *The Dain Curse*, *Red Harvest*, and, finally, in 1930, *The Maltese Falcon*.

The Maltese Falcon, whose main character Sam Spade carries the author's first name, was first published in *Black Mask*. Unlike Hammett's Continental Op stories, which were written in the first person and conveyed the nameless main character's thoughts, Falcon is presented in the more conventional third person in which thoughts are not expressed, only actions. The name may be Spade's only connection with the author. Wrote Hammett in a preface to the 1934 reprint, "Spade . . . is a dream man in the sense that he is what most of the private detectives I worked with would like to have been, and, in their cockier moments, thought they approached."

The *Falcon*'s success led Hammett to a successful writing career that would grow to include *The Thin Man* series and dozens of additional detective stories. As Hammett's tuberculosis became worse, so did his drinking, he found himself unable to write. It may be noted that his most prolific creative period was a scant twelve years from 1922 ("The Parthian Shot," *Smart Set* magazine) to 1934 ("This Little Pig," *Collier's*).[3] One reason Hammett may have turned down Jack Warner's $5,000 to write a sequel to *The Maltese Falcon* was that he could no longer write.

A prolific lothario, he eventually settled down with writer Lillian Hellman (whom he first met in Hollywood where they were both under writing contracts) on her Hardscrabble Farm in Upstate New York. (*Settled* might be the wrong word inasmuch as he continued to philander even while involved with Hellman. But so did she.) When writing no longer sustained his interest, he coached Hellman into being a successful playwright (*The Children's Hour*, *The Little Foxes*, *Toys in the Attic*, etc.).

Despite Hammett's insistence that he was not Sam Spade, the two share ethics: you do your job and you keep your word no matter who around you does neither. In a world that demands and even celebrates compromise, the man who holds to the moral course is to be respected. Hammett and Spade also share a devotion to duty.

And there is another link between the two Samuels. In *The Maltese Falcon*, Spade tells Brigid a story that could well have had its roots in Hammett's Pinkerton days. It's the story of Charles Flitcraft.

As Spade tells it, Mrs. Flitcraft hired him to find her husband. He had simply disappeared from their home in Tacoma, Washington in 1922.[4] There was no indication that he had committed a crime or had fallen out of love with his wife and children; indeed, he left them in good financial stead. Spade managed to locate Flitcraft in Canada in 1927 where he had become, as he was in the States, a successful businessman. What had happened to him in the States was that, one day, when he was returning from lunch, a beam came loose from a construction site and just missed him as he walked on the street. This shocked Flitcraft into evaluating his life and, after doing so, he deemed that he had not lived it to its fullest. He moved elsewhere, remarried, and lived a life that was essentially the same as the one he had abandoned. The banality of this case stuck with Spade and made him realize that people don't change, they just think they do.

Did Dashiell Hammett change after leaving his home, leaving his family, leaving one profession, and leaving another? On September 16, 1942, with America at war, he began serving in the US Army. He was fifty-one, well beyond service age, and yet compelled to start life anew even while knowing the futility of it. Until June 27, 1945, he was stationed in the Aleutian Islands off Alaska.[5] There he edited the camp newsletter, *The Adakian*. On his discharge he returned to New York and assumed the presidency of the New York Civil Rights Congress. His earlier membership in the Communist Party led to his being subpoenaed in July 1951 to testify in court about the Civil Rights Congress's bail fund. The fund had been established in 1946 to facilitate people who had been jailed for political reasons and the government wanted to know where the money came from. Hammett refused to testify and was jailed for contempt of court; he served five months. In retrospect, it was revealed that Hammett never had the names that the court demanded. He kept his mouth shut as a matter of principle.

In 1953 he was subpoenaed by the House Un-American Activities Committee who questioned him about Communist membership. Once again, he refused to testify and was blacklisted. (His name appears on page 71 of *Red Channels*.) Said Hellman at Hammett's funeral (she too had refused to name names before HUAC and had been blacklisted), "he had come to the conclusion that a man should keep his word."

Hammett died on January 10, 1961, of lung cancer but had already been weakened by tuberculosis and decades of drinking and smoking. He was sixty-seven.

Sam Spade has proved to be more than durable, he seems indestructible. Besides the written stories there have been movies, television adaptations, extended radio series (placing Spade into any number of non-Hammett mysteries), comic books, and foreign adaptations. What distinguishes Spade is his ability to not only see but also to observe (a distinction Sherlock Holmes always stressed), collect data, play the thug when necessary and the lover where required, and never to trust anyone (except perhaps his secretary Effie who sees him for what he is). He is human and flawed and tough and cynical, but not so cynical that he has forgotten that there are things a man must stand for. In that regard, Hammett cut Spade from his own cloth and sent him on a journey he knew he did not have the ability to complete himself. In a strange way, Sam Spade was the stuff that Dashiell Hammett's dreams were made of.

APPENDIX B

The Rat Pack

Devotees of the famous Rat Pack of the 1960s—Frank Sinatra, Dean Martin, Sammy Davis Jr., Joey Bishop, and Peter Lawford being its prime members—may be unaware that that collection of famous hipsters actually began in 1955 with a slightly different, and far more culturally diverse, cast of characters.

On June 3 of that year, the Master, otherwise known as British theatrical legend Noël Coward, was booked into Las Vegas's Desert Inn.[1] As a friend and one of his greatest fans, Frank Sinatra, his own legend restored after his 1953 Oscar for *From Here to Eternity*, organized a trip for himself and his friends to attend Coward's opening. The group included, according to collected sources, Sinatra, Humphrey Bogart, Lauren Bacall, Angie Dickinson, restaurateur Mike Romanoff and his wife Gloria, David and Hjordis Niven, super-agent Irving "Swifty" Lazar, composer Jimmy van Heusen, writer George Axelrod and his wife Joan, agent Charles Feldman and actress Capucine, writer Charles Lederer, and Judy Garland and her husband, producer Sid Luft.

Sir Noël was a smash, and the delegation that came to see him also got smashed. After four days of partying, Bacall, who was not a big drinker, supposedly picked her way through the detritus-filled hotel suites and declared, "You look like a god damn rat pack." Someone must have been sober enough to hear her, because it stuck.

Although the Pack gathered often at the Bogarts' home at 232 South Mapleton Drive in the Holmby Hills section of Los Angeles, the Pack's more public hangout was Romanoff's, the restaurant at 306 North Rodeo Drive in Beverly Hills (later moved to 104 South Rodeo Drive) owned by Hollywood's faux "Prince" Mike Romanoff. Romanoff was fake royalty but a great restaurateur who openly despised his well-heeled guests, a trait that endeared him to Bogart, who similarly took sport in puncturing egos.[2]

When the Pack members weren't working, they would gather for lunch at Romanoff's where Bogart's chief gambit was finding someone to expense his luncheon tab, most often Irving Lazar or a cooperating reporter. Romanoff was clever enough to sit the celebrities in the center of the room and the tourists at its perimeter so everyone could get a clear view of the stars without contriving to pass their tables on the way to the loo.

It was at a meeting at Romanoff's sometime after returning from the Coward opening that the Rat Pack appointed its officers: Sinatra was the leader and Bogart was the Director of Public Relations (although even Sinatra acknowledged Bogart was the real leader). Sid Luft was Acting Cage Master, Nathaniel Benchley (who had missed the Las Vegas gambit) was Honorary Recording Secretary, and Bacall was Den Mother. "I was not a drinker," she explained. "I mean, how did I ever get mixed up with Bogart? I'll never know because I hated to drink. I finally had to learn how to drink something in order to stay awake and keep all those hours and do what they did. But I could never do it well."[3]

The Rat Pack's motto was "never rat on a rat," and its coat of arms was a rat gnawing on a human hand.

The Rat Pack has been compared to the Algonquin Round Table, that collection of columnists, dramatists, and wits who held a ten-year lunch between 1919 and 1929 at the 59 West 44th Street hotel in New York. Certainly the levels of celebrity are comparable; America's literati were as prized during their heyday in the 1920s as ring-a-ding-ding society was followed in the 1960s. The Algonquins rose to fame because they wrote about each other, whereas the Rat Pack secured notoriety because other people wrote about them. In fact, the general public knew nothing of the Rat Pack until 1960 when they filmed the heist movie *Ocean's Eleven*. The film (remade in 2001) starred Sinatra, Dean Martin, Sammy Davis Jr., Peter Lawford, and Joey Bishop. The entertainers, top-billed to a man, had shot it in and around performing their shows at the Sands Hotel and Casino.[4] As the story goes, one night Sammy Davis Jr.'s act in the Copa Room of the Sands was running too long—too long, that is, for Frank Sinatra, who was waiting for him. Sinatra walked on stage to give him the velvet hook, and the room went wild. The next night, Dean Martin did the same thing. It's hard to know who had more fun, the guys or the audience (or perhaps the casino owners), but it caught on.[5]

When Bogart died, Sinatra inherited the mantle of leadership and he exploited it by bringing Martin, Davis, Lawford, and at various times Shirley MacLaine, Spencer Tracy, Cary Grant, Audrey Hepburn, Juliet Prowse, Marilyn Monroe, and Nat "King" Cole into the nest. At one point Sinatra tried changing the name of the Rat Pack to "The Clan," which proved awkward considering the presence of Davis, so he changed it again to "The Summit."

There were some reports that John Huston was a member of the Rat Pack, but these are unverified. Not only was he usually traveling around the world making movies, but he was also not a man who joined retinues. Perhaps he stopped by the Bogarts' for a drink or three, but consorting with the rest of the Pack seems highly unlikely. Moreover, Lauren Bacall, in her memoirs *By Myself* and *By Myself and Then Some*, barely mentions the Rat Pack.

Peter Lawford's 1954 marriage to Patricia Kennedy brought the illustrious Kennedy family into the fold, and when John Fitzgerald Kennedy ran for president in 1960, he had the support not only of the Rat Pack but, according to legend, personal access to some of its members.

With the passing of members of the Rat Pack, the Rat Pack itself passed into legend. Their responsibility for building the reputation of Las Vegas cannot be overstated.[6]

No report on the Rat Pack would be complete without Den Mother Lauren Bacall's performance at the New York Friar's Club roast of her husband in 1955. Women weren't allowed because the language was, to say the least, a tad rough, so Bacall made her appearance by audio. The roast exists today as a bootleg. Bacall is introduced by host Red Buttons:

> Yeah, this is Lauren Bacall. Mrs. Bogart, the uninvited guest. You rat bastards. I was delighted, but when Bogie told me that I couldn't attend because it was a stag, I sure was disappointed. I said, 'Bogie, why can't I go?' He said, 'baby it's gonna be a little rough. You know how men act at a stag and that's why women aren't allowed.' I was furious. In fact, I was goddamn mad. What the hell could anyone say that you haven't called me? I must tell you of an incident that happened to Bogie before I met him. He was keeping company with a girl and one day while he was waiting in front of her house, she wanted Bogie to go to the store for her so she opened the window and called out, 'Humphrey? HUMP-FREE!' and twenty guys ran up to her room.
>
> Boys, don't think this guy Bogie is easy to live with. When Bogie gets his script for a picture, especially where he plays a tough guy, he studies his part with so much sincerity you'd think our home was a hideout and he was really on the lam. When he has his script memorized, he puts so much realism into it, he really believes that he's the tough guy. Bogie even fights in his sleep. He wakes me up three or four times a night and says, "baby hold my gun."[7]

Acknowledgments

This book has been an adventure for which I want to thank many people, here and gone, who gave me guidance before, during, and after: Ernie Anderson, Jeanie Braun, Elizabeth Cathcart, David Chapman, Christopher Darling, Derek Davidson, Marsha Hunt, Todd Ifft, Larry Jackson, Pancho Kohner, Eric Lax, Howard Mandelbaum, Roger C. Memos, John Milius, Danny Peary, A. M. (Ann) Sperber, Cass Warner Sperling, Bill Weber and, at the Margaret Herrick Library, Matt Severson, Howard Prouty, Ben Del Vecchio, Ben Friday, Christine Ha, Mona Huntzing, Daniel Jasso-Hernandez, Francesca Krampe, Genevieve Maxwell, Cole McCabe, and Elizabeth Youle.

I also want to thank Lauren Bacall whether she wants me to or not.

Special thanks to Lee Sobel, my agent and friend, for kicking me in the slats (just like Charlie Allnutt kicked the *African Queen*) to set me back on course when I veered. I am also grateful to my fellow writers Lawrence Grobel, Daniel Kremer, David Morrell, James Robert Parish, Jon Winokur, and Michael Scott for their sympatico. My love and appreciation to Liane Brandon for her friendship and talent.

Particular thanks to Claiborne Hancock, Jessica Case, Nicole Maher, Dan O'Conner, Mike Richards, and Maria Fernandez of Pegasus Books for their excitement and expertise in bringing this book from page to reality.

Lastly, I want to thank Batel and Noam Nizzani, and Ami, Ivanna, Adam, and Joseph Benjamin Lahmani for leading Louie, my Italian greyhound, to me four years ago. Those who do not have a dog have no idea what it means when he pokes his nose under your typing hand and wants to go walkies just when you've finally figured out how to break that writing logjam. Louie is a used dog and I am a used human. We need each other.

Selected Bibliography

Academy of Motion Picture Arts and Sciences (AMPAS®).
Amadeo, Kimberly. "Six Problems with NAFTA," June 25, 2019. history.iowa.gov/sites/default/files/primary-sources/pdfs/history-education-pss-trade-NAFTA-source.pdf.
American Film Institute Catalog, aficatalog.afi.com/.
Bacall, Lauren. *By Myself.* New York: Alfred A. Knopf, 1978.
Behlmer, Rudy. *Inside Warner Bros. 1935–1951.* New York: Simon & Schuster, 1985. Studio correspondence reproduced in the Behlmer book are from the Warner Bros./USC Archives.
Black, Megan. "Scene/Unseen: Mining for The Treasure of the Sierra Madre's Critique of American Capitalist Exploitation in Mexico," *Modern American History* 2, no. 1, (2019).
Corbett, Steinberg. *Reel Facts: The Movie Book of Records, Updated Edition.* New York: Vintage Books, 1982.
Doherty, Thomas. *Show Trial: Hollywood, HUAC, and the Birth of the Blacklist.* New York: Columbia University Press, 2018.
Daniel, Douglass K. *Tough as Nails: The Life and Films of Richard Brooks.* Madison: University of Wisconsin Press, 2011.
Finler, Joel. *The Hollywood Story.* New York: Crown Publishers, 1988.
Forester, C. S. *The African Queen.* New York: Bantam, 1949.
Grobel, Lawrence. *The Hustons.* New York: Charles Scribner's Sons, 1989.
Hartnett, Vincent et al. *Red Channels: The Report of Communist Influence in Radio and Television.* New York: Counterattack, June 1950.
Helen, Tapio. "B. Traven's Identity Revisited." Historiallisia Papereita 12, *Historiallinen Yhdistys* (translated from Finnish). web.archive.org/web/20111205034425/http://www.helsinki.fi/hum/hist/yhd/julk/traven01/traven.html.
Hepburn, Katharine. *The Making of The African Queen: Or, How I Went to Africa with Bogart, Bacall, and Huston and Almost Lost My Mind.* New York: Alfred A. Knopf, 1987.
Hirschorn, Clive. *The Warner Bros. Story.* New York: Crown Publishers, 1980.

Huston, John. *The African Queen* (United Artists, 1951). 1951. MS Hollywood, Censorship, and the Motion Picture Production Code, 1927–1968. Margaret Herrick Library. Archives Unbound.

Huston, John. *An Open Book*. New York: Alfred A. Knopf, 1980.

Huston, John. *Key Largo* (Warner Bros., 1948). 1948. MS Hollywood, Censorship, and the Motion Picture Production Code, 1927–1968. Margaret Herrick Library. Archives Unbound, link .gale.com/apps/doc/SC5106204685/GDSC?u=gdscacc1&sid=bookmark-GDSC&pg=1.

Huston, John. *The Treasure of the Sierra Madre* screenplay, Burbank, California: Warner Bros., 1947 (three drafts, undated).

Hyams, Joe. *Bogie: The Humphrey Bogart Story*. New York: New American Library, 1966

Internet Broadway Database (IBDB.com).

Kazan, Elia. *A Life*. New York: Alfred A. Knopf, 1988.

Kohner, Pancho. *No Green Bananas: The Life and Times of a Filmmaker* (unpublished).

Lax, Eric. commentary track for *The Treasure of the Sierra Madre* DVD, 2010.

Margaret Herrick Library of the Academy Foundation of the Academy of Motion Picture Arts and Sciences.

Naremore, James, ed. *The Treasure of the Sierra Madre*. Warner Bros. Screenplay Series, Madison: University of Wisconsin Press, 1979.

Peary, Danny. *Cult Movies 2*. New York: Dell, 1983.

Rossen, Robert. *The Treasure of the Sierra Madre* screenplay. Burbank, California: Warner Bros., January 1, 1947 (unpublished).

Segaloff, Nat. *Big Bad John: The John Milius Interviews*. Sarasota, Florida, BearManor Media, 2021.

Segaloff, Nat. *Mr. Huston/Mr. North: Life, Death, and Making John Huston's Last Movie*. Albany, Georgia: BearManor Media, 2015.

Silverman, Rich. *Discovering Treasure: The Story of The Treasure of the Sierra Madre*. Turner Entertainment Company/DVD Special Features, 2003.

Sperber, A. M. and Eric Lax. *Bogart*. New York: William Morrow and Company, 1997.

Sperling, Cass Warner and Cork Millner with Jack Warner Jr. *Hollywood Be Thy Name: The Warner Brothers Story*. California: Prima Publishing, 1994.

Stone, Judy. *The Mystery of B. Traven*. Los Altos, California: William Kaufman, 1977.

Tovar, Lupita. *The Sweetheart of Mexico: A Memoir as Told to Her Son, Pancho Kohner*. Xlibris Corporation, 2011.

Traven, B. *The Treasure of the Sierra Madre* New York: Alfred A. Knopf, 1935.

Warner Bros.-University of Southern California Archives (WB-USC).

Wiley, Mason and Damien Bona *Inside Oscar*. New York: Ballantine Books, 1993.

Wyatt, Will. *The Secret of the Sierra Madre: The Man Who Was B. Traven*. New York: Doubleday & Company, 1980.

Wyatt, Will, and Robert Robinson. *B. Traven: A Mystery Solved*. United Kingdom: British Broadcasting Corporation, 1978.

Notes

Prologue: On the Twentieth Century

1   A. M. Sperber and Eric Lax, *Bogart* (New York: William Morrow and Company, 1997).
2   Message exchange with author July 6, 2024.
3   *The Dick Cavett Show*, February 21, 1972, Daphne Productions/ABC-TV.

1. Becoming Bogie

1   Sperber and Lax, *Bogart*.
2   Jeffrey Meyers, *Humphrey Bogart: A Life in Hollywood* (London: Andre Deutsch, 1997).
3   Interviewed in "Humphrey Bogart: Here's Looking at You, Kid," *The South Bank Show*, London Weekend Television, January 5, 1997.
4   When it started to come in, he squirreled away a stash of cash he called his "fuck you" fund to tide him over if he rejected a distasteful employment offer.
5   The legend among studio publicists was that Bogart didn't mind when they signed his name to restaurant tabs, and they returned the favor by making sure his name got in the columns.
6   "Raoul Walsh's idea of a tender love story is to set fire to a whorehouse"—A widely quoted comment from Twentieth Century-Fox's Darryl F. Zanuck.

2. The Impossible John Huston

1   Huston did, in later years, undergo surgery to repair an aortic arterial aneurysm. His father, Walter Huston, died from an aortic aneurysm.
2   *The Dick Cavett Show*, February 21, 1972.
3   In 1938 Walter Huston, by then established on both stage and screen, famously introduced Kurt Weill-Maxwell Anderson's "September Song" on Broadway in *Knickerbocker Holiday*.

4	John Huston, *An Open Book* (New York: Alfred A. Knopf, 1980).
5	Huston described *The Lonely Man* as a what-if story in which Abraham Lincoln lived to free not only the slaves but the working man. It was produced by the labor federation, the Congress of Industrial Organizations.
6	The prolific Ben Hecht and Charles MacArthur received screen credit.
7	Huston to Wallis quoted in Lawrence Grobel, *The Hustons* (New York: Charles Scribner's Sons, 1989).
8	A treatment is more than a story condensation; it describes how the story will be told on screen.
9	It may be pushing the symbolism, but there is irony in someone named "Mad Dog" being betrayed by a loving dog. The story was durable enough to inspire two remakes: the western *Colorado Territory* (1949) with Joel McCrea and Virginia Mayo, directed by *High Sierra*'s Raoul Walsh, and *I Died a Thousand Times* (1955) starring Jack Palance and Shelley Winters.

3. The Ornery Jack L. Warner

1	Roy Newquist, *Conversations with Joan Crawford* (Secaucus, NJ: Citadel Press, 1980).
2	Neal Gabler, *An Empire of Their Own: How the Jews Invented Hollywood* (New York: Crown Publishers, 1988).
3	The average ticket price through most of the 1930s was 25 cents. boxofficemojo.com.
4	One early filmmaker, Alan Dwan, carried a gun to shoot back.
5	boxofficemojo.com and the Motion Picture Association of America.
6	This allowed Jack to ascend to production chief and consolidate his power. Zanuck subsequently joined with producers Joseph Schenck and William Goetz, wangled a silent investment from MGM's Louis B. Mayer and Loew's Nicholas Schenck, and formed Twentieth Century Pictures, which merged with William Fox's moribund company in 1935 to form Twentieth Century-Fox.
7	In 1937 the Mob sent gangster Willie Bioff from Chicago to Hollywood. Bioff maneuvered his flunky George Browne into the presidency of the IATSE, the industry's chief labor union. He then began to shake down the studios for protection money to make sure the IATSE did not strike. The scheme fell apart, but not before money was paid and people were jailed.
8	Huston, *An Open Book*.
9	Cass Warner Sperling and Cork Millner with Jack Warner Jr., *Hollywood Be Thy Name: The Warner Brothers Story* (California: Prima Publishing, 1994).

4. The Black Bird

1	$2.2 million on a budget of $350,000. ultimatemovierankings.com/1940-top-grossing-movies/.

2	The same thing happened when the studio wanted to rerelease *The Public Enemy* and *Little Caesar*. Surprisingly, *Little Caesar* was given a Code seal because it was considered a period piece, but *The Public Enemy* was denied a seal because it seemed more contemporary. Both films had been released in 1931.
3	Michael Sragow, "On its 75th anniversary, John Huston's The Maltese Falcon is still a marvel of tough, sardonic suspense." The Moviegoer, Library of America, October 6, 2016. loa.org/news-and-views/1125-on-its-75th-anniversary-john-hustons-the-maltese-falcon-is-still-a-marvel-of-tough-sardonic-suspense/.
4	Raft to Warner, June 6, 1941. WB-USC.
5	Rudy Behlmer, *Inside Warner Bros.* (New York: Simon & Schuster, 1985).
6	"Bogart: Here's Looking at You, Kid," *The South Bank Show*.
7	Exchange with the author, July 6, 2024.
8	The AFI Catalog also lists (without citation) Loretta Young, Paulette Goddard, Brenda Marshall, Janet Gaynor, Joan Bennett, and Betty Field as possible Brigids. https://aficatalog.afi.com/.
9	Ever the practical joker, John Huston had his father repeat the fall until he was bruised.
10	Huston, *An Open Book*.
11	AFI Catalog.
12	Eve Arden, whose wisecracking persona gave her a career, was also considered for Effie. Other casting also-rans were Ben Weldon as Miles Archer, Frankie Darro as Wilmer, and both Alan Hale and Charles Wilson as detective Polhaus. AFI Catalog.
13	This and Effie's remark to Spade that Cairo's business card smells of gardenias, indicate his homosexuality, something that the censors forbade to be mentioned.
14	Hammett moved into a small apartment at this same address when doctors feared that his tuberculosis would infect his children. This was before he abandoned his family, although he kept in contact with his daughters Mary Jane and Josephine. It was at this address that he wrote *The Maltese Falcon* and other works.
15	Grobel, *The Hustons*.
16	Huston, in his memoir, maintained that if an actor tried to stretch and play a different kind of role, audiences resented it.
17	This must be a coincidence since the bird was a tribute to Spain, not France.
18	Grobel, *The Hustons*.
19	Warner wire to Wilk, February 14, 1942. WB-USC.
20	Warner wire to Wilk, May 19, 1942. WB-USC.
21	Warner wire to Wilk, June 17, 1942 WB-USC.

5. All This and World War Two

1. At this point in history, Chiang Kai-skek had been forced by the Chinese Communists to fight against Japan, despite his having tried to oust the Communists themselves from China.
2. *New York Times*, December 20, 1941.
3. AFI Catalog.
4. This is the climactic scene in which all the spies save Totsuiko leave to prepare the torpedo plane.
5. Mark H. Glancy, "Warner Bros Film Grosses, 1921–51: the William Schaefer Ledger," *Historical Journal of Film, Radio, and Television*, 1995.
6. Joe Hyams repeats the legendary story of how Peter Lorre made a bet that he could have the battling Bogarts fighting within one minute. He simply walked between them and said softly, "Douglas MacArthur." Within moments the couple's political differences (he against, she for) became fisticuffs.
7. Grobel, *The Hustons*. Gibson's credit does not appear on *Moby Dick* or anywhere else.
8. youtube.com/watch?v=lnxyCgdhSBw&t=40s.
9. Released July 30, 1943. youtube.com/watch?v=EVUyg-L28tA.
10. Huston, *An Open Book*.
11. In this memoir, Huston writes more passionately about his Aleutian adventures than about practically anything else in his storied career.
12. Released May 3, 1945. The veracity of the documentary has been challenged; certain scenes may have been staged for the camera. youtube.com/watch?v=3OLJZvgIx5w.
13. Jack Matthews, "Huston Documentaries: Only Following Orders," *Los Angeles Times*, September 11, 1985.
14. William L. O'Neill, *A Democracy at War: America's Fight at Home and Abroad in World War II*, (New York: The Free Press, 1993).
15. Huston, *An Open Book*.
16. Peter Maslowski, *Armed with Cameras: The American Military Photographers of World War II*, (New York: The Free Press, 1993).
17. Capra's *Why We Fight* series is credited with educating the public about the war and it remains an instructive perspective on the time period.
18. Huston, *An Open Book*.
19. Huston, *An Open Book*.
20. Sperber and Lax, *Bogart*.
21. Huston, *An Open Book*. Bogart was famous for saying, "The whole world is three drinks behind. If everyone in the world would take three drinks, we would have no trouble. If Stalin, Truman, and everybody else in the world had three drinks right now, we'd all loosen up and we wouldn't need the United Nations." (Widely attributed.)

22	Todd McCarthy, *Hollywood Reporter*, August 14, 2014.
23	Lauren Bacall, *By Myself* (New York: Alfred A. Knopf, 1978).
24	youtube.com/watch?v=PvcE9D3mn0Q&t=30s.
25	American Film Institute Catalog.
26	youtube.com/watch?v=uiD6bnqpJDE&t=25s.
27	*Let There Be Light*, Army Pictorial Service, Signal Corps, US War Department, 1946.
28	youtube.com/watch?v=KKSAGjceSKs.
29	Huston, *An Open Book*. Another version of the story includes Humphrey and Betty Bacall, who had also been drinking, accompanying the couple.
30	Sperber and Lax, *Bogart*.
31	Grobel, *The Hustons*.
32	Joe Hyams, *Bogie: The Humphrey Bogart Story* (New York: New American Library, 1966).
33	Hyams, *Bogie*.
34	Both interviewed in *John Huston: The Man, the Movies, the Maverick*, Turner Network Television, 1988.
35	Bacall, *By Myself*.

6. *The Treasure of the Sierra Madre*

1	"The Big Picture," *New York Times*, March 20, 2005.
2	The book—or at least its English translation—was copyrighted by Traven and publisher Alfred A. Knopf, Inc. in 1935 and renewed by B. Traven in 1965. How Traven renewed his copyright without signing the US Copyright Office form is a mystery, unless he worked through a legal proxy.
3	Obringer to Wallis, November 14, 1941. WB-USC/Behlmer.
4	Obringer to Ebenstein, January 15, 1942. WB-USC/Behlmer. Under Copyright law, the translation of a work is separate from the copyright in the original work; for example, the French language writing of Jules Verne is now in the public domain, but a new English translation would not be.
5	Jack L. Warner by this time had been given an honorary military commission for his services in the war, and he insisted on being addressed by that rank.
6	Kohner quoting Traven in a June 18, 1941, letter to Commons. Commons was apparently a client of the Kohner Agency but efforts to find any produced screen credits for David Commons have been unsuccessful.
7	Traven to Kohner, June 22, 1942.
8	Kohner to Traven, July 28, 1942.
9	Traven to Kohner, October 28, 1942.
10	October 28, 1942 letter from Traven to Kohner.
11	The offer, of course, had to be a bluff.

12	Eric Lax commentary, *The Treasure of the Sierra Madre* DVD, 2010. Curtin is the name assigned to the character of Lacaud in the novel. Huston advised Traven of this in a December 30, 1946, letter. Traven questioned changing Lacaud to Cody, but Huston would explain that Lacaud sounded foreign. When spoken, however, "Cody" and "Lacaud" sound similar.
13	A Rossen draft dated January 1, 1947, with changes made June 9, 1947, survives among collectors. It is nearly word-for-word the script that is credited to John Huston published by the University of Wisconsin in 1979 noted as coming from the files of the motion picture Academy. Two drafts by Huston are in the Academy's Huston collection. They are undated, but one contains inner pages with changes made March 20, 1947, and June 9, 1947. The minor revisions to Huston's draft give his father more lines but otherwise there are no substantive differences. Rossen's credit is nowhere on either script.
14	Grobel, *The Hustons*. Raoul Walsh directed the 1943 film. Huston is not credited.
15	Warner Bros. Publicity Dept, Academy of Motion Picture Arts and Sciences (AMPAS).
16	Warner Bros. Publicity Dept, AMPAS.
17	Lax commentary, *The Treasure of the Sierra Madre* DVD. Even though Holt had acquitted himself reasonably well in Orson Welles's *The Magnificent Ambersons* (1942), he clearly lacked the acting chops to hold his own against Bogart and Walter Huston in *Treasure*. Alas, this needs to be said. In a letter to Huston on January 4, 1947, Traven said he wasn't familiar with Reagan's work. WB/USC.
18	kids.britannica.com/students/article/John-Huston/311771.
19	Grobel, *The Hustons*.
20	These are expertly done, although one can observe a slight mismatch in contrast between background and foreground in these scenes. Additionally, when the camera moves in on the actors, it moves in equally on the background, which would not happen in an actual outdoor setting. Process scenes include meetings on park benches, campfire scenes, and occasional reaction shots between Dobbs and Curtin. The plates and were shot by Hans Frederick Koenekamp, ASC and the main scene by Ted McCord. On location shots where Dobbs is seen from behind or at a distance, Bogart's double, Joseph Smith, appears. H. F. Koenekamp was father of Frederick James Koenekamp, ASC.
21	This refers to the train robbery that was significantly changed by the time the film was shot.
22	Warner Bros., like the other studios, had done well during the war. They were flush with $21.1 million revenue in 1947 and assets worth $270 million. Lax commentary, *The Treasure of the Sierra Madre* DVD.
23	Production Code files, AMPAS.
24	Production Code files, Margaret Herrick Library, AMPAS.

25 Grobel, *The Hustons*.
26 Lax commentary, *The Treasure of the Sierra Madre* DVD.
27 This was also Traven's dig at American industrialists who were exploiting Mexico's resources and its cheap labor force.
28 While in Mexico, both Hustons partook of marijuana. Walter enjoyed himself, but John reportedly had a bad reaction and swore it off for the rest of his life.
29 The final budget would be approximately $2,600,000 which included between 35 percent and 40 percent studio overhead attached to the budget. (Kohner to Traven care of Martinez, January 30, 1948. Courtesy Pancho Kohner.
30 Hyams, *Bogie*.
31 Grobel, *The Hustons*.
32 Bacall, *By Myself*.
33 Apropos this, when John Milius, who wrote *The Life and Times of Judge Roy Bean* (1972), which John directed, asked what the best part of being a director is, Huston answered, "Sadism."
34 Hyams, *Bogie*.
35 Bacall, *By Myself*.
36 *The Dick Cavett Show*, February 21, 1972.
37 Grobel, *The Hustons*. The author heard an explanation that Huston sought to adopt a Mexican national because he collected pre-Colombian art and, as an American, he was prohibited from bringing artifacts out of the country, but a Mexican could. This could not be verified. In later years, Huston's and Pablo's relationship reportedly broke down.
38 Production Code Administration files, Margaret Herrick Library, AMPAS.
39 Production Code Administration files, Margaret Herrick Library, AMPAS.
40 Warner Bros financial information in The William Shaefer Ledger. Appendix 1, *Historical Journal of Film, Radio and Television*, (1995).
41 *Weekly Variety*, January 7, 1948.
42 *Daily Variety*, January 6, 1948.
43 *Hollywood Reporter*, January 6, 1948.
44 Bosley Crowther, *New York Times*, January 24, 1948.
45 *New York Daily News*, January 25, 1948.
46 *New York Herald Tribune*, January 25, 1948.
47 *The Nation*, January 30, 1948.
48 Mason Wiley and Damien Bona, *Inside Oscar* (New York: Ballantine Books, 1993).

7. Comparing Script and Novel of *The Treasure of the Sierra Madre*
1 The book is set in 1920, the year the Mexican revolution ended. The shooting script begins August 5, 1924, and the film begins (as shown on a posting

of winning lottery numbers) on February 14, 1925. In 1924, troops loyal to President Álvaro Obregón defeated rebels led by Adolfo de la Huerta. The American military had also arrived to protect American interests in Mexico. Huston originally included a scene of Dobbs encountering this, but he removed it before filming. Megan Black, "Scene/Unseen: Mining for *The Treasure of the Sierra Madre*'s Critique of American Capitalist Exploitation in Mexico," *Modern American History* 2, no. 1 (2019).

2   The film cuts the panhandlings to three; Aristotle established the rule of three in drama.
3   Dobbs at first resists the boy's entreaties, apparently out of irritation, but more likely because he lost in the last lottery as the film begins.
4   Megan Black notes this and expands upon it in her paper, "Mining for *The Treasure of the Sierra Madre*'s Critique of American Capitalist Exploitation in Mexico."
5   Moulton is combined into the character of Curtin in Huston's script, and Dobbs encounters Curtin on a Tampico park bench.
6   The script places Curtin in this scene with Dobbs.
7   Not only does this set out the moral of the novel, it symbolizes the greed of the capitalist system that Traven so despises.
8   The date is not given but this began in 1518.
9   Although Howard doesn't tell the Green Water Mine story in the film, his apparent expertise makes him attractive to Dobbs and Curtin. In the book, Howard is more seductive and seems to want to lure his flophouse audience into a scheme to return and try again. Howard is vague about whether he took part in torturing Tilton. Note that later he will have no hesitation voting to kill Lacaud (Cody in the film).
10 There is no discussion of crime in the film, and Curtin is more complex in the way he discusses it in the book. The greatest change is that, in the book, Dobbs learns of his winnings in the newspaper where, in the film, the boy who sold him the ticket returns to tell him the news.
11 Traven makes it clear that he trusts the Mexican government but not the bureaucrats who run it.
12 Significantly, in the film, Curtin hesitates before saving Dobbs after the cave-in, then does so, and Dobbs is grateful. One is led to believe that these men are becoming close. Traven specifically says that they do not; Huston shows that they do (until Dobbs turns).
13 The film has Howard and Curtin saying they'll be satisfied with $25,000 apiece. Dobbs has his sights set on $75,000 or more. It is also at this point that Dobbs begins descending into paranoia and threatens Curtin for seeking his hiding place. In the film, these feelings emerge before Lacaud arrives; in the book, after.

14	It is never mentioned that the men are fur trappers, yet at the end the bandits who kill Dobbs speculate that the bags of "sand" he is carrying are designed to increase the weight of the furs in his pack.
15	People of mixed Spanish and European heritage.
16	Huston combined Gold Hat's backstory with the train attack that Dobbs, Curtin, and Howard survive *en route* to Durango, having Dobbs and Gold Hat make eye contact that seals their connection in the story. He also cut Traven's accusation that the Church was complicit in crime.
17	National security force (versus city police).
18	This was shortened and cleaned up significantly for Alfonso Bedoya to speak. The Spanish translates to "you god-damned bastard and fuck your mother." Traven explains that the Church empowered the bandits and taught them torture based on methods during the Inquisition.
19	There is no gun battle between the bandits, and the prospectors Dobbs and Gold Hat do not continue their face-off.
20	In the film, of course, Cody/Lacaud is killed by the bandits and the partners discover a letter from his wife in Texas begging him to return home and raise their daughter, portraying Cody as a dreamer driven to succeed for personal, rather than material, motives. This foreshadows Dobbs's breakdown and states the moral of the story.
21	This cautionary tale about the duplicity and linkage of the church and the nobility is not in the film.
22	This repeats Traven's continuing excoriation of the inequities of capitalism.
23	None of this is in the movie.
24	In the film, Dobbs shoots Curtin only the first time.
25	Gold Hat is not among the trio of bandits. It was Huston's idea to bring Gold Hat into the story for the third time, making a point about Fate that Traven appreciated.
26	The film treats their executions with more ritual: they dig their graves, Gold Hat's sombrero blows off and he is allowed to fetch it, then he is shot offscreen and his hat blows back into frame.
27	This explains how Curtin recovers.
28	Howard's laugh is in the book, and Walter Huston said he used the laugh he had used when his stage production of *Othello* bombed.
29	In the film, there is no remaining gold, an irony that Huston introduced and with which Traven enthusiastically agreed.
30	In the film, Curtin takes his share of the money realized from selling their burros and supplies and intends to travel to Texas to report Cody's death to the man's family.
31	To its discredit, Huston's script describes the tonsorial result as "His head shines like a n____r's heel."

32. As a point of expert exposition, it is fifteen minutes before we learn the names of Dobbs and Curtin, although Curtin says "Dobbsie" earlier.
33. Wiley & Bona, *Inside Oscar*.
34. Jack Warner ordered a total destruction of this apparently scurrilous film; no copies are known to exist.
35. Two of which (*Let There Be Light* and *The Battle of San Pietro*) were so powerful that the Army suppressed them.
36. Worldwide rentals of $2,375,000 on a budget of $576,000. Warner Bros financial information in The William Shaefer Ledger.
37. Commentary, DVD/Blu-ray edition.
38. Howard does, however, compare communism to capitalism in a speech cut from the film or script that follows Dobbs's declaration that he deserves more because he staked more money to the expedition.
39. The train attack occurs in a sidebar tale from Lacaud (Cody) in the book not involving Curtin, Dobbs, or Howard.
40. A speech to this effect by an unemployed rigger in the Oso Negro sleeping quarters was cut from the film.
41. One would be hard pressed to find many Hollywood films that deal with labor movements. One thinks of *Norma Rae*, *F.I.S.T.*, *Hoffa*, *Whistle at Eaton Falls*, *9 to 5*, *The Irishman*, and *On the Waterfront* but few others emanated from the studio system.
42. This is an example of the classic Kuleshov Effect (Lev Kuleshov) in which a close-up off an expressionless actor is intercut, first with a bowl of soup, and then with a child, and audiences infer that, in the first, he is hungry and, in the second, he is affectionate.
43. Huston used this technique on *The Maltese Falcon* (released October 1941), perhaps because Bogart was 5'9" and needed screen prominence. It also meant that Arthur Edeson's camera could include ceilings, a device supposedly innovated by Orson Welles in *Citizen Kane* (May 1941), although John Ford, for one, had used them in 1939's *Stagecoach*.
44. James Naremore, ed., *The Treasure of the Sierra Madre*, Warner Bros. Screenplay Series (Madison: University of Wisconsin Press, 1979).
45. John Huston, *The Treasure of the Sierra Madre* screenplay, Burbank, California: Warner Bros., 1947. It occurs in Scene 13 between Howard and one of the men in the flophouse.

8. *Key Largo*, HUAC, and Betrayal

1. No report was ever issued.
2. The first meeting was held at Ira Gershwin's house. Among the 500 eventual CFA members were Gershwin, Katharine Hepburn, Henry Fonda, Richard Conte, John Garfield, Paul Draper, Alexander Knox, Canada Lee, Philip

NOTES

Epstein, Julius Epstein, June Havoc, Sterling Hayden, Philip Dunne, Marsha Hunt, Gregory Peck, Danny Kaye, Lauren Bacall, Humphrey Bogart, Paul Henreid, Norman Corwin, Frank Sinatra, Evelyn Keyes, Gene Kelly, Jane Wyatt, William Wyler, Oscar Serlin, John Huston, William Goetz, and Cornel Wilde.

3   Lew Wasserman of the powerful agency MCA lent his office to the organizers of the broadcast but insisted that his support be kept secret.
4   Ring Lardner Jr., remarks accepting an ACLU award, December 15, 1999.
5   The broadcasts were written by Norman Corwin and Robert Presnell Jr. Presnell was later blacklisted as was his wife, actress Marsha Hunt.
6   Karina Longworth, "Bogie and the Blacklist," slate.com, March 4, 2016.
7   The meeting is the subject of the speculative play *The Waldorf Conference* (1993) by Nat Segaloff, Daniel M. Kimmel, and Arnie Reisman.
8   Bessie had written *Northern Pursuit*, *Hotel Berlin*, and *Objective Burma*. Maltz had written *Pride of the Marines* and even a bit of *Casablanca* (uncredited) for the studio.
9   Sperber and Lax, *Bogart*.
10 "Katherine Hepburn," Katherine [sic] Hepburn, HUAC (National Archives and Records Administration file, cited in Thomas Doherty, *Show Trial* (New York: Columbia University Press, 2018).
11 Edward G. Robinson with Leonard Spigelgass, *All My Yesterdays* (New York: Hawthorne Books, 1973).
12 Sperber and Lax, *Bogart*.
13 Longworth, "Bogie and the Blacklist."
14 Bacall, *By Myself*.
15 Both quotes: Sperber and Lax, *Bogart*.
16 Hyams, *Bogie: The Humphrey Bogart Story*.
17 Marsha Hunt, *Marsha Hunt's Sweet Adversity*, directed by Roger C. Memos, 2015.
18 Grobel, *The Hustons*.
19 McCloud tells them that George died heroically in Monte Cassino, Italy, near San Pietro, an allusion to Huston's World War II documentary, *The Battle of San Pietro*.
20 When Bogart bought his own vessel, he christened it *Santana*. In the film he clearly knows his way around a boat.
21 Douglass K. Daniel, *Tough as Nails: The Life and Films of Richard Brooks* (Madison: University of Wisconsin Press, 2011).
22 Huston, *An Open Book*.
23 Vincent Hartnett et al., *Red Channels: The Report of Communist Influence in Radio and Television* (New York: Counterattack, June 1950).
24 Nevertheless, DeMille cast him as Dathan, the Hebrew turncoat who enslaved his own people.

25	Various letters from the Production Code Office, John Huston Collection, Margaret Herrick Library, the Academy Foundation of the Academy of Motion Picture Arts and Sciences.
26	Author interview for *Mr. Huston/Mr. North: Life, Death, and Making John Huston's Last Movie*, Albany, Georgia: BearManor Media, 2015.
27	Glancy, "Warner Bros Film Grosses, 1921–51."
28	Sperling and Millner with Jack Warner Jr., *Hollywood Be Thy Name*.
29	Several sources, among them Clive Hirschorn, *The Warner Bros. Story* (New York: Crown Publishers, 1980).
30	The case was not solely about vertical integration but against discriminatory practices ("clearances") in licensing films to competing theaters. The US Department of Justice revisited the case in 2019 and determined that the circumstances no longer warranted the Consent Decree and it was allowed to sunset by 2022. Many current observers believe that the conditions persist because of the conglomeratization of communications companies.
31	Warner spun off its chain of twenty theaters, Stanley Warner Theatres, selling many of them to Pacific Theatres.
32	By comparison, the studio that became MGM had been created by Loew's Theatres in 1924 as a means of assuring themselves of a flow of product, and Paramount Pictures in 1925 bought a controlling interest in Chicago's Balaban and Katz circuit to likewise guarantee an automatic outlet.

9. *The African Queen*

1	Paperwork seen in the documentary by Nicholas Meyer, *Embracing Chaos: Making "The African Queen,"* 2010.
2	Later prints of *The African Queen* restore his name to Sam Spiegel.
3	Elia Kazan, *A Life*, New York: Alfred A. Knopf, 1988.
4	Kazan, *A Life*.
5	Despite this apparent insecurity, Jones had won the Academy Award six years earlier for *The Song of Bernadette* (1943).
6	The $1.2 million budget yielded $2.1 million returns. Scott Eyman, *Lion of Hollywood: The Life and Legend of Louis B. Mayer* (New York: Simon and Schuster, 2005).
7	Lilian Ross, *Picture* (New York: Reinhardt, 1962).
8	Breen to Warner, April 16, 1947. AMPAS.
9	Hyams, *Bogie: The Humphrey Bogart Story*.
10	Huston, *An Open Book*.
11	Hepburn, *The Making of The African Queen*.
12	Rudy Behlmer, *Behind the Scenes* (New York: Samuel French, 1990).
13	Liam Gaughan, "The African Queen Set Experience Led to a Lawsuit," *Collider*, March 28, 2024. collider.com/the-african-queen-lawsuit/.

NOTES

14 Interviewed in Meyer, *Embracing Chaos: Making "The African Queen,"*
15 Huston, *An Open Book*.
16 dailyscript.com/scripts/African%20Queen,%20The%20(1951).txt.
17 Huston told several version of this story over the years.
18 *A Death in the Family* was adapted for the stage by Tad Mosel as *All the Way Home* in 1960. It won the Pulitzer Prize in 1961. It is one of only two instances of the Pulitzer Prize being given to an original and its dramatic adaptation. The other is James Michener's *Tales of the South Pacific* and the Broadway musical *South Pacific*. I'm telling you this because I lost a bet to Tad Mosel because I didn't know it.
19 As a technical note, the rapids sequence is a combination of dummies in a full-sized boat, stand-ins in the boat, and intercuts of studio blue screen process shots which, in the three-strip Technicolor system, were extremely complicated.
20 C. S. Forester, *The African Queen* (New York: Bantam, 1949).
21 Breen to Spiegel, April 2, 1951.
22 Spiegel wire to Breen, October 22, 1951. The film was awarded Code seal #15611 on March 7, 1952. Given that the film had premiered on December 26, 1961, no explanation is given for how it played over two months without a seal. The Catholic Legion of Decency rated the film A-II, "suitable for adults and adolescents."
23 The Bogarts also welcomed a daughter, Leslie, named in honor of Leslie Howard, on August 23, 1951.
24 Steve Rose, "Anjelica Huston: My Father John's Wildest Shoot," *The Guardian*, England, May 11, 2010.
25 Hepburn, *The Making of The African Queen*.
26 *City Lights* interview with Brian Linehan, City TV, Canada, 1979.
27 Hepburn, *The Making of The African Queen*.
28 *The Dick Cavett Show*, September 1987, Daphne Productions-ABC-TV. The airdate cannot be determined, but it was during the week after Huston's death on August 28, 1987.
29 Hepburn, *The Making of The African Queen*.
30 Grobel, *The Hustons*.
31 Interviewed in Meyer, *Embracing Chaos: Making "The African Queen."*
32 She tells it more fully in Hepburn, *The Making of "The African Queen."*
33 Grobel, *The Hustons*.
34 *The Dick Cavett Show*, February 21, 1972.
35 *The Dick Cavett Show*, February 21, 1972.
36 *Daily Variety*, October 22, 1952. Also Gaughan, "*The African Queen* Set Experience Led to a Lawsuit."
37 *Hollywood Reporter*, February 18, 1953.

38	*Daily Variety*, November 20, 1955.
39	Wiley and Bona, *Inside Oscar*.
40	Academy of Motion Picture Arts and Sciences.

10. Beat the Devil

1	Danny Peary, *Cult Movies 2* (New York: Dell, 1983).
2	In 1949, Rita Hayworth married Prince Aly Khan, making world headlines and providing a current event reference. Rita and Aly divorced in January 1953, ten months before the film's premiere.
3	In another inside joke, "Jack Clayton" is the name of the film's associate producer. Bernard Lee, of course, memorably played "M" in the James Bond films.
4	This is why Bogart was so concerned when his remarks following the HUAC gambit threatened to shake his investors.
5	Hyams, *Bogie: The Humphrey Bogart Story*.
6	AFI Catalog.
7	Hepburn wanted to make *Miss Hargreaves*, based on Fletcher Markle's fantasy novel originally produced live on CBS-TV's *Studio One* in 1952.
8	Huston would receive $175,000 for his directing and writing services. IMDb.com.
9	Lawrence Grobel, *Conversations with Capote* (New York: New American Library, 1985) and Grobel, *The Hustons*.
10	Interview with the author March 21, 2024.
11	This was being generous; Huston was a homophobe, evidenced by the way he badgered Montgomery Clift during the filming of *Freud* (1962), after apparently accepting him on *The Misfits* (1961).
12	*The Dick Cavett Show*, February 21, 1972.
13	Restaurateur Dave Chasen, referring to Bogart's drinking, said, "He's a hell of a guy until 11:30. The only thing about Bogie is, he thinks he's Bogart." Cameron Shipp, "Humphrey Bogart's Dark Side," *Saturday Evening Post*, August 2, 1952. This has been refined over the years into, "The trouble with Humphrey Bogart is that, after three drinks, he thinks he's Humphrey Bogart."
14	Interview with the author July 9, 2024.
15	Bacall, *By Myself*.
16	Undated, but probably 1980 when Huston was publicizing his memoir, *An Open Book*, in Canada. *Cinephilia and Beyond*; youtube.com/watch?v=MxlfPUAVngQ. In some versions of the story Bogart's teeth were only loosened.
17	Bill DeMain, "10 Things You Might Not Know About Peter Sellers," *Mental Floss*, September 8, 2018. He may also have dubbed the voice of the ship's purser, whom Huston discovered playing piano in an Italian restaurant. ("Rick's Flicks," steynonline.com, April 30, 2022.) It is largely unknown that Sellers was a superb mimic as well as a legendary comic actor.
18	"Humphrey Bogart: Here's Looking at You, Kid," *The South Bank Show*.

19	"1954 Box Office Champs," *Weekly Variety*, January 5, 1955.
20	Vincent Porter, "The Robert Clark Account." *Historical Journal of Film, Radio and Television*, 20, no 4 (2000).
21	*Daily Variety*, April 23, 1964.
22	Hyams, *Bogie: The Humphrey Bogart Story*.
23	The film's most famous line has an impatient Peter Lorre musing, "Time. Time! What is time? Swiss manufacture it. French hoard it. Italians squander it. Americans say it is money. Hindus say it does not exist. Do you know what I say? I say time is a crook."
24	This is a romantic notion worthy of comment. As Robert Altman said, "What's a cult? It just means not enough people to make a minority." There is a penchant among some film critics and scholars to glom onto an "under-appreciated" (their term) film the way animal lovers will adopt and raise the runt of a litter. This is done to boost attention for the critic more than for the film.
25	*The Dick Cavett Show*, February 21, 1972. In that same interview, Cavett remarked, quite perceptively, that "even if you come in at the beginning, you feel like you came in at the middle."
26	Interview with the author, July 9, 2024.
27	He did wind up making a film for David O. Selznick after all—*A Farewell to Arms* (1957)—from which he was fired and replaced by Charles Vidor after he and Selznick had a falling out.

11. Life After Death

1	Vindobona Awstriae; youtube.com/watch?v=9EoWIJ2xUUk&list=WL&index=8.
2	Hepburn, *The Making of The African Queen*.
3	Grobel, *The Hustons*. In Huston's memoir, *An Open Book*, there is a notable lack of information about Bogart and a restraint, even coldness, in discussing what was believed to be a deep friendship.
4	Lauren Bacall, "Introduction" to Hyams, *Bogie*.
5	Warner and Lou Chesler, head of AAP's parent company PRM, Inc., were having lunch at New York's "21" restaurant and when he was asked his price for the library, J. L. answered with the bistro's name, monumentally underestimating the value of his library.
6	Interview with author, July 9, 2024.
7	*The Dick Cavett Show*, February 21, 1972.
8	Interview with the author, March 21, 2024.
9	One aberration is the musical *Annie* (1982). As with *Key Largo*, however, it is tempting to think that Huston made the film because the play celebrated President Franklin Roosevelt, a man whom Little Orphan Annie's right-wing creator, Harold Gray, hated, as did *Key Largo*'s Maxwell Anderson. It seems an elaborate way to get even, but producer Ray Stark's money surely helped.

Appendix 1. Henry Blake: A Filmmaker's Secret Weapon

1. Producer John Houseman said it perfectly: "In the old days, they used to help a producer make a movie. Now they dare him." Told to the author.
2. Ayn Rand to Blanke, thank you letter, June 26, 1948, The Ayn Rand Institute, aynrand.org/archives/letters/letter-341/.
3. Huston, *An Open Book*.

Appendix 2: Walter Huston Appreciation

1. The author has always heard it said *Hewston* by family members.
2. Michael Caine spoke of the one piece of direction that Huston gave him when they made *The Man Who Would Be King* (1975): "He never said anything to you; he never gave you any direction. I was doing a take, and it was a long monologue, and halfway through—I hadn't done anything wrong—he went, 'Cut.' And he gave me my character in one line. He went, 'You can speak faster, Michael; he's an honest man.' And I've been very suspicious of people who talk slowly ever since." Thomas Leatham, *Far Out Magazine*, January 10, 2023. Note that this is also the probably direction that Huston gave to his father during *The Treasure of the Sierra Madre*.
3. Obituary, *Orangeville Banner,* Toronto, Canada, April 13, 1950.

Appendix 3. The Gold Standard

1. Music believed to be derived from Stephen Foster ("Camptown Races") and Frank Shay ("Iron Men" and "Wooden Ships") and popularized by the Hutchinson family in their 1855 songbook.
2. Ian Fleming's villain was named Auric Goldfinger.
3. "Gold," UC Berkeley's Rausser College of Natural Resources, nature.berkeley.edu/classes/eps2/wisc/gold.html.
4. This refers to the use of electricity to separate metals, not hair removal.
5. gold.org/gold-supply/gold-mining-lifecycle.
6. Nothing in this chapter should be taken as investment advice.
7. Martha C. White, "The Simple Reason Investors are Going Nuts for Gold Right Now," *money.com*, July 27, 2020.
8. An annual conference of anonymous European and North American business leaders who have been meeting since 1954 to discuss world financial and social agendas.
9. The 1944 convocation in Bretton Woods, New Hampshire, among forty-four countries to align the value of the US dollar on gold. This was voiced in 1970 by President Richard M. Nixon after which the US dollar could no longer be exchanged for gold.

Appendix 4. The Elusive B. Traven

1. Will Wyatt, *The Secret of the Sierra Madre: The Man Who Was B. Traven* (New York: Doubleday and Company, 1980).
2. Did Huston keep his hotel room door unlocked in a strange country? Or is he feeding a legend—his own as well as Traven's?
3. Will Wyatt, *B. Traven: A Mystery Solved*, United Kingdom: BBC, 1978.
4. Wyatt, *B. Traven: A Mystery Solved*.
5. Unsourced (and rather cryptic), "The Mystery of Sierra Madre," *Movies! Reel Variety*, September 16, 2022. moviestvnetwork.com/stories/the-mystery-of-sierra-madre. It was also reported that producer Henry Blanke had offered Traven $1,000 a week to advise the film, but only if he showed up. He refused and sent Croves, who received the lower rate. This would prove contentious.
6. Wyatt, *B. Traven: A Mystery Solved*.
7. Wyatt, *B. Traven: A Mystery Solved*.
8. Lupita Tovar, *The Sweetheart of Mexico: A Memoir, as Told to Her Son, Pancho Kohner* (Xlibris Corporation, 2011).
9. B. Traven letter, February 27, 1946(?).
10. Tovar, *The Sweetheart of Mexico*.
11. Briefly, a young man, Gerald Gales, travels through a succession of jobs and living conditions, each of which allows the author to comment on the politics and morality of the task as well as explain how each is performed.
12. An intriguing premise: a sailor without identification papers sails on a ship that is marked to be destroyed for the insurance coverage.
13. How he legally signed his contracts is a matter of conjecture unless they can be examined. Any agreements that were inspected for this book were with proxies and were unsigned.
14. Maria Luce Martinez.
15. Wyatt, *The Secret of the Sierra Madre*.
16. James Goldwasser, "Ret Marut: The Early B. Traven," *Germanic Review*, June 1993.
17. B. Traven, *Land des Fruhlings* (Land of Springtime), Zurich, Switzerland: Büchergilde Gutenberg, 1936.
18. Wyatt, *B. Traven: A Mystery Solved*.
19. With the exception of Pancho Kohner's comments and Lupita Tovar's memoir, this is a profoundly condensed narrative of an odyssey traveled by many curious investigators. The author recommends consulting the works of both Will Wyatt and Judy Stone in the bibliography as well as numerous other books researching the mystery.

Appendix 5. John Huston, B. Traven, and the Mexican Connection
1. Huston, *An Open Book*.
2. Huston, *An Open Book*.

Appendix 6. *The Bridge in the Jungle*
1. Pancho Kohner, *No Green Bananas: The Life and Times of a Filmmaker* (unpublished at this writing).
2. Interview with the author, April 6, 2024.
3. The author viewed a private copy courtesy of Mr. Kohner.

Appendix 7. Dashiell Hammett and Sam Spade
1. The proper pronunciation is "da-SHEEL," referencing his mother's French maiden name, De Chiel, but it was Americanized over the years to "DA-shul" or, to his friends, "Dash."
2. *The Maltese Falcon* (serialized in five parts from September 1929 to January 1930 *Black Mask* magazine); "A Man Called Spade" (*American Magazine*, July 1932); "Too Many Have Lived" (*American Magazine*, October 1932); "They Can Only Hang You Once" (*Collier's*, November 19, 1932); and "A Knife Will Cut for Anybody" (published posthumously in 2013).
3. Several later stories were reworked versions of earlier stories.
4. Remember that the novel is set in 1928 but the Huston movie is set in 1941.
5. This was the same outpost where John Huston and his film crew made "Report from the Aleutians" in 1943 but there is no indication that the two men met there if, in fact, they ever met at all.

Appendix 8. The Rat Pack
1. Coward called it the most successful booking of his career. He was paid $40,000 a week to perform his cabaret show, and his musical director was Peter Matz (*Life* magazine, June 20, 1955).
2. Writer-director Preston Sturges, who owned a competing restaurant, The Players, was a particular burr under Romanoff's saddle. One night, as a prank, Bogart and actor Robert Coote got Sturges drunk and deposited him in Romanoff's living room.
3. *The Dick Cavett Show*, September 1987.
4. Not all of them were booked at the Sands, but as their contracts expired with other casinos, they consolidated at the Sands.
5. youtube.com/watch?v=UeJJnWUYqpE.
6. See the worship site: theratpack.com/about/.
7. youtube.com/watch?v=Lf-0Z-fWH0o. This is digitized from a reel-to-reel recording given to the father of poster Marc Snader in 1955.

Index

A
Academy Award, 82, 107, 127–128, 151–152, 180. *See also* Oscar
Academy Theatre, 67
Across the Pacific (1942), vii–viiii, 38–52, 84, 145
Adakian, The (newsletter), 185
Adam Solitaire (play), 13
Adventures of Robin Hood, The (1938), 151
African Queen, The (1951), vii–viii, 67, 111–128, 134, 146
African Queen, The (Forester), 114–117, 119–120
Agee, James, 67, 107, 116–117, 120, 128
Ahern, Brian, 16
Albarran, Pablo, 64
Alémán, Miguel, 174
All My Yesterdays (Robinson), 97
All That Money Can Buy (1941), 153
Allied Artists, 140
Amazing Dr. Clitterhouse, The (1938), 9
American Madness (1932), 153
American Mercury (journal), 13
Amsterdam Theatre, 65
Anderson, Ernie, x
Anderson, Maxwell, 99, 103–105, 108, 153
Andrews, Dana, 48
Andy Hardy (series), 57
Angels with Dirty Faces (1938), 8
Antonioni, Michelangelo, 142
Asphalt Jungle, The (1950), 50, 113
Asphalt Jungle, The (Burnett), 113
Associated Artists Productions (AAP), 143
Astaire, Fred, 28
Astor, Mary, 29–31, 36, 38–39, 41, 43, 154

Atayde, Gilberto Ramos, 179
Axelrod, George, 187
Axelrod, Joan, 187

B
B. Traven: A Mystery Solved (1978), 167
Baby Face (1933), 83
Bacall, Lauren
  Big Sleep and, 52
  children of, 49, 122
  Dark Passage and, 95–96
  To Have and Have Not and, 46, 52, 99
  How to Marry a Millionaire and, 133
  HUAC and, 93–98
  Humphrey Bogart and, ix–xi, xiii, 2, 46–52, 61–62, 93–108, 122, 128, 136, 142, 187–190
  Key Largo and, 93–108
  Mr. North and, ix, 145
  Rat Pack and, 187–190
Background to Danger (1943), 56
Bad Men of Missouri (1941), 28
Baird, Michael, 116, 127
Barnard, Ivor, 129, 133
Barnes, Howard, 67
Barrymore, Lionel, 101, 105, 107–109
Bartlett, Sy, 41–42
Basshe, Emjo, 13
Battle Circus (1953), 128
Battle of San Pietro, The (1945), 45–46
Beat the Devil (1953), vii–viii, 2, 129–141, 144, 146
Beat the Devil (Cockburn), 132–133
Bedoya, Alfonso, 64, 80
Belasco, David, 22
Benchley, Nathaniel, 188

Bennett, Bruce, 80, 87
Bergman, Ingrid, 29, 142
Bessie, Alvah, 95
Beverly Hills Hotel, 99, 136
Bible: In the Beginning (1966), 50, 144
Bierce, Ambrose, 167
Big Sleep, The (1946), 52
Biograph Studios, 22
Birth of a Nation (1930), 153
Bischoff, Sam, 150
Bishop, Joey, 187–189
Black, Lesley, 15–16, 30
Black Legion (1937), 8
Black Mask (magazine), 183–184
blacklist, 95–99, 180, 186
Blake, Robert, 60, 79
Blanke, Henry, 27, 29, 34, 49, 52, 56–58, 68, 149–151, 164
Blanke, Ursula, 151
Blanke, Wilhelm, 150
Blondell, Joan, 5
Blue, Monte, 101
Bogart, Belmont DeForest, 1–3, 5
Bogart, Catherine Elizabeth (Catty), 1
Bogart, Frances (Pat), 1
Bogart, Humphrey
  Across the Pacific and, vii–viii, 38–52, 84, 145
  African Queen and, 115–128, 134, 146
  Amazing Dr. Clitterhouse and, 9
  Angels with Dirty Faces and, 8
  appearance of, 28
  background of, vii–xi, 1–10
  Battle Circus and, 128
  Beat the Devil and, vii–viii, 2, 129–141, 144, 146
  Big Sleep and, 52
  birth of, 1
  Black Legion and, 8
  Broadway's Like That and, 5
  Bullets or Ballots and, 8
  Caine Mutiny and, 88, 141
  Casablanca and, 49, 52, 84, 143
  children of, 49, 122
  Dancing Town and, 5
  Dark Passage and, 95–96
  Dead End and, 8, 105
  Deadline U.S.A. and, 128
  death of, 140, 142, 189
  Desperate Hours and, 141
  early years of, 1–5
  final days of, 141–142
  funeral of, 142
  Harder They Fall and, 141
  To Have and Have Not and, 46, 52, 99
  Helen Menken and, 4–5
  High Sierra and, 8–10, 16, 25, 30
  HUAC and, 93–98
  illness of, 141
  Jack Warner and, xiv–xv, 6–10, 17–18, 23–37, 52–67, 83–84, 91–115, 134, 143
  John Huston and, vii–xi, xiv–xv, 9–10, 17–68, 78–147, 149, 155, 178, 182, 187–189
  Key Largo and, vii, 50, 96–110, 146
  Knock on Any Door and, 96
  Lauren Bacall and, ix–xi, xiii, 2, 46–52, 61–62, 93–108, 122, 128, 136, 142, 187–190
  legacy of, vii, 141–146
  Maltese Falcon and, vii–viii, 18, 26–37, 53, 82, 84, 86–87, 133, 143, 145, 182–186
  Marked Woman and, 7
  marriages of, 4–8, 10, 30, 43–44, 46–52, 61–62, 93–108
  Mary Philips and, 5–8
  Mayo Methot and, 7–8, 10, 30, 43–44, 46
  nickname of, xi, 2
  Oklahoma Kid and, 8
  parents of, 1–5
  Passage to Marseilles and, 52
  Petrified Forest and, 6–7, 99
  Rat Pack and, 187–189
  Roaring Twenties and, 8
  Sabrina and, 141
  Sahara and, 52
  San Quentin and, 8
  They Drive by Night and, 17

In This Our Life and, 42, 51, 55
Treasure of the Sierra Madre and, vii, 49–50, 52–68, 78–89, 104, 116, 143, 146, 178
Up the River and, 5, 141
Wagons Roll at Night and, 17, 25
We're No Angels and, 141
Bogart, Maud Humphrey, 1–2, 5
Bogart, Stephen, 49, 122
Bogie: The Humphrey Bogart Story (Hyams), 98, 138
Bond, Ward, 31
Borzage, Frank, 68
Boston Herald, The (newspaper), x
box-office returns, 20, 43, 66–67, 92, 109–110, 138
Boyer, Charles, 104
Brady, Alice, 4
Brady, William A., 4
Brando, Marlon, 28, 142
Brattle Theatre, 143
Breen, Joseph I., 27, 58–59, 65, 105–106, 114–115, 121–122, 133
Breen Office, 27, 58–59, 65, 114–115, 133
Brewer, Roy, 98
Bridge in the Jungle, The (1970), 144, 178–181
Bridge in the Jungle, The (Traven), 171
Bridge on the River Kwai, The (1957), 111
Broadhurst Theatre, 6
Broadway's Amsterdam Theatre, 65
Broadway's Like That (1929), 5
Broder, Jack, 127
Bronfman, Edgar, 180
Bronson, Charles, 180
Brooks, Richard, 97–98, 103–107, 141
Brown, Clarence, vii
Buck, Joyce, 47
Buck, Jules, 47, 97
Bull, Peter, 119
Bullets or Ballots (1936), 8
Burnett, W. R., 8–9, 16, 113
Burton, Richard, 140
Buttons, Red, 190

By Myself (Bacall), 51, 189
By Myself and Then Some (Bacall), 189

C

Cagney, James, 8–9
Caine, Michael, 140
Caine Mutiny, The (1954), 88, 141
Calhern, Louis, 113
Camacho, Manuel Ávila, 174
Cameron, Kate, 67
capitalism, 53, 85–86, 91–92
Capote, Truman, 134–137
Capra, Frank, vii, 45–47, 153
Capucine, 187
Carranza, Venustiano, 174
Carreta, The (Traven), 176
Carson, Robert, 40–41
Casablanca (1943), 49, 52, 84, 143
Cascade Theatre, 20
Cavett, Dick, 126, 139
censorship, 27–29, 34–36, 57–61, 65–66, 83–84, 105–107, 114–115, 121–122, 133
Challee, William, 99–100
Chase, The (1966), 111
Chinatown (1974), 61, 144
Clasa Films Mundiales, 180
Clayton, Jack, 138
Cockburn, Claud, 132–133
Cohan, George M., 7, 153–154
Cohn family, 19
Cole, Nat "King," 189
Collier, John, 117, 128
Collier's (magazine), 184
Columbia Pictures, 60, 110, 115, 138, 140
Committee for the First Amendment (CFA), 93–98
Commons, David, 54–55
communism, xiii–xiv, 86, 91–99, 104–105, 113, 186
Conklin, Peggy, 6
Connery, Sean, 140
Consent Decree, 110–111
Convention City (1933), 83, 149

Cook, Elisha Jr., 31
Cotton-Pickers, The (Traven), 167, 171
Covarrubias, Miguel, 60
Cowan, Jerome, 31
Coward, Noël, 187–188
Crane, Stephen, 113
Craven, Richard, 59
Crawford, Joan, 19, 153
Croves, Hal, 164–171, 174–177, 180. *See also* Traven, B.
Crowther, Bosley, 67
Crump, Owen, 44
Cukor, George, vii
Cult Movies 2 (Peary), 129, 144
Curtis, Tony, 142
Curtiz, Michael, 92, 142

D

Daily Variety (trade paper), 67
Dain Curse, The (Hammett), 184
Dancing Town, The (1928), 5
Dangerous Female (1931), 26–27
Dark Passage (1947), 95–96
Davies, Joseph E., 92, 153
Davis, Bette, 6–8, 15, 114–115
Davis, Sammy Jr., 187–189
De Havilland, Olivia, 29–30, 51, 138
Dead, The (1987), 51, 144
Dead End (1937), 8, 105
Deadline U.S.A. (1952), 128
Dean, James, 28
Death in the Family, A (Agee), 117
Death Ship, The (1959), 174
Death Ship, The (Traven), 167, 170, 172
Del Rio, Delores, 166
DeMille, Cecil B., 105, 149
Desert Inn, 187
Desire Under the Elms (play), 153, 155
Desperate Hours, The (1955), 141
Deutsch, Adolph, 36
Devil and Daniel Webster, The (1941), 152–153
Diaz, Porfirio, 173–174, 176
Dickinson, Angie, 187

Dieterle, William, 16
Dietz, Howard, 107
Dillinger, John, 8
Dodsworth (1936), 152–154
Dodsworth (Lewis), 154
Don Juan (1926), 22
Douglas, Kirk, 28
Dracula (1931), 13–14
Drifting (play), 4
Dunne, Philip, 93

E

Ebenstein, Morris, 53–54
Edeson, Arthur, 30, 41
Edison, Thomas A., 21
Edwards, Anthony, 145
Eighteenth Amendment, 3
Elmer the Great (1933), 154
Empire of Their Own, An (Gabler), 19
Epstein, Julius, 92
Essanay Studio, 22
Ethel Barrymore Theatre, 10
Etting, Ruth, 5
European Film Fund, 151

F

Farrell, Charles, 5, 9
Fat City (1972), 144
Feige, Adolf, 170–171
Feige, Hermine, 170–171
Feige, Otto, 170–171
Feldman, Charles, 187
Fellini, Federico, 142
Ferrer, José, 99–100
film budgets, 13–14, 20–23, 27, 30, 43, 52–53, 58–65, 83–84, 92, 109–110, 115–116, 132, 138–139, 149, 179–180
Film Foundation, The, 139
film grosses, 20, 43, 66–67, 92, 109–110, 138
film noir, 30, 37, 113
film rights, 6, 22, 26, 41, 53–55, 99, 114, 138, 140, 154, 169, 178–180
First Amendment, 93–98

INDEX

Fitzgerald, Geraldine, 29
Flynn, Errol, 56
Ford, John, vii, 5
Foreman, Carl, 47
Forester, C. S., 114–117, 119–120
Fountainhead, The (1949), 149–150
Fox, 5, 20, 23, 156
Frankenstein (1931), 13–14
Freud (1962), 144
Freund, Karl, 109
Friars Club, 190
From Here to Eternity (1953), 187
Fu, Lee Tong, 40
Furies, The (1950), 156

G

Gable, Clark, 140
Gabler, Neal, 19
Galindo, Alejandro, 166
Galindo, Marco Aurelio, 166
Garbo, Greta, vii
Gardner, Ava, 48
Garfield, John, 9, 56, 113
Garland, Judy, 187
Garson, Greer, 128
General From the Jungle (Traven), 176
George, Gladys, 31
Gerard, James W., 21
Gershwin, Ira, 43, 47, 97
Gibson, Charlie, 43–44
Girl of the Golden West (1938), 22
Godard, Jean-Luc, 142
Gold Rush, 157–158
gold standard, 157–161
Golden Age of Hollywood, 11, 20, 142, 149
Goldwasser, James, 169
Goldwyn, Samuel, 8, 13, 16, 19, 149, 154
Gomez, Thomas, 101
Gone with the Wind (1939), 15, 48
Gore, Rhea, 11–12
Got, Roland, 38
Government (Traven), 175
Gramercy Park Hotel, 4

Grant, Cary, vii, 189
Granville-Barker, Harley, 14
Grayson, Charlie, 49
Great Depression, 5, 7, 13, 23, 61, 92, 160
Great Experiment, 3
Great McGinty, The (1940), 26
Great Sinner, The (1949), 156
Great War, 3
Green Pastures, The (1936), 151
Greenstreet, Sydney, 29, 32, 35, 38–39, 133
Gregory, James, 99
Griffith, D. W., 152–153
Grimes, Tammy, 145
Grobel, Lawrence, xv, 28, 35, 125, 134–135, 144–145

H

Haade, William, 101
Haft, Steven, x
Hagen, Jean, 113
Hagen, Uta, 99–100
Halliday, Bryant, 143
Halton, Charles, 40
Hamilton, Guy, 122
Hamilton, John, 33, 38, 125
Hammett, Dashiell, 18, 26–29, 35–36, 182–186
Harder They Fall, The (1956), 141
Harris, Averell, 100
Hartley, Alice, 122
Harvard University, 143
Harvey, Cy, 143
Harvey, Dorothy Jeanne, 14–15
Hawks, Howard, 27, 46, 142
Hayden, Sterling, 113
Hayes, Gabby, 154
Hayworth, Rita, 29, 131
Hearst organization, 95
Hell is for Heroes (1962), 149
Hellinger, Mark, 132
Hellman, Lillian, 184–186
Helvick, James, 132
Hemingway, Ernest, 113
Hepburn, Audrey, 189

Hepburn, Katharine, vii–viii, 96, 116–126, 134, 141
Hernandez, Maricela, 51, 145
High Sierra (1940), 8–10, 16, 25, 30
Hill, Gladys, 121–122
Hitchcock, Alfred, vii
Hitler, Adolf, 112, 151
Hobart, Rose, 4
Holliday, Doc, 153
Hollywood Bowl, 44
"Hollywood Fights Back," 93–94
Hollywood Reporter (magazine), 67
Hollywood Ten, 94–98, 180
Holm, Celeste, 68
Holmstrom, Axel, 54–55
Holt, Jack, 60
Holt, Tim, 56, 60–61, 65, 79, 88–89
Hopkins, Arthur, 6
Horizon Pictures, 113–115, 127
Hotel Barner, 164
Houghston, Elizabeth, 153
Houghston, Robert, 153
House Divided, A (1931), 14
House Un-American Activities Committee (HUAC), xiii–xiv, 91–110, 186
Housman, Laurence, 14
How to Marry a Millionaire (1953), 133
Howard, Leslie, 6
Howard, Sidney, 154
Hoy (magazine), 168
Huerta, Victoriano, 174
Hughes, Hatcher, 12
Humphrey, Maud, 1–2, 5
Hunt, Marsha, 98–99
Huston, Allegra, 50, 152
Huston, Anjelica, 50–51, 122–123, 145, 152
Huston, Danny, ix–x, 50, 145, 152
Huston, John
    Across the Pacific and, vii–viii, 38–52, 84, 145
    African Queen and, vii–viii, 67, 114–128, 134, 146
    Asphalt Jungle and, 50, 113
    background of, vii–xi, 11–18

    Battle of San Pietro and, 45–46
    Beat the Devil and, vii–viii, 2, 129–140, 144, 146
    Bible: In the Beginning and, 50, 144
    birth of, 11
    Bridge in the Jungle and, 144, 178–181
    children of, 50–51, 122–123, 145, 152
    Chinatown and, 61, 144
    Dead and, 51, 144
    death of, x, 51, 144–145
    early years of, 11–14
    Fat City and, 144
    father of, 10–15, 29, 48, 53, 56–57, 60, 65, 67–68, 92, 144, 152–156
    final days of, 144–145
    Freud and, 144
    HUAC and, 93–98
    Humphrey Bogart and, vii–xi, xiv–xv, 9–10, 17–68, 78–147, 149, 155, 178, 182, 187–189
    illness of, x, 11–12, 144–145
    Jack Warner and, xiv–xv, 15–18, 23–37, 52–67, 83–84, 91–115, 134, 143, 184
    Jezebel and, 15, 24, 27, 150
    Juarez and, 16
    Key Largo and, vii, 50, 96–110, 146
    legacy of, vii, 141–146
    Let There Be Light and, 45, 48
    Maltese Falcon and, vii–viii, 18, 26–37, 82, 84, 86–87, 145, 150–151, 182–186
    Man Who Would Be King and, 140, 144
    marriages of, 14–16, 30, 48–51, 62, 64
    Mexican connections, 13, 163–166, 172–177
    in military service, 13, 41–48, 56–57
    Misfits and, 140, 144
    Moby Dick and, 43–44, 140, 144
    Moulin Rouge and, 128, 132
    Mr. North and, ix, 145
    Night of the Iguana and, 144
    Other Side of the Wind and, 144
    Prizzi's Honor and, 144–145
    Red Badge of Courage and, 113–114
    Report from the Aleutians and, 44–45

In This Our Life and, 42, 51, 55
Treasure of the Sierra Madre and, vii–viii, 13, 49–50, 52–90, 104, 116, 143, 146, 149–158, 161–171, 173, 176, 178
Tunisian Victory and, 45–46
Under the Volcano and, 144
We Were Strangers and, 50, 113
Wind and the Lion and, 144
Wise Blood and, 144
Huston, Pablo, 51, 64
Huston, Rhea Gore, 11–12
Huston, Tony, 50, 152
Huston, Walter, 10–13, 15, 29, 48, 53, 56–57, 60, 65, 67–68, 92, 144, 152–156
Hustons, The (Grobel), 144–145
Hutton, Betty, vii
Hyams, Joe, 3, 49, 98, 138

I

I Am a Fugitive from a Chain Gang (1932), 83
In This Our Life (1942), 42, 51, 55
In Time to Come (play), 42
International Alliance of Theatrical Stage Employees (IATSE), 98
Internet Movie Database (IMDb), 61
Invisible Man, The (1933), 13–14
Ivens, Joris, 47

J

Jack Benny Program, The (1953), 128
Jaffe, Sam, 113
Jazz Singer, The (1927), 22
Jezebel (1938), 15, 24, 27, 150
John Huston: The Man, the Movies, the Maverick (1988), 51
Johnsrud, Harold, 100
Johnston, Eric, 95
Jones, Jennifer, 113, 130, 133–134, 144
Juarez (1939), 16

K

Kalmanson, Benny, 66
Kaye, Danny, 97
Kazan, Elia, 112

Kennedy, John Fitzgerald, 189
Kennedy, Patricia, 189
Kerr, Deborah, 68
Key Largo (1948), vii–viii, 50, 91, 96–110, 146
Key Largo (play), 99–101
Keyes, Evelyn, 48–51, 62, 64, 176
Keystone Studios, 22
Killers, The (1946), 132
Kipling, Rudyard, 140
Knickerbocker Holiday (1938), 153
Knock on Any Door (1949), 96
Know Your Enemy: Japan (1945), 47
Koch, Howard, 42, 92
Kohner, Pancho, 166–167, 171, 178–180
Kohner, Paul, 16, 26, 52–56, 151, 156, 162, 165–167, 178
Koster, Henry, 151
Kurnitz, Harry, 50
Kurosawa, Akira, 142

L

labor riots, 92, 150
labor unions, 23, 86, 92, 98, 179, 183
Laemmle, Carl, 13, 19
Laemmle, Carl Jr. "Junior," 13–14
Lakeside Country Club, 9, 30
Lanchester, Elsa, 115
Land of Springtime (Traven), 175
Lang, Fritz, 150
Lardner, Ring Jr., 94, 154
Lasky family, 19
Laughton, Charles, 115
Lawford, Peter, 187–189
Lawrence, Marc, 103
Lawrence of Arabia (1962), 111
Lax, Eric, 3, 84–85
Lazar, Irving "Swifty," 187–188
Lederer, Charles, 187
Lee, Bernard, 132
legacies, vii, 141–146
Leigh, Vivien, 15
Let There Be Light (1946), 45, 48
Lewis, Harry, 101
Lewis, Sinclair, 154

Life of Emile Zola, The (1937), 151
Lincoln, Abraham, 152–153
Little Caesar (1931), 6, 16, 83
Litvak, Anatole, 45
Lollobrigida, Gina, 130, 133, 139, 144, 146
London, Jack, 167
Lonely Man, The (play), 15
Longworth, Karina, 97
Lord, Robert, 132
Lorre, Peter, 29, 31, 129, 133, 139
Love Happy (1949), 113
Loy, Myrna, 93
Lubin Company, 22
Lubitsch, Ernst, 150–151
Luce, Claire, 5
Luft, Sid, 187–188
Luján, Rosa Elena, 167–171, 174
Lupino, Ida, 9, 16–17, 49
Lyceum Theatre, 154

M

Macaulay, Richard, 40–41
MacKenzie, Aeneas, 16
MacLaine, Shirley, 189
MacLane, Barton, 31, 79
Maddow, Ben, 113
Madero, Francesco I., 173–174
Madsen, Virginia, 145
Magee, Frank, 41
Major and the Minor, The (1942), 26
Making of the African Queen: Or How I Went to Africa With Bogart, Bacall and Huston and Almost Lost My Mind (Hepburn), 123
Malden, Karl, 99
Maltese Falcon, The (1941), vii–viii 18, 26–37, 53, 82, 84, 86–87, 133, 143, 145, 149–151, 153, 182–186
Maltese Falcon, The (Hammett), 18, 26–29, 35–36, 184–186
Maltz, Albert, 95, 180
Man Who Came Back, The (1931), 5, 9
Man Who Would Be King, The (1975), 140, 144

Man Who Would Be King, The (Kipling), 140
Mañana (magazine), 168, 174
Mansfield Theatre, 42
Mantz, Paul, 49
Manuel, Alvin, 116, 127
Marc, Javier, 179
March to the Monteria (Traven), 176
Marked Woman (1937), 7
Marks, Owen, 67
Marshall, George, 45
Marshall, James, 157
Martin, Dean, 187–189
Martinez, M. L., 167
Marut, Ret, 169–170, 172, 175. *See also* Traven, B.
Marx Brothers, 113
Masterson, Mary Stuart, 145
Mateos, Adolfo Lopez, 167
Maximilian, Emperor, 16
Mayer, Louis B., 15, 19
McCallum, John, 116
McClintic, Guthrie, 99
McCord, Ted, 86–87
McDermid, Finlay, 105, 114
McDowell, David, 117
McLane, Barton, 60–61
Mencken, H. L., 13
Menken, Helen, 4–5
Meredith, Burgess, 145
Methot, Mayo, 7–8, 10, 30, 43–44, 46
Metropolis (1927), 150
Metropolitan Museum of Art, 175
MGM, 15, 22, 57, 92, 105, 110, 113
Midsummer Night's Dream, A (1935), 151
Miller, Gilbert, 6
Mirisch, Walter, 140
Misfits, The (1961), 140, 144
Mission to Moscow (1943), 92, 153
Mister 880 (1950), 156
Mr. Huston/Mr. North: Life, Death, and Making John Huston's Last Film (Segaloff), x
Mr. North (1988), ix, 145
Mitchum, Robert, 145

Moby Dick (1956), 43–44, 140, 144
Mondale, Walter, 48
Monroe, Marilyn, 113, 189
Morgan, Dennis, 41
Morgan, Mrs. Percy T., 7
Morin, Alberto, 101–102
Morley, Robert, 117, 129, 133
Morros, Boris, 112
Motion Picture Association of America, 48, 95
Motion Picture Patents Company, 21
Moulin Rouge (1952), 128, 132
Movietone, 23
Muhsam, Erich, 169
Muni, Paul, 9, 16, 99–100
Murders in the Rue Morgue (1932), 14
Murphy, Audie, 114
Museum of Modern Art (MoMA), 45, 48
musical scores, 36, 55, 65, 86, 89, 106–107, 153, 157, 187
Mutual Film Corporation, 22
My Four Years in Germany (1918), 21

N
Naremore, James, 87
Nation, The (magazine), 67
New York Daily News (newspaper), 67
New York Herald Tribune (newspaper), 67
New York Times (newspaper), 67
New Yorker (magazine), 114
Newman, Paul, 142
Niblo, Fred Jr., 17
Night of the Iguana (1964), 144
Night Unto Night (1948), 109
Niven, David, 187
Niven, Hjordis, 187
No Exit (play), 57
Nun's Story, The (1959), 149

O
Obringer, Roy J., 53–54
Ocean's 11 (1960), 188
Oklahoma Kid, The (1939), 8
Old Acquaintance (1943), 151

Olimbrada, José, 172
On Our Merry Way (1948), 50
On the Waterfront (1954), 111–112
O'Neill, Eugene, 153, 155
Open Book, An (Huston), ix
Oscar, 49, 67–69, 82, 107, 127–128, 151–152, 156, 180, 187
Othello (play), 65, 153
Other Side of the Wind, The (2018), 144
O'Toole, Peter, 140
Outlaw, The (1943), 153

P
Page, Geraldine, 142
Pantages Theatre, 128
Paramount, 5, 22–23, 26, 110–111
Passage to Marseilles (1944), 52
Passenger to Bali (play), 10
Pasternak, Joe, 151
Peary, Danny, 129, 136, 140, 144
Pegler, Westbrook, 95
Perrone, Mario, 131
Perske, Betty Joan, xi, 47, 122, 136. *See also* Bacall, Lauren
Petrified Forest, The (1936), 6–7, 99
Petrified Forest, The (play), 6
Philbin, Regis, 141
Philips, Mary, 5–8
Phillips Academy Andover, 2–3
Photophone, 23
Picker, David, 179
Picture (Ross), 114
Pinkerton's National Detective Agency, 183–185
Plaza Hotel, ix
Polonsky, Abe, 97
Preminger, Otto, 42
Prizzi's Honor (1985), 144–145
Production Code, 27, 34–36, 57–59, 65–66, 83–84, 105–107, 114–115, 121–122
production schedules, 7, 27, 30, 42–44, 58–65, 125–127, 149–150
Provincetown Players, 12

Prowse, Juliet, 189
Public Enemy (1931), 83
Pulitzer Prize, 117

R

Raft, George, 8–9, 17, 28
Rain (1932), 153
Rainger, Ralph, 107
Rand, Ayn, 150
Rankin, John, 95
Rat Pack, The, 187–190
RCA, 23
Reagan, Ronald, 56
Rebellion of the Hanged (Traven), 176
Red Badge of Courage, The (1951), 113–114
Red Badge of Courage, The (Crane), 113–114
Red Channels (report), 98–99, 104, 186
Red Harvest (Hammett), 184
Reinhardt, Gottfried, 111
Reinhardt, Wolfgang, 16
Remmick, Lee, 142
Report from the Aleutians (1943), 44–45
Rheiner, Samuel, 112
Riskin, Robert, 156
Rivera, Diego, 60
RKO Pictures, 23, 56, 110, 115
Roach, Janet, x, 145
Roaring Twenties, The (1939), 8
Robinson, Charles, 178
Robinson, Edward G., viii, 6, 8–9, 56, 97, 101–109
Robinson, Robert, 167
Rodney, John, 101
Romanoff, Gloria, 187
Romanoff, Mike, 49–50, 187–188
Romanoff's restaurant, 49–50, 188
Romulus Films, 116, 128, 132, 138
Roosevelt, Eleanor, 125
Roosevelt, Franklin D., 23, 41, 46, 57, 91–92, 104–105, 108, 125
Rose, Fanny Elmina, 154
Rose, Steve, 123
Ross, Lilian, 114
Rossen, Robert, 56

Rough Sketch (Sylvester), 113
Roulien, Raul, 15
Roulien, Tosca, 14–15
Royal Films, 138–139
Ruint (play), 12

S

Sabrina (1954), 141
Sagittarius Productions, 180
Sahara (1943), 52
St. Joseph, Ellis, 10
Sallis, Zoe Ishmail, 50
Samuel Goldwyn Productions, 13. *See also* Goldwyn, Samuel
San Quentin (1937), 8
Sands Hotel and Casino, 189
Santana (yacht), 63, 103
Santana Productions, 96, 132–133, 138, 140
Sartre, Jean-Paul, 57
Satan Met a Lady (1936), 26–27
Saturday Evening Post (magazine), 40–41
Saturday's Children (1940), 5
Scarface (1932), 9
Schoenfeld, Herm, 67
Scorsese, Martin, 139
Scott, Zachary, 56
Screen Actors Guild, 8
Selig Company, 22
Sellers, Peter, 137
Selznick, David O., 133–134, 149
Sergeant York (1941), 27
Serrano, Manuel, 131
Seymour, Dan, 101
Shamark Enterprises, 127
Shane, Celeste "Cici," 51
Shaw, Joseph Thompson, 184
Shaw, Tommy, 51
Sheridan, Ann, 41, 59
Sherman, Vincent, 42, 56
Sherman Anti-Trust Act, 110
Sherwood, Robert, 5–6
Shingelton, Wilfred, 122
Shurlock, Geoffrey, 57–58
Siegel, Don, 41

silent films, 4–5, 29, 150, 153
Silvani, Aldo, 130
Silvi, Roberto, x
Simmons, Jean, 133
Sinatra, Frank, 28, 187–189
Slate (magazine), 97
Smart Set (magazine), 184
Smith, Bernard, 167–168
socialism, 77, 85–86, 169
Soma, Enrica Sonia "Ricki," 50–51, 122, 156
Sony Pictures, 139
Sound Services, Inc., 115
sound-on-film system, 23
Spanish Civil War, 99–100, 104
Sperber, A. M., 3, 84, 98
Sperling, Milton, 24
Spiegel, Lynn, 127
Spiegel, Sam, 111–127
Spota, Luis, 167–168, 174
Stanton, Harry Dean, x, 145
Stanton, Paul, 39
Steiner, Max, 65, 86, 89
Stewart, James, vii, 44
Stone, Lewis, 57
Storm, The (1930), 14
Sturges, Preston, vii, 26
Stuyvesant, Pieter, 153
Suddenly, Last Summer (1959), 111
Summer Holiday (1948), 156
Sunderland, Nan, 154
Supreme Court, 110
Sutter, John, 157
Sylvester, Robert, 113

T

Tales of Manhattan (1942), 112
talking pictures, 5, 22–23
Ten Commandments, The (1956), 105
Theodore, Ralph, 100
Theophilus North (Wilder), x
They Drive by Night (1940), 17
Thin Man, The (Hammett), 184
Thomas, J. Parnell, 91–94

To Have and Have Not (1944), 46, 52, 99
Tong, Kam, 40
Torsvan, Traven, 167–169, 172–176. *See also* Traven, B.
Tovar, Lupita, 165–167, 171
Tozere, Frederic, 100
Tracy, Spencer, 5, 141–142, 189
Traven, B., 52–57, 61, 66, 72, 85–88, 162–180
Treasure of the Sierra Madre, The (1948), vii–viii, 13, 49–50, 52–90, 104, 116, 143, 146, 149–158, 161–171, 173, 176, 178
Treasure of the Sierra Madre, The (Traven), 52–57, 61, 66, 69–90, 162–171
Trevor, Claire, 101, 105, 107–109
Trilling, Steve, 29, 95
Trivers, Barry, 17
Trozas (Traven), 176
Truffaut, François, 142
Tulli, Marco, 129, 133
Tunisian Victory (1944), 45–46
Turner, Ted, 143
Twentieth Century-Fox, 84, 110, 115, 133

U

UFA studios, 150
Under the Volcano (1984), 144
Underdown, Edward, 130, 139
United Artists, 110, 116, 127, 132, 138, 143, 179, 181
United States v. Paramount et al (court case), 110
Universal Pictures, 13, 22, 24, 110, 112
University of Vienna, 111
Up the River (1930), 5, 141
Urzi, Saro, 131

V

Vagrant, The (Sturges), 26
Valenti, Jack, 48
Van Heusen, Jimmy, 187
Veiller, Tony, 132–133
Viertel, Peter, 113, 117, 123, 128, 132–133
Vietnam War, 160

Villa, Francisco "Pancho," 173–174
Vitagraph Studios, 22
Vitaphone, 5, 22
Vizzard, Jack, 121

W

Wagons Roll at Night, The (1941), 17, 25
Wald, Jerry, 99
Waldorf-Astoria Hotel, xiii, 95
Wallace, Henry, 96
Wallis, Hal, 9, 16–17, 25–26, 30, 53, 83–84, 149–151
Walsh, Raoul, 9, 17, 142
Walter F. Heller Company, 116
Warner, Albert, 20–23, 95
Warner, Harry, 20–23, 91–92
Warner, Jack L.
  Across the Pacific and, 41–44, 49, 84
  African Queen and, 111–115, 121–122, 134
  background of, 7–9, 19–25
  Beat the Devil and, 134
  birth of, 20
  early years of, 20–21
  HUAC and, 91–110
  Humphrey Bogart and, xiv–xv, 6–10, 17–18, 23–37, 52–67, 83–84, 91–115, 134, 143
  John Huston and, xiv–xv, 15–18, 23–37, 52–67, 83–84, 91–115, 134, 143, 184
  Key Largo and, 96–110
  Maltese Falcon and, 18, 26–37, 53, 84, 184
  Treasure of the Sierra Madre and, 56–67, 83–84, 104, 169
  See also Warner Bros.
Warner, Rose, 20–21
Warner, Sam, 20–23
Warner Bros., viii–ix, xiii–xv, 3, 5–10, 15–37, 41–44, 49, 52–68, 83–84, 91–115, 121–122, 134, 143, 149–151, 169, 178, 184
Wayne, John, vii
We Were Strangers (1949), 50, 113
Weekly Variety (trade paper), 67
Weill, Kurt, 153

We're No Angels (1955), 141
Whipple, Bayonne, 154
Whistler, James McNeill, 2
White Hunter, Black Heart (Viertel), 123, 132
Whitely, Chris, 109
Whitmore, James, 113
Why We Fight (series), 45, 47
Wild Boys of the Road (1933), 83
Wilder, Billy, 26, 111, 140, 151
Wilder, Thornton, x
Wilk, Jacob, 36
Wind and the Lion, The (1975), 144
Winning Your Wings (1942), 44
Winsten, Archer, 84
Wise Blood (1979), 144
Withers, Googie, 116
Wonskolaser, Benjamin, 20
Wonskolaser, Jacob, 19
Woodward, Joanne, 142
Woolf, James, 116, 128, 132, 138
Woolf, John, 116, 126, 128, 132, 138
Woollcott, Alexander, 4
World War I, 3, 21, 27, 114, 150, 160, 183
World War II, viii, 15, 23, 38–51, 54, 82–83, 91–92, 101, 104, 107, 114, 149, 160, 162, 169
Writers Guild, 23–24
Wuthering Heights (1939), 16
Wyatt, Will, 162, 167, 170–171
Wyler, William "Willy," 8, 14–15, 24, 93, 140, 150–151

Y

Yankee Doodle Dandy (1942), 153
York, Alvin, 27
Yost, Elwy, 136
Young, Collier, 49–50
Young at Heart (1954), 149
Yung, Victor Sen, 39

Z

Zanuck, Darryl F., 20–21, 23, 84, 150
Zapata, Emiliano, 174
Ziegelbrenner (newspaper), 169, 171